The Psychology of Culture

Edward Sapir
The Psychology of Culture
A Course of Lectures

Reconstructed and edited by
Judith T. Irvine

Mouton
de Gruyter
Berlin · New York
1994

Mouton de Gruyter (formerly Mouton, The Hague)
is a Division of Walter de Gruyter & Co., Berlin.

♾ Printed on acid-free paper which falls within the guidelines
of the ANSI to ensure permanence and durability.

Library of Congress Cataloging-in-Publication Data

Sapir, Edward, 1884 – 1939.
  The psychology of culture : a course of lectures / Edward Sapir ;
reconstructed and edited by Judith T. Irvine.
    p.   cm.
  Includes bibliographical references and index.
  ISBN 3-11-012920-5 (pbk. : alk. paper)
  1. Culture. 2. Ethnopsychology. 3. Personality and culture.
I. Irvine, Judith T. II. Title.
GN506.S26   1993   93-38287
306 – dc20   CIP

Die Deutsche Bibliothek — Cataloging-in-Publication Data

Sapir, Edward:
The psychology of culture : a course of lectures / Edward Sapir.
Reconstructed and ed. by Judith T. Irvine. — Berlin ; New York :
  Mouton de Gruyter, 1994
  ISBN 3-11-012920-5

Disc conversion and printing: Arthur Collignon GmbH, Berlin
Binding: Lüderitz & Bauer, Berlin
Printed in Germany

Table of Contents

Part I: The Concept of Culture

Part II: The Individual's Place in Culture

Part III: Symbolic Structures and Experience (1933–34)

Acknowledgements

The work that follows is a reconstruction of a course of lectures Edward Sapir gave at Yale University, lectures that were to have been the basis of a book he had contracted to publish with Harcourt, Brace. Most of the material used for the reconstruction comes from student notes, collected and microfilmed shortly after Sapir's death with a view toward eventual publication.

In embarking on this task I was initially somewhat daunted by the temerity of constructing a text in which, inevitably, I must put words in Sapir's mouth. I am much indebted, therefore, to the late Fred Eggan, the principal custodian of this material over the decades, who encouraged me to interweave the notes, put them in narrative form, and treat the whole as a Sapir "manuscript". I was also encouraged by the example of Charles Bally and Albert Sechehaye, without whose efforts we would never have seen Ferdinand de Saussure's *Course in General Linguistics*. Nevertheless, I have marked my own insertions so that readers will have some basis for judging for themselves degrees of certainty in the reconstruction.

There are many people who have contributed materials, encouragement, or assistance to this project. J. David Sapir first drew me in to the plans for publishing a new edition of Edward Sapir's work; he has remained a source of encouragement, as has Dell Hymes, himself a historian (as well as eminent practitioner) of linguistic anthropology and, like David Sapir, my former teacher. Both were members of the Sapir Centenary joint committee of the Linguistic Society of America and the American Anthropological Association, which selected the editorial board for *The Collected Works of Edward Sapir* (CWES). An edition of the present work appears in CWES, volume III.

For source materials I am indebted, first of all, to David Mandelbaum and Fred Eggan, who initially collected and preserved eleven sets of student notes from Sapir's course at Yale. Fred Eggan gave me a copy − perhaps the only one extant − of the microfilm on which the notes were recorded. Both he and David Mandelbaum also provided me with access to their own notes on all courses they took with Sapir, as well as relevant correspondence. Just before his death, Mandelbaum very kindly answered my questions about Sapir and invited me to look at his files in his office at Berkeley. I am grateful to Ruth Mandelbaum for her help in following through on that invitation and for sharing her own recollections of the Yale student cohort. The Anthropology Department of the University of California at Berkeley hospitably assisted my work in their offices.

Several other students whose notes were assembled on the Yale microfilm were still available to help me. I am grateful to Irving Rouse, Mary Mikami Rouse, Weston LaBarre, and Walter Taylor for permission to use their notes and for helpful responses to my inquiries. Walter Taylor further provided for me to consult his papers for the originals of his class notes and related correspondence. Two Yale students whose notes on Sapir's course were not included in the microfilm located them and lent them to me: Beatrice Blyth Whiting and Edgar Siskin. I am also indebted to them (and to John Whiting and Allan Smith, as well) for sharing recollections of the Yale years, and to Siskin for lending me — as well as encouragement — additional notes on other courses he took from Sapir.

Copies of notes taken by the late Stanley Newman and Frank Setzler, from an earlier version of the course given at the University of Chicago, were kindly provided by Richard Preston. Preston has studied most of the class notes material himself (see Preston 1986) and his interpretations of it contribute much to my own.

I owe a considerable debt to Philip Sapir, Editor-in-Chief of *The Collected Works of Edward Sapir*, for providing me with copies of Edward Sapir's correspondence with Harcourt, as well as other correspondence relating to the *Psychology of Culture* notes and to the 1949 volume, *Selected Writings of Edward Sapir*; for permission to publish Sapir's chapter outline and a previously unpublished excerpt from Sapir's correspondence; for identifying and obtaining for me a further set of sources, the student notes from the Rockefeller Seminar on "The Impact of Culture on Personality"; for helping me get funds for archival work and research assistance; and for many other forms of assistance and encouragement.

Regna Darnell, my co-editor on the CWES volumes, *Culture* (vol. III) and *Ethnology* (vol. IV), has read the manuscript at many stages and provided helpful advice throughout. John Lucy and Victor Golla have also read and commented upon the manuscript or portions of it. Michael Silverstein provided me with notes from his own research on Sapir, and brought Eggan's microfilm and other notes to me so that we did not have to entrust them to the mails.

Mary Catherine Bateson gave permission to use the Rockefeller Seminar materials, on file with the Margaret Mead papers in the Library of Congress. I would also like to acknowledge the Peabody Museum of Harvard University for permission to consult the Walter Taylor papers, then housed in their archives (now at the Smithsonian), and the Bancroft Library of the University of California at Berkeley for access to the Kroeber papers.

My efforts in the early stages of the process of reconstructing a text owe much to the assistance of Sue Woodson-Marks. Jane Goodman, Somervell Linthicum, Jacqueline Baum, and Elizabeth Martin made preliminary reconstructions of portions of the text and contributed (as did Laurie Rothstein and Gregory Button) to thinking through how the reconstruction should be done.

Last but not least, I am grateful for the help, advice, and moral support of Marie-Louise Liebe-Harkort of Mouton De Gruyter, and for the encouragement and forbearance of my family, Stephen L. Pastner and Deborah and Rebecca Pastner.

Judith T. Irvine

Editor's Introduction

In 1928, after a conversation with Alfred Harcourt on the Twentieth-Century Limited out of Chicago, Edward Sapir wrote to Harcourt, Brace proposing to publish a book on "The Psychology of Culture". Estimated at about 100,000 words in length, the book was to be based upon a graduate course of the same title which Sapir had been giving for three years at the University of Chicago. The course had attracted a considerable audience, drawing in psychologists as well as anthropologists and sociologists. Sapir hoped that the book, too, might appeal to a wide circle of non-professional readers.[1] The book proposal and the chapter outline accompanying it were well received, and Harcourt contracted to publish the work.

Despite Harcourt's enthusiasm for the project and Sapir's sense of its potential importance, the book was not to be. Other projects intervened, including duties which Sapir undertook for financial or administrative reasons. But the idea for the book was not merely a momentary flash of enthusiasm conceived in a heady train conversation and forgotten as soon as the train pulled into the station. Although Sapir's interest in the project appears to have fluctuated, he continued to teach and to rework the course on which it was to be based, and to refer to his intention to complete the book, until almost the end of his life. He gave the course several times after his move to Yale in 1931, and materials from the last version of the course (1936–37) suggest new ideas and a renewed excitement about the project, especially toward the end of the academic year.

The following summer (1937), after a strenuous eight weeks' teaching at the Linguistic Institute in Ann Arbor, Sapir suffered a serious heart attack and had to curtail his work effort and travel plans for his sabbatical year (1937–38). Still, in a hopeful mood in October 1937 he wrote that "it is my plan to work at 'The Psychology of Culture' during this sabbatical."[2] As it turned out, recurrent illness made it impossible to carry out this plan. Though he again mentioned the work in a letter of October 1938 as "a book that I have still to write",[3] by that time it was all too clear that his physical strength was waning. Sapir died in February 1939, this project and many others remaining unfinished.

Many of Sapir's unfinished works were edited and completed by his students and colleagues after his death. As early as May 1939 Sapir's widow, Jean McClenaghan Sapir, and Leslie Spier initiated plans to fulfill the Harcourt contract, so that "The Psychology of Culture" could be published posthumously.[4] The enterprise differed from other efforts to edit Sapir's work, because no actual manuscript in Sapir's hand had been found, other than the chapter outline and correspondence he had sent to the publisher.[5] What was proposed, therefore, was to collect sets of notes from the students who had attended the course of lectures on which the book was to have been based, and from these to "present the gist of it" as an essay.[6]

Sapir's students responded with alacrity. Under the leadership of David Mandelbaum, who had emerged as organizer of the *festschrift* eventually published as a memorial volume,[7] eleven sets of notes were assembled and microfilmed.[8] Elizabeth Herzog, then the wife of the ethnomusicologist George Herzog, was to have attempted the reconstruction. Although the notion of fulfilling the Harcourt contract was soon abandoned, there was considerable enthusiasm for including some version of this material in a collection of Sapir's writings (the collection published in 1949 as *Selected Writings of Edward Sapir*, edited by Mandelbaum). Commenting, for example, on a proposed table of contents for that volume, the linguist Zellig Harris assigned the highest priority on the list of Sapir's works to "The Psychology of Culture; The Outline of Sapir's course, supplemented by an integrated transcript of students' notes". "Please, as full as possible," Harris wrote.[9]

By 1946, however, it had become evident that the class notes material could not be included in *Selected Writings* after all. The task of reconstructing a text from the notes was much larger than it had seemed at first, and the resulting text would have been too long to be added to an already sizeable volume. Although, in succeeding years, many people expressed interest in seeing the notes and hoped that a synthesis would still be done, nothing came of the idea until the Sapir Centenary in 1984.[10] With renewed interest in Sapir and the initiation of a new publication project, *The Collected Works of Edward Sapir*, which was to include as much of Sapir's academic work — published or unpublished — as possible, an attempt to integrate the student notes looked worth undertaking.

The present work is the result. It is an attempt to fulfill the hope Sapir's students, colleagues, and family have expressed over the years: that a set of lectures making a major contribution to anthropology and psychology should be made public. Though Sapir is justly renowned for the importance of his work in linguistics — and his interest in the details of linguistic analysis was almost always greater than his interest in the details of ethnological work — the extent of his commitment to rethinking theory and method in anthropology and psychology has tended to be underestimated. It is not to be measured by the number of his actual publications.[11] Sapir saw himself as a central contributor to the social sciences, and many of his contemporaries would have agreed. *The Psychology of Culture* was to have been an important work.

A synthesis of classroom presentations is not, of course, the same thing as the polished, carefully thought-through manuscript Sapir would himself have produced had he lived to complete this book. His class lectures must often have included spontaneous flashes of insight, tentative explorations of ideas, and off-the-cuff examples, all of which he would have meticulously checked, developed, and evaluated before presenting them in print as final intellectual judgements.[12] When these lectures were given, Sapir's ideas were still evolving, and a classroom presentation to students differs from a formal presentation to colleagues. One notices, for instance, that these lectures include a few comments on Sapir's anthropological contemporaries that are sharper in tone than any he ever allowed to appear in print. Moreover, student lecture notes — which make up the vast preponderance of the source materials for the reconstruction — must surely differ from what was actually said, both in inclusiveness and in subtlety.

Nevertheless, the notes include so many passages in which one seems to hear the echo of Sapir's voice, and so many topics unrepresented or only hinted at in his published writings, that Sapir's students and others from 1939 on have seen this material as a significant part of his intellectual legacy. Most important, perhaps, is the broad scope of the lecture course and book, as compared with the essay format of his actual publications in cultural anthropology and psychology. *The Psychology of Culture* affords us a glimpse of how Sapir would have sketched a broad vista of anthropological and psychological issues. Although some of those issues are perhaps of less interest today than they were in the 1930's, on the whole Sapir's conception of culture, of anthropological method and theory, and of individuals and their relationships remains fresh and relevant. The work is not only a document of historical interest, but a contribution to contemporary culture theory and psychological anthropology.

The Evolution of Sapir's Course

Since the material drawn upon for reconstruction comes from several different versions of Sapir's course, the resulting text necessarily masks what those differences are and in what ways the course shifted over time. It may be useful, therefore, to summarize the kinds of changes that appear in the source materials as the course evolved.[13] The most interesting changes are those that suggest new directions in Sapir's thinking. Not all the differences among versions of the course are likely to be due to changed ideas, however. Some are more likely related to practical and pedagogical concerns.

I shall pay most attention to the Yale period, since it provides most of the material I have used in reconstructing the text. But by the time Sapir presented the course at Yale he had already given several versions of it elsewhere. The earliest was a summer course at Columbia in 1925; no detailed records of this remain, as far as I know. At the end of that summer Sapir moved to Chicago, where (in the fall of 1925) he offered a set of ten lectures derived from the Columbia course to a popular audience, a group headed by the Chicago lawyer Clarence Darrow. Following that condensed version came the regular University course on "The Psychology of Culture", first given in the winter term of 1926 and repeated several times. Since Chicago was on a quarter system, the course there occupied only 30 one-hour class meetings over ten weeks, a much shorter format than at Yale, where it was spread over a full academic year.

Arriving at Yale in 1931, Sapir did not offer the "Psychology of Culture" course immediately. Instead, he first presented portions of this material during the international seminar on "The Impact of Culture on Personality" sponsored by the Rockefeller Institute and held at Yale in 1932 – 33.[14] The students in the seminar were young scholars in the social sciences from a variety of different countries. The idea was that these scholars, representing different cultural traditions, would combine the roles of informant and analyst, and the result would be a social science transcending the limitations of any one set of cultural assumptions. In leading the seminar Sapir was assisted by John Dollard, as well as a long list of visiting speakers.

Although the Rockefeller Seminar had the same title as Sapir gave to his lecture course in the following year, its format and emphasis were different. In the seminar Sapir did not attempt to lecture on the full range

of topics he had discussed at Chicago and planned for the book. Participants' activities included a "nuclear course" of two lectures per week,
but apparently Sapir did not give many of these lectures himself until the
second semester. Concerned more with psychology than with culture per
se, most of his presentations that spring relate only to portions of the
second half of his book outline and the Chicago course.

It was not until 1933 – 34, then, that Sapir first offered a two-semester
regular graduate course on the material for his book. Retaining for the
time being the Rockefeller Seminar title, "The Impact of Culture on
Personality", Sapir expanded his Chicago course but devoted a considerable amount of course time to student reports and discussion. Several
class meetings in the fall were given over to exercises in the description
and analysis of two common American cultural patterns: smoking and
piano-playing.[15] There were also assignments on definitions of "culture"
and the concept of "the social", on devising cultural inventories,[16] and
(in the spring term) on the investigation of etiquette. Later versions of
the course apparently abandoned these pedagogical exercises, expanding
the lecture component instead, at least as regards classroom hours. In
1935 – 36 and 1936 – 37 Sapir also changed the course title back to "The
Psychology of Culture".

These pedagogical changes affect several portions of the reconstructed
manuscript. Because the 1933 exercises on smoking and piano-playing
were self-contained, easily isolated from the rest of the course, and never
repeated, I have removed them from the main body of the text. The other
assignments were not so easily isolated, and since Sapir seems to have
integrated their discussion into his lecture material, I have included them
likewise. Chapter 2 in particular, with its leisurely exploration of the term
"social", reflects the dynamics of classroom give-and-take, as (to a lesser
extent) does Chapter 12's treatment of etiquette. Although a shift from
class discussion to lecture presents some difficulties for the editorial
process, differences between versions of the course on these topics cannot
be attributed solely or even largely to changes in Sapir's thinking.

Another difference between the 1933 and later versions of the material
in Chapter 2, "The Concept of Culture in the Social Sciences", involves
disciplinary issues. Perhaps because of his involvement in the interdisciplinary Rockefeller Seminar the previous year, as well as his recent
experiences with the interdisciplinary activities of the Social Science
Research Council, Sapir's discussion of Chapter 2's topic in 1933 has
relatively little to say about the special disciplinary concerns of anthropology, preferring a more diffuse orientation to the social sciences in

general. In 1935 and 1936 Sapir seems, instead, to speak to an audience of anthropologists about their own field and its problems, such as methodological difficulties in cross-cultural ethnography. The sense of anthropological audience is again apparent in Chapter 5, where the later versions of the course include a lengthy excursion into Sapir's own Nootka ethnography to illustrate cultural configurations and methods of investigating them.

Given the hazards of student attendance and note-taking, it is probably unwise to draw many inferences from omissions in topical coverage. Still, one might notice that in Chapter 3, "'Causes' of Culture", a section on economic causes discussed in 1933 does not occur in the records for later years. The putative "causes" of cultural form discussed in this chapter − the others are race, geography, and an aprioristic psychology − are raised here only to be thoroughly and finally dismissed; conceivably, Sapir may have decided that the role of economics in culture is a different, more complicated kind of problem. Did he also change his mind as to whether economic determinants were to be entirely dismissed? The answer remains unclear. What he did say on economic "causes" in 1933 does not appear to be out of line with his published statements of later years, and he certainly never changed his mind so radically as to become an economic determinist. Yet, the 1936−37 notes show a discussion later on in the course (see Chapter 10, "The Adjustment of the Individual in Society") that closely follows a portion of his argument in the 1939 paper, "Psychiatric and Cultural Pitfalls in the Business of Getting a Living", where large-scale economic organization appears as an independent social force impinging on the individual.[17]

With the exception of the matters mentioned so far, and some expansion of lectures in later years to fill class time no longer taken up by discussion of student assignments, the contents and organization of the first two thirds of the course − the material represented in Chapters 1 through 8 − remain quite stable during the Yale years. Evidently Sapir had settled on the view of culture he wanted to present (Part I, chapters 1−6), and on what he wanted to say about the concept of personality (chapters 7 and 8 in Part II). Up to this point in the book, culture and the individual are discussed rather separately. It is the remaining chapters that explore their nexus and clinch the argument; and the three Yale versions of this discussion differ considerably. Sapir's ideas in this culminating portion of the course seem still to have been evolving. In the later versions of the course he revised the organization of the last two months' lectures and added new material.

These changes had major implications for the thrust of Sapir's book. They also created editorial problems. Because the student notes from different years are not compatibly organized, and because Sapir's new ideas are represented only in the 1936−37 notes, the final chapters of the book proved difficult to reconstruct. I have had to rely more heavily than elsewhere on Sapir's published writings and letters of the same period (1937−39) − and on my own interpretation − to fill in the gaps. Material with which Sapir had concluded the course in earlier years, including much of his discussion of symbolism, could not be smoothly integrated into the 1937 discussion.

My solution was to move the earlier material out into separate chapters (12 and 13). Thus the final (1937) version of the course ends with Chapter 11. Part III is an addendum, representing earlier conclusions. It is not that Sapir had come to disagree with the details of what he had then said, but that he did not use them to conclude the course. Unfortunately, the evidence as to how he actually did conclude it in the final lecture of 1937 is relatively scanty. Only a few sketchy notes on that lecture survive.

The Plan and Purpose of the Book

Because of the lack of a strong concluding statement in the reconstructed text, it may be worthwhile to summarize the book's argument here.

There can be little doubt that Sapir envisioned his proposed book as a major theoretical statement of Boasian cultural anthropology. Many of the book's concerns were shared by fellow members of the Boas school, and some of the material in chapters 3 and 4 (the discussion of culture, race, and geography, and the critique of culture-trait inventories) overlaps substantially with statements by others. But although not all the ideas in the book are unique to Sapir, it is perhaps insufficiently recognized today how much he contributed to their discussion. For example, his conception of cultural patterning and configuration, and their relation to function, were developed prior to the appearance of Benedict's *Patterns of Culture*, but not published in detail until now (see Chapter 5), although he had presented them in letters, lectures, and colloquia. And as Benedict's book did in 1933, Sapir's 1928 plan for *The Psychology of Culture* was to explore the relationship between the patterns of culture and the psychology of individuals − though with a different conception of what the relationship was, as his critique of Benedict's work reveals (see Chapter

9). Thus the fact that Sapir's sense of cultural anthropology's agenda was shared with some of his fellow Boasians does not diminish the originality of his contribution.

As his contemporaries often recognized, Sapir's expertise in linguistics gave him a special perspective that extended into the rest of his anthropological work. One way in which language occupies an important place in his cultural anthropology is that he so frequently cites it as a prime example of a cultural phenomenon. Indeed, in the present book discussions of language appear again and again, for that reason. Linguistic examples are drawn upon to illustrate arguments about culture; the organization of cultural patterns is deemed analogous to the organization of grammatical forms, with lexicon providing a key to the patterns' psychological reality (see, especially, Chapter 5); and conversational interaction emerges as the locus of cultural dynamics (Chapter 10). One might also suspect that Sapir's understanding of language's systematicity, and the relation between form and meaning in language, contribute at a more subtle level to his ideas about cultural configurations and function – even to his ideas about the processes of cultural change (Chapter 6). Yet, the originality of the book does not stem only from the influence of linguistics in it, but also from Sapir's conceptions of "culture" and "psychology" themselves and the epistemological issues relating to them.

To explore "the psychology of culture", the Yale course material divides into two roughly equal parts: a discussion of the concept of culture and a discussion of psychology. The rationale for this organization may perhaps be best understood by a glance at Sapir's 1930 Hanover Conference paper, which seesaws between culture and personality in order to show that an exploration of the one necessarily leads to a consideration of the other. They are two poles of analytical interest – two approaches to the same observational subject matter, namely human behavior. Like the conference paper, the book points to the theoretical and methodological problems that arise if "culture" and "individual psychology" are contrastively understood. Instead, each is to be understood in ways that lead toward the other.

In the first half of the book Sapir defines "culture" in terms of ideas and values, organized in conceptual systems. From the beginning he bases this view of culture on an argument that – in any society – individuals will represent society's values differently. Culture rests, therefore, on selective valuation, and on an imaginative projection of ideals and wishes which some social subgroups will appear to fulfill more than others do (Chapter 1). While a psychological approach to culture is of course a hallmark of Boasian anthropology, Sapir's presumption of intra-societal variation as basic to the very concept of culture is clearly his own, as is his emphasis on imagination.

The methodological and theoretical importance of individual variation is a subject Sapir had been exploring at least since 1917 (in "Do We Need the 'Superorganic'?", his reply to Kroeber [1917]), and it occupies much of the present work as well, especially Chapter 2. There, in an argument clearly continuous with his 1917 paper, Sapir points out the problematic methodological abstractions involved in moving from the observation of individuals' behavior to a statement of cultural pattern pertaining to society. It is a fallacy, he contends, to identify culture with physical phenomena, such as material objects or outward behavior. Instead, culture resides in the *significance* of these, and in the conceptual pattern underlying them. It is also a fallacy to identify culture with society, in the sense of some aggregate of people. Despite the fact that anthropologists must consider cultural meanings to have a social (as opposed to a private) frame of reference, Sapir warns that "society" is not a physical or observational given, but a conceptual construct. As such it influences the behavior of even the most isolated individual.

Despite its social frame of reference, then, culture must not be assumed to be uniformly shared among some aggregate of people. Everyone does not know the same things, and the significance they attribute to those things will not be identical, since it must always depend in part on individual experience. Yet, the systems of symbols through which people interact operate with reference to a community and its sanctions. These symbols enable people with quite different personal experiences to participate in the life of the larger group. Through symbols an individual can come to benefit from other participants' special knowledge, and even, sometimes, to believe that everyone shares understandings of the meanings of symbols when they actually share only the forms (see Chapter 9).

If Sapir's conception of culture points inward, toward the psychology of the socialized individual interacting with others, his conception of individual psychology points outward, toward socialization and interaction. It is as much a fallacy, to him, to study psychology as if the individual existed in isolation, as it is to study culture as if individuals had no relevance. Sapir concedes that an individual's temperament may be influenced by factors of biology or prenatal experience, in ways not yet well understood. From the beginning, however, the child interacts with and adapts to a social world, and his or her psychology cannot be understood without reference to its cultural patterns and symbolism.

Much of Chapter 7's discussion of "personality" clearly parallels the 1934 encyclopedia article of the same title (Sapir 1934b). Chapter 8's discussion of Jung, however, is not represented in any of Sapir's work published elsewhere, apart from a brief book review (Sapir 1923b) written much earlier. Like many other intellectuals of the 1920's and 1930's Sapir had become interested in psychology and psychiatry, and this interest has been well known; but the depth of his intellectual appreciation of Jung has not been obvious heretofore. Jung describes personality as a system, a psychological organization interacting with and adapting to an external world. This view of psychology must have appealed to Sapir as he searched for a conception of culture that would be realistic in terms of the individual. Despite the close attention Sapir gives to Jung's work in Chapter 8, however, he does not in the end rest content with Jung's analysis, or even with his own revised version of it. The psychology Sapir arrives at in *The Psychology of Culture* is a synthesis that derives not only from Jung, but also from Koffka's Gestalt psychology, from Sullivan's interpersonal psychiatry, and from his own studies of linguistic symbolism.

"Personality", in Sapir's usage, is as much a cognitive organization as an emotional one. Chapters 9 and 10 explore the relationships this organization has with culture. There are three:

(1) **Personality as model, or metaphor, for culture.** As he wrote in 1934 ("The Emergence of the Concept of Personality in a Study of Cultures"), "the more fully one tries to understand a culture, the more it seems to take on the characteristics of a personality organization." If personality is understood as a systematic psychological organization depending on constellations of symbols — an organization in which each part is interconnected with other parts, and which interacts with an external world — then, in these respects, it is analogous to the concept of culture Sapir had presented in earlier chapters. At a time when some anthropologists still thought of culture as an assemblage of traits, a psychiatry that emphasized the systematicity of personality must have seemed a useful model.

More specifically, Jung's typology of personalities according to the nature of their organization and their interaction with their environment provides Sapir with an analogy for a typology of cultures. The two levels are not to be confused, however. In a society having an "introverted" culture there is no special reason to suppose individuals have introverted personalities (see Chapter 9).

(2) **"As-if" personalities: cultural systems provide normative standards for behavior.** The patterns of culture conventionalize the forms of behavior deemed acceptable, within a community, for its particular range of social occasions. In so doing, Sapir argues, the cultural patterns suggest a normative personality (or personalities) — the kind of person who would behave in that way even if not required to by convention. The individual who conforms to these behavioral conventions thus behaves *as if* he or she had that personality, or those motives, regardless of what the actual motives or opinions might be (see Chapter 9 and Sapir's 1926 conference presentation, "Notes on Psychological Orientation in a Given Society"). Just as cultures differ in their behavioral conventions, so they differ in "as-if" personalities. These "as-if" personalities must not be confused with an individual's actual personality, Sapir insists (attributing that error to Benedict and Mead). The "as-if" personality is merely an external standard, a frame of reference that is part of the environment to which an individual must adapt.

(3) **Personalities' actions and interactions give rise to cultural meanings.** Without subscribing to a "great man" theory of history, ever since the 1917 debate with Kroeber Sapir had emphasized the role of the creative individual in culture. A personality is both an organized system and an integrative mechanism, he argues. Shaped in terms provided by the patterns of culture, a personality contributes, in turn, to the re-shaping of the patterns themselves. From his or her experience each individual extracts significant uniformities, systematizes them, and bases actions on them. In the process, personal significances may influence cultural ones, depending on an individual's circumstances and opportunities to affect the experiences of others.

Though I have summarized it only roughly, this argument appears many times in Sapir's work, from 1917 to the several versions of the "Psychology of Culture" course. In 1933 – 34, the emphasis is on symbols as mediators between individual and society (Chapter 12). The constellations of meanings conveyed by a symbol shift, he suggests, between different individuals as well as between different cultural systems. Yet, private symbolisms may come to take on a wider, hence social, significance. In 1933 Sapir says little about how this influence can come about; in 1937, he situates it in the specific social interactions of individuals — thus inserting a situational, interactional level of analysis between the psychology of individuals and the abstracted patterns of societies (Chapter 10). Influenced by Harry Stack Sullivan's interpersonal psychiatry, Sapir now argued that what we can consider "culture" emerges from the interactions of specific individuals, and the symbols involved in those interactions. In a discussion partly replicated in his 1937 publication, "The Contribution of Psychiatry to an Understanding of Behavior in Society" (a paper given in a symposium of psychiatrists including Sullivan), Sapir seems to have told his 1937 class:

> Cultural considerations alone can never explain what happens from day to day — they are inadequate for predicting or interpreting any particular act of an individual. The reason for this, in a nutshell, is that in those particular acts the individual is not adjusting to "society", but to interpersonal relationships. Faced, therefore, with the difficulty of segregating the psychological and the social systems, and convinced that the gap between the sociological approach and the psychological approach must be filled and both systems must be used, I find that I am particularly fond of Dr. Harry Stack Sullivan's pet phrase of "interpersonal relations"...
>
> The study of "interpersonal relations" is the problem of the future. It demands that we study seriously and carefully just what happens when A meets B — given that each is not only physiologically defined, but each also has memories, feelings, understandings, and so on about the symbols they can and must use in their interaction... In any [specific] situation when two people are talking, they create a cultural structure. Our task, as anthropologists, will be to determine what are the potential contents of the culture that results from these interpersonal relations in these situations.[18]

Sapir did not end the 1937 course with that statement. Instead, as in earlier years and in his 1928 chapter outline (the prospectus for Harcourt), he took up a subject then prominent in some schools of psychiatry and anthropology: the concept of "primitive mentality" (Chapter 11). A work on the "psychology of culture" in the 1930's could scarcely omit discussing the influential notions of Freud, Lévy-Bruhl, and Malinowski, authors whose work must have dominated many readers' conceptions of what culture and psychology might have to do with one another. Although he had discussed Freudian psychiatry elsewhere (see, for instance, his 1917 reviews of Freud and Pfister), the critiques of Lévy-Bruhl and Malinowski have no equivalent in Sapir's previously published work.

As the end of Chapter 11 shows, Sapir shifted away from the concept of "primitive mentality" to make a concluding statement for the 1937 course as a whole. He seems to have alluded to the individual's creative integration of cultural forms — "the springs for art in every human being", as the class notes put it — and returned to the argument that the individual's tendency to expression may, under certain conditions, give rise to or influence cultural patterns. Regrettably, very few notes on this concluding passage survive.

In sum, although some of the ideas in this book can also be found in Sapir's published essays, these lectures provided him with an opportunity to explore some of them more fully and to place them in a broadly comprehensive argument. Other ideas, and the breadth of the terrain he covers here, are not to be found in his previously available work, and so must add to our sense of his contribution. Examining the evolution of the course sheds light on the development of his ideas in the last decade of his life, for he was still actively engaged in thinking about the "psychology of culture" right up to the end. Whether he had finally arrived at a formulation that really satisfied him, however, we shall never know.

Sources and Editorial Procedures

The principal source materials for this project were fifteen sets of student notes taken in Sapir's course on "The Psychology of Culture". Eleven sets were available on the Yale microfilm, a copy of which was given me by Fred Eggan. Eggan had been given the microfilm by Louis Wirth, who had received it (or copies of the actual notes) from Elizabeth Herzog sometime before June 1942.[19] Apparently, there was some possibility at that time or in the next few years that Wirth might have the notes mimeographed, or that Eggan might look them over and do the synthesis himself.

Sapir gave the course at Yale three times: in 1933 – 34 (when it was titled "The Impact of Culture on Personality"), in 1935 – 36, and in 1936 – 37. Students from all three years contributed notes to the microfilm. Of the eleven students, nine can be firmly identified:

Ernest Beaglehole (PhD 1931 from the London School of Economics; a postdoctoral visitor at Yale before completing his major fieldwork on Pukapuka later in the 1930's; a native of New Zealand, he returned there in 1937 to hold the first chair in Psychology; died in 1965): notes 1933 – 34.

Willard W. Hill (PhD Yale 1934; for many years chair of Anthropology at the University of New Mexico; known for his studies of peoples of the southwestern U.S., especially the Navajo; died in 1974): notes 1933 – 34.

Weston LaBarre (PhD Yale 1937; Professor emeritus of Anthropology at Duke University; noted for studies of psychology and religion, particularly the Peyote cult): notes 1933 – 34.

David Mandelbaum (PhD Yale 1936; taught briefly at the University of Minnesota and then for many years at the University of California at Berkeley; fieldwork among the Cree and in India; editor of *Selected Writings of Edward Sapir*, 1949; died in 1987): notes 1933 – 34.

Walter W. Taylor (transferred to Harvard for his PhD, which he received in 1943; primarily an archaeologist, often cited for his interest in the sociocultural implications of archaeological data; Professor emeritus at the University of Southern Illinois, Carbondale): notes 1935 – 36.

Lyda Averill Taylor (wife of Walter Taylor; died in 1960): notes 1935 – 36.

Anne M. Cooke, later Smith (PhD Yale 1940; she and Erminie Voegelin were the first women to receive anthropology PhD's from Yale; conducted ethnographic research on the Ute; taught at Franklin and Marshall College; now deceased): notes 1936 – 37.

Irving Rouse (PhD Yale 1938; a specialist in New World culture history, especially in the Caribbean and surrounding areas; Professor emeritus at Yale): notes 1936 – 37.

Mary Mikami Rouse (PhD from Yale in Sinology; wife of Irving Rouse): notes 1936 – 37.

Two other notetakers from the microfilm cannot be identified. One, who took notes in 1936 – 37 (the final year of the course), may be Erminie Voegelin; the other, who took notes in 1933 – 34, may be Willard Park.[20] Among other possibilities for the '33-'34 note-taker are Verne Ray, Walter Dyk, Pearl Beaglehole, or Dorothy Hill (wife of Willard). This set of notes is almost in complementary distribution with Willard Hill's.

In addition to the notes on microfilm, two other students in Sapir's course at Yale were kind enough to give me their notes:

Edgar Siskin (PhD Yale 1941; a rabbi, after early fieldwork in North America he moved to what was then Palestine; now head of the Jerusalem Center for Anthropological Studies): notes 1933 – 34; and

Beatrice Blyth Whiting (PhD Yale 1942; noted for her work in the cross-cultural study of socialization and education; Professor emerita of Educational Anthropology, School of Education, Harvard University): notes 1935 – 36.

Notes from earlier versions of the course, given in 1927 and 1928 at the University of Chicago, were obtained from Richard Preston via Regna Darnell. The Chicago notetakers were:

Stanley Newman (PhD Yale 1932; a graduate student who accompanied Sapir on the move to Yale, Newman's first major research was a grammar of Yokuts; though best known for his studies of North American linguistics, he also worked in educational psychology; taught for many years at the University of New Mexico; died in 1984): notes 1927; and

Frank M. Setzler (after graduate work at Chicago, he held a position as archaeologist and museum curator at the U.S. National Museum in

Washington; author of many works in North American archaeology; died in 1975): notes 1928.

Another source of material derives from the Rockefeller Seminar (1932 – 33). The student participants wrote up summaries of each session. I have drawn upon the summaries for the sessions led by Sapir during the second semester, sessions that evidently included lectures as well as discussions. The participants' summaries are on file in the Margaret Mead papers in the Library of Congress. Those whose notes concerned Sapir's sessions were: Theodore P. Chitambar (India); Walter Beck (Germany); Bingham Dai (China); Leo Ferrero (Italy/Geneva); Ali Kemal (Turkey); Henry Halvorsen (Norway); and Robert Marjolin (France).[21]

I have also drawn upon Sapir's own outline prospectus for *The Psychology of Culture*, sent to Harcourt in 1928.[22] Additional sources, used only where appropriate and necessary to flesh out an argument, are Sapir's correspondence, his published writings, the unpublished transcripts of his presentations at the Hanover conferences of the Social Science Research Council (1926 and 1930), and student notes from other courses and lectures given by Sapir. Besides the notes on Sapir's lectures to the Friday Night Club (1933; notes taken by David Mandelbaum) and the Medical Society (1935 – 36; notes taken by Weston LaBarre), which are included in the Yale microfilm, notes on several other courses Sapir gave at Chicago and Yale were generously lent to me by their notetakers: David Mandelbaum, Fred Eggan, and Edgar Siskin.

As a lecturer, Sapir had an inspiring, even electrifying effect on his audience. Describing what it was like to be a student in Sapir's class, David Mandelbaum wrote (1941: 132 – 34), "he was more than an inspired scholar, he was an inspiring person. Listening to him was a lucid adventure in the field of ideas; one came forth exhilarated, more than oneself... He could explain his explorations so clearly, in such resplendent phrases, that we felt ourselves, with him, heroes in the world of ideas. An eminent psychiatrist recently remarked that Sapir was an intoxicating man. That he was."[23] Ironically, however, the awe and excitement Sapir aroused in his students seems sometimes to have interfered with note-taking. As Walter Taylor remarked, "Sapir's command of English was itself quite hypnotic and ... resulted in my listening to him talk and not to what he was saying! And note-taking merely interfered with the flow of language and the intricacies of Sapir's thinking. In fact, if I remember correctly, I stopped taking notes altogether toward the end of the course – but I did not stop being fascinated and excited about the ideas he was presenting."[24] In a similar vein – and out of modesty – several notetakers I spoke or corresponded with expressed doubts about the usefulness of their own notes as compared with others'.

That Sapir's lecture style was complex, polished, and compelling is amply evident not only from students' recollections but also from the existing transcripts of his conference presentations to the Social Science Research Council (n.d. [1926], n.d. [1930]). It is easy to see how a notetaker might feel that his or her notes could not adequately represent the actual performance, and that essential ideas or statements had been left out. But with regard to the notes' value for reconstructing the gist of Sapir's arguments, the note-takers' doubts were quite unfounded. While any one set of notes is necessarily only a partial record, when several sets are compared the record becomes that much more complete. Each note-taker omits different things. Although the brilliance of Sapir's performance cannot be fully recaptured, the essentials of his argument usually can be. In fact, many interesting points emerged only as a result of the detective work of comparing and integrating the various sets of notes.

For these reasons the option of simply reproducing the notes themselves for publication, without synthesis, has never been seriously entertained. It is only through careful comparison that one can get a sense of an individual note-taker's omissions (of passages, wording, or whole lectures), of note-cards out of order (mistakes probably introduced in the microfilming process), of repetitions resulting from a note-taker's having copied another student's notes to supplement his or her own, and so on.

The editorial procedure, therefore, has been to compare, select among, and interweave the various sets of notes in order to reconstruct Sapir's text as closely as possible. Obviously, the result will differ from Sapir's written style, and it cannot display the vividness and wit for which his spoken style was so often lauded. But the contents of the notes overlap sufficiently with each other, while remaining sufficiently different from Sapir's published writings, to make it worthwhile to attempt some approximation of these lectures that influenced so many eminent anthropologists and linguists, and which Sapir himself envisioned as a book.

The task of reconstruction was complicated by the fact that the notes come from several versions of the course. There is no single Sapir oral "text" to be reconstructed — no single course of lectures; instead, there are several overlapping courses. Had there been more material from the final (1936—37) version, I might simply have reconstructed a text for that presumably most mature stage of his thinking. Indeed, I began this project with that intention. But the 1936—37 material was not adequate for reconstruction by itself, and it omitted or only hinted at many interesting topics for which notes existed from the earlier years.

The solution was to incorporate all the notes from the Yale period, while giving greater weight to those representing the latest version of the course. That is, where the versions differ, either in the order in which topics are introduced or (which is less often) in the content or implications of a discussion, the 1936—37 version takes priority. These Yale materials, both from the "Psychology of Culture" course and from the Rockefeller Seminar, are represented in their entirety,[25] interwoven for narrative presentation. Sapir's own 1928 outline is also incorporated almost entirely, because it comes to us as his own typescript, unmediated by notetakers; but because of its earlier date it bears less organizational weight in the reconstruction than do the later materials.

Other sources, including the notes from the Chicago versions of the same course, are drawn upon only when necessary to flesh out or clarify a passage. Although the Chicago notes — especially Newman's — are very interesting, they differ more substantially from the Yale versions than the latter differ among themselves. The course was much shorter at Chicago, and Sapir seems to have reworked it considerably when he moved to Yale. Only a few excerpts from the Newman and Setzler notes are included in the reconstructed text, therefore.

Once the content and organizational decisions were made, putting the material into narrative form required further editorial decisions. The notes vary in format: some are largely narrative (Cooke, Mandelbaum, Beaglehole, Irving Rouse, the unidentified notetaker of 1936—37); some are largely in outline form (Hill, Mary Mikami Rouse, Whiting, Siskin, the unidentified notetaker of 1933—34); others are in paragraphs of telegram-like prose (the Taylors, LaBarre). In reconstructing a text, where I had only to supply connectives, articles, auxiliary verbs, and the like in order to turn "telegram style" and outlines into narrative, I have done so without so indicating in the draft. Similarly, for smoothness of flow I have sometimes altered the syntactic structure of a sentence in the notes. But wherever I have had to supply a content word or a content-filled connecting passage, I have marked my own additions in brackets.

Since some of these bracketed additions are lengthy, I have supplied a number of footnotes that try to explain my rationale for inserting what I did.[26] It is not always possible, however, to identify a single source or articulate a specific reason for these insertions. Some of them derive from the implications of a notetaker's spatial organization of notes — such as placing one point below another, or placing a notation in the margin, or drawing connecting arrows. Other insertions I can only attribute to my own interpretation, after immersion in the material, of what Sapir meant.

Where notetakers' wording of a passage differs in ways that are not easily reconciled, an option I have often taken is to include both versions. Lecturers often repeat a statement in slightly different wording to emphasize a point; there is no reason to suppose Sapir did not do so. Still, the reconstructed text may sometimes be rather more repetitive than Sapir's actual lecture would have been. In this as in other respects the reconstruction differs from what Sapir might have wished to see in print. His written style was carefully polished, closely argued, and seldom redundant.

In sum, the editorial procedures and mode of presentation of the reconstructed "text" have had the aim of staying as accountable to the sources as possible while offering a synthesis that would be accessible to the reader. Although I cannot hope to have represented exactly the book Sapir would have published himself, I hope I have come somewhere close to his intentions, as those were represented in his course of lectures.

A Note on the Paperback Edition

This reconstruction of Sapir's work was originally prepared for inclusion in volume 3 of *The Collected Works of Edward Sapir* (CWES). It seemed appropriate, however — and consistent with Sapir's original intentions — also to publish a separate version of *The Psychology of Culture* that would make the work more widely accessible.

The CWES version of the text differs from the paperback version mainly in including a large number of annotations, codes, and explanatory footnotes whose purpose is to show how the editorial reconstruction was done. Each reconstructed passage is coded so that the reader can see which individual note-taker, or other source, was drawn upon, and in what order of importance. Differences between note-takers' renderings of a passage are indicated. Editorial insertions, where substantial, are explained. The reconstructed text is thereby made more accountable to its sources. Moreover, an interested reader can track the contribution of any particular note-taker to the whole.

Although these annotations are useful for scholarly purposes, they are potentially distracting for the general reader who is more interested in the flow of Sapir's argument. For that reason they have been omitted from the paperback edition.

Also included in the CWES edition are Sapir's own (1928) chapter outline, and three appendices, namely: (1) a reconstruction of classroom discussions in 1933 on the study of American culture — on smoking and piano-playing, as cultural patterns; (2) David Mandelbaum's notes on Sapir's lecture to the Friday Night Club, October 13, 1933; (3) Sapir's lists of suggested readings for the 1933–34 and 1935–36 versions of his course.

Judith T. Irvine

Notes

1. Edward Sapir to Alfred Harcourt, 27 June 1928.
2. Edward Sapir to David Mandelbaum, 15 October 1937.
3. Edward Sapir to Philip Selznick, 25 October 1938.
4. Jean Sapir to David Mandelbaum, 19 May 1939.
5. It is not clear whether any manuscript materials, such as lecture notes, ever existed. Sapir's students differ in their recollections of whether he brought papers with him to class. Judging from students' documentation, some of the lectures remained very similar from one year to the next — perhaps suggesting the use of notes — but other lectures did not.
6. Jean Sapir to David Mandelbaum, 19 May 1939.
7. Leslie Spier, Alfred I. Hallowell and Stanley S. Newman, eds. (1941) *Language, Culture and Personality: Essays in Memory of Edward Sapir.*
8. According to Irving Rouse (pers. comm.), Willard Park may also have played a central role in assembling notes from students still at Yale.
9. Zellig Harris to Philip Sapir, 20 July 1942.
10. At the Centenary Conference in Ottawa, Sapir's prospectus and the corpus of class notes were discussed in print for the first time (Preston 1986).
11. Thus Jean Sapir wrote to David Mandelbaum (30 January 1950) thanking him for giving a major place in *Selected Writings* to Sapir's contributions "in the culture and personality field, about which Edward thought so much but wrote so little. The very dates of what he did get into print tell the whole story."
12. I owe this comment to Allan H. Smith, a student in the 1935–36 Yale course.
13. See also Preston (1986).
14. For further information on the Impact seminar see Darnell (1990), chapter 17.
15. See Appendix 1 of the CWES edition for a reconstruction of the class discussions on smoking and piano-playing.
16. The idea seems to have been for the students to discover that it was impossible to devise any cultural inventory in advance of ethnographic investigation.
17. Sapir's criticisms of the discipline of economics, in the 1939 paper, tend to concern the methodological individualism according to which some economists posit a typical individual, an "economic man" and his behavior, in order to explain the workings of an economic system. They do not concern the study of economic systems as such.

18. I quote from my reconstructed text; see Chapter 10. The reconstruction here is on pretty firm ground.
19. Elizabeth Herzog to Louis Wirth, 19 July 1942.
20. I owe these suggestions to Irving Rouse.
21. Other participants in the Seminar included: Andras Angyal (Hungary), Wilhelm Gierlichs (Germany), Michiji Ishikawa (Japan), Jan Krzyzanowski (Poland), Niilo Maki (Finland), and Max Weinreich (Poland). For further information on the Seminar participants see Darnell (1990).
22. Sapir's 1928 outline is published in the CWES edition of *The Psychology of Culture* as a companion piece to the reconstructed text — a companion of special importance, since it is Sapir's own writing.
23. David Mandelbaum (1941), "Edward Sapir" (an obituary appearing in *Jewish Social Studies* 3: 131 – 40). See also the recollections of other former students of Sapir at the Ottawa centenary conference (Cowan, Foster, and Koerner, 1986).
24. W. W. Taylor to J. T. Irvine, 18 February 1987.
25. Except the classroom exercises on smoking and piano-playing, which may be found in Appendix 1 of the CWES edition of this work.
26. Most of these explanations may be found in the CWES edition of the text.

Part I

The Concept of Culture

Chapter One

The Term "Culture"

There are certain terms that have a peculiar property. Ostensibly they mark off specific concepts, concepts that lay claim to a rigorous objective validity. In practice, they label vague terrains of thought that shift or narrow or widen with the point of view of whoso[ever] makes use of them, embracing within their gamut of significance conceptions that not only do not harmonize but are in part contradictory. An analysis of such terms soon discloses the fact that underneath the clash of varying contents there is unifying feeling-tone. What makes it possible for so discordant an array of conceptions to answer to the same call is, indeed, precisely this relatively constant halo that surrounds them.[1]

[Suppose we ask ourselves, then,] what is "culture"? [I propose to show you that here is a term of the very type just mentioned: a label that seems to mean something particularly important, and yet,] when the question arises of just where to put the label, trouble begins,[2] for the uses of the term "culture" have varying connotations. We cannot take culture for a rigidly defined thing. [But perhaps there are nevertheless some common themes we might identify and thence arrive at our own idea of] the meaning of the concept of culture.

1. The Traditional English Use

There seem to be three reasonably distinct ways of defining [the term] "culture". First of all, consider its meaning in the phrase, "a man of culture". This is the traditional English use, a conventional idea of culture [referring to an] ideal of individual refinement [and implying] a normative ascription of value — a preconception that one type of behavior is superior to another, and that certain customs are best. [When we speak of "a man of culture" we mean a man whose conduct and qualities are those considered better and more valuable than those of other men.] There is a highly evaluative [connotation to the term, and an] emphasis on selectivity [among the various forms of] behavior [practiced] in a civilization,[3] [such that the selected behaviors seem to endow their practitioners with an aura of] unanalyzed excellence and nobility. [There is nothing specially English about the evaluative process, however.] The ascription of value to every type of behavior is a natural [impulse, so fundamental an expression of human psychology that we may reasonably expect to find some idea resembling this sense of the term "culture" among peoples otherwise widely different.]

"Culture", so defined, implies a standard pertaining to an individual or group. To be "a man of culture" involves participation in special social values clustering around tradition. [It is not the particular content of those traditions that is vital in distinguishing the cultured person from others — for all too] often the culture ([in this sense of the term]) of an advanced civilization is a [mere] rehash of traditional, staid subjects — [but the fact that they *are* traditional and valued.] Everyone who is cultured lives in a certain realm of specific feeling, [deriving not only from those attitudes and typical reactions traditionally prescribed for him, but also from] a feeling of security that comes to the person within the cultured circle. Because of this personal and group security, one's relation with the out-group becomes easy or supercilious. Aloofness of some kind is generally a *sine qua non* of [this] type of culture.[4] It is an idea of culture that depends largely on class, more often hereditary class [than class of any other kind], and it centers upon a literary tradition and a practical tradition, be it church, military, or business.

What is it that validates class stratification in any society? [Although this question is a difficult one, let us approach it by comparing a few examples. We might start by] examining the culture of the English country gentleman of the eighteenth century. [What characterizes] this cultured class? In 1750 it was necessary for the cultured gentleman to quote Horace. [It was quite unnecessary for him to engage in activities of an immediately practical kind;] the tendency, instead, was to deny that the exigencies of nature [had any bearing on one's behavior.] The elite of 1750 had freed themselves from the natural urgencies and hence could be casual and free from care. Thus sport developed in England as one of the earmarks of the gentleman, as was hunting. There were few occupations for him to [take up, but it was quite] definite [which ones would be suitable: they were limited to political and military activities, such as being a member of] Parliament or [an officer in the] navy, or [being a member of] the clergy — and it is rather peculiar [to England, perhaps,] that the gentry and clergy were so [closely] associated. [In sum,] this cultured class [is distinguished by] its economic security, wealth, and leisure, its education in the classics, its engagement in hunting and sport, and [its involvement] in public activities such as politics and the established church.

So, enjoying freedom from care (in a collective sense), living a gracious life, and preoccupied with conventional literary values, these English gentlemen held a common stock of cultural goods from [whose] extreme conventionality [they gained] a feeling of essential security. [That form of] collective anxiety which arises from a lack of participation in known cultural goods was relatively absent; instead, the common fund of cultural symbols enabled [this class to enjoy] a margin of dissent and a certain emotional freedom. ([In contrast,] there is so much collective anxiety in cultural groups in America that adventurousness is not permitted except in the form of humor. American society is anxiety-ridden because we have not defined a cultural group which has meanings in common, nor have we universally accepted [a set of] customs as a stereotyped ideal.)

One sense of "culture", then, is "cultivation". [The idea that some members of society are more cultivated than others,] and the ideal that certain customs are best, [can be found in civilizations exhibiting the widest differences in other respects.] Yet, the method of arriving at the cultured state is different, in different civilizations. Consider, for instance, the old Chinese gentleman of the mandarin class, who need not be wealthy but who had to pass stiff examinations on the philosophy of the Chinese poets, and who must himself be able to write poetry and paint exquisite characters. Literary ability was the great thing: passing examinations on the Chinese classics gave him a right to receive a good government post, and joined him with others who had done the same thing. A developed aesthetic attitude, and the gracious side of life, were emphasized. Thus the Chinese elite was different [from the English] in particular, but remarkably similar in kind, for although the principle of selection of this cultured group differed from that of the eighteenth-century English group in that the mandarin class was more democratically chosen, it was a selection nevertheless; and several [other] features were rather similar. Again graciousness characterized the class, and membership was dependent upon familiarity with the literary tradition. One [within the privileged circle] was very secure in the symbolic system of knowledge and in the special cultural tradition, and the cultural ideal was calmly accepted by elite and folk alike. There was very little strain between the cultural tradition and the folk mind.

The Athenian gentleman of scholarly tendency, with his interest in government, is another case in point. Here too is an economically secure class; [and in addition to] economic freedom, the criteria [for membership] again [emphasize acquaintance with] an enshrined literature. [This is part of the gentleman's] preoccupation with [materially] useless things − [the other side of the coin being] freedom of thought and [the opportunity for] bold speculations. [So if you start with the English gentleman,] compare the Chinese gentleman, next the Athenian gentleman, and go on to examine your gentlemen of all cultures, primitive or civilized, [you will find that] there will be something of a parallelism in their respective "cultures".

[At this point you may wish to object that it seems somewhat odd to speak of "gentlemen" in any but the higher civilizations. Let me remind you, however, that] we have no rigid definition of culture nor an absolute concept according to which we could say who is more or less cultured among a people. [And for the same reasons it is] difficult to determine which cultures are "higher" or "lower". A primitive people may have a much more complex and more highly developed system of kinship terminology, for example, than have we, or of seating prerogatives [at a feast. Nor could we depend on our own sense of what constitutes fine manners, for] the system of etiquette [also] differs among different peoples. [Even though some form of etiquette convention may characterize the elite in many different societies, we cannot say much in advance about its content: even] belching, sneezing, and so on [may have quite different evaluations. So let us not hesitate to examine the characteristics of elites even in cultural groups where application of the label "gentlemen" might seem, to some, quite surprising.]

In Orthodox Jewish society, culture [(in this first sense) pertains to] a traditional rabbinical group. Their special culture, [just as in the Chinese and English cases, involves a] literary tradition, consisting of the Old Testament scriptures, which are accepted literally as an inspired document, plus the body of oral tradition codified in about 200 A. D. Erudition in these texts and the scholastic tradition [is valued because of the] belief that everything important is contained therein, although there is some freedom of interpretation. This is a theocratic society, [then, although we might also consider it] democratic, [since membership in the rabbinical class] has little to do with birth or economic or military status − it depends only on learning. Manipulation of this vast mass of tradition, and application of it to practical [concerns] in everyday life, are the marks of membership in the cultured group. One becomes a member of this class not through family or economic status, but by acquiring [the appropriate] erudition. Although great social prestige attaches to the [rabbinical] group, membership in it is informal. It is a republic of religious letters, [based upon a] lineage of spirit [rather than a lineage of birth; and] a humble snobbery, with a feeling of personal responsibility to God's word, [characterizes the scholarly elite].

There are several similarities [between the rabbinical group and] other groups of cultured persons. First, the elite is a comparatively small group, looked up to without strain by the people at large; second, their culture is built around a literary tradition — the rabbinical group takes as their class symbol a literary document; third, the cultured group has freedom, in at least a psychological sense, from mundane economic care. The scholars' world was perhaps a substitute for the drab everyday struggle. They were excused from common [duties] when they wished, and could contribute their studies or meditation instead.

In primitive society, too, there are "cultured" groups accepted as such by the folk. In Northwest Coast society, for example (that is, among the Indians on the west coast of British Columbia), there are definite classes: chiefs, commoners, and slaves.[5] The elite are the nobles, who marry among themselves, and are the repository of the tribal lore, an oral tradition [comprised of] ancestral legends, impersonal myths, folklore, and songs. [So strong is these nobles'] connection with the glorious past that they speak of an ancestor [in the first person, as] "I" — as if they feel they are the dramatic impersonators of tradition. [Like our other examples, these nobles] too are removed from the necessity of earning a living and are highly respected by the people as a whole. [So although the Northwest Coast Indians are] a non-agricultural people, [subsisting by] hunting, fishing, and gathering, [even] here the cultured class has a special economic and social position, determined at least in part by family lineage. [The special valuation of literature as representing the stock of cultural goods has its parallel here as well, even though] there is no writing; for the noble has a special [crest symbolically] bearing [a load of] oral tradition — the ancestral legends connected with the nobles' names. The name is the emblem of a glorious past. But again there is a certain mobility [between classes], and no fast line between the noble class and the rest.[6] [So in several respects the nobles of the Northwest Coast] show similarities with [the other examples we have considered. Like those others,] they are a selected group, whose members are conscious of belonging, and [who are expected to display a certain] graciousness. A gracious attitude is shown in a tradition of liberality, about which there is much ado, [despite the fact that on the whole] this is a cruel and relentlessly snobbish society.

[Another example from primitive society is] the Navajo, although the elite [category] among the Navajo is less formally [defined] and less sharply segregated [from the rest of society than is the elite among] the Northwest Coast Indians, with their hierarchy and strong class distinction which depend on the doings of ancestors.[7] In Navajo [society] class distinction [based on birth] is not strong, so practicality [of achievement] is at a premium. The Navajo elite are the "chanters" (as the native term [describes them]) or medicine men, highly versed experts in ritual and the accompanying lore, songs, and so on. It is a greater honor [to be a chanter] than to be a chief, and once an individual is a chanter he is in the "in-group".

[The chanters' performances,] elaborate ritual chants accompanied by dramatic representations of origin legends, are used in curing disease by way of pleasing angry gods. The chanter must learn the legends, [along with all] details of the ceremony and prayers. The set of rituals involves a large number of sand paintings, which he manufactures, and an even larger number of different songs, which must be done absolutely without mistake. Yet, the chanters are sometimes employed for a deliberately faked illness: if a long time has passed with no one sick, someone makes believe he is sick so that the ceremony may be performed. Apparently, the rituals have a transcendental value [causing them to be performed even if it is only] in an effort to keep the knowledge of them alive. The rituals are not entirely for practical use, then; they are appreciated for their beauty, just as in the other cultures mentioned.

Because the Navajo rituals [require] exact knowledge [on the part of] the chanters, they involve a great deal of memory, [both verbal and] visual. It may take ten years to learn one chant.[8] [But the chanter's cumulative store of traditions transforms him into something much more than a mere repeater of memorized material, for] the knowledge of chants, legends, and rituals builds up into a theological and aesthetic doctrine. Thus the chanters are a group of professors of theology, the aristocrats of the Navajo, prestigious persons for whom the average Navajo has great respect. They are the repositories of the load of theological tradition; and this world of holiness is a closed world, as it is for the Orthodox Jews. For the Navajo, there are no more miracles, no more communications with the gods.

[So] the elite of all cultures are somehow alike in that they are all the keepers of the traditional lore, be it classics, folklore, or songs. That is, all [six] of these groups cluster their values around tradition, as laid down in literature, documents, or oral legend. All six, too, show a real desire for a transcendent ideal of life — a mystic insight, a feeling for something beyond the necessities of the day. The cultured man is one who participates in this ideal world of traditional values. This one notion of culture is not rare or accidental, then; it is something more profound and universal than restricted to certain classes of Western society. Probably every society possesses some sort of ideal tradition around which people's emotions cluster, and where people select, out of the possible behavior patterns of their group, certain ones that bring [prestige.][9]

[Now,] the elite [in all these cases are also alike in that] they are all more or less economically free and consequently leisured. They [have both the time and the freedom to] preserve and dramatize the glorious past, whence [comes] their esteem by the masses. But what is the universality of this phenomenon due to? What is it that universally causes peoples to support such a leisured class and respect it? [About this interesting problem I can only offer speculation; but perhaps] the explanation of [the support of] elites [lies in some form of] wish-fulfillment on the part of the masses. In a [process of] transference similar to the transfer of ambition from father to son, the [common people] transfer [their wishes onto] the elite; and it is because of this unconscious identification that the elite are so easily accepted. The dream life [of the masses] is embodied in the elite, to which they consequently pay homage. [We should not simply dismiss this psychological process as delusionary and self-defeating, for it surely represents] a desire to transcend our own stubborn humanity, that is present in all normal individuals.

This orthodox [concept of] culture is highly evaluative, [then, and it is even plausible to think of] culture [in this sense] as an evaluative attempt to shirk the problem of life, through an artificial security and feeling of well-[being]. The manifestation of [such] culture is [supposed to be] the arrival at human excellence; [yet in each case it turns out that human excellence] is to be arrived at through the culture of that particular group, [and we should look in vain for any logical reason to choose between the excellence of the Navajo chant and the excellence of quoting Horace.] There is really no difference, [in this moral realm,] between the value of a written and an unwritten literature.

[In light of the claim to universal superiority through the preservation of indispensable spiritual heirlooms,][10] perhaps the most extraordinary thing about the cultured ideal is its selection of the particular treasures of the past which it deems worthiest of worship. This selection, which might seem bizarre to a mere outsider, is generally justified by a number of reasons, sometimes endowed with a philosophic cast, but unsympathetic persons seem to incline to the view that these reasons are only rationalizations *ad hoc*, that the selection of treasures has proceeded chiefly according to the accidents of history.[11] [Were rationality the only guide] a case could be made for teaching Eskimo in the public schools instead of Greek or Latin; [but the languages of the classical world are not, for us, merely grammatical schemes for our intellectual exercise. Their importance rests primarily on their value as symbols of our tradition.] In the acceptance of social symbols one must not be too logical.

2. The German 'Kultur'

The foregoing has defined one conception of culture – the contrast between the cultured group and the folk. This idea of culture is the evaluational term referring to the activities of the elite. A second definition of culture is the German *kultur*, which even when used by German anthropologists seems always to have something mystical in its meaning. It somehow embraces the idea of the *geist* of a people, the underlying soul or spirit. The German philosophers' idea was that there were general and absolute values which transcended trivialities and could be said to be characteristic of a group. [If we wish to try to put this less mystically we might say that] *kultur* is a unified or integrated conception of culture, [emphasizing] its complex of ideas, [its sense of] the larger values of life, and its definition of the ideal (for example, the Greek ideal of calmness and the perfect, static image). Though wider [than the first conception of culture it is] still a selective or evaluating use of the term, as applied to larger groups. Thus *kultur* belongs to a whole people and includes [their notion of] those things that are fine and that differentiate the human race from the animal world – and, often, from humans [considered] more primitive. Certain societies have definite ideals, and anything contrary to the ideal, [they believe,] is not cultured but barbaric.

Distinguishing *kultur* from *natur*, Rickert makes the statement that primitive peoples have no culture.[12] The distinction seems to be based on the supposed self-consciousness of the spirit [among "civilized" peoples as opposed to the "primitives",] such as Hottentots, who do not have it. A good conception of this meaning can be obtained from Spengler's *Untergang des Abendlandes* ('*The Decline of the West*'). [Rickert's statement about primitive peoples must be rejected, however, for] there is no such thing as a state of nature, or a man without cultural conditioning. [If this conception of culture has any usefulness it will be found to be as suitably applied to the Hottentots as to ourselves.][13]

It is not easy to define the *geist* of a culture (or people, rather) — to estimate a whole civilization in terms of these archetype values. [Still, let us try some examples and, for each, consider its] culture from the standpoint of basic ideas. For instance, French culture might be characterized by the ideal of the golden mean: nothing in excess. There seems to be a pervading formality, [an emphasis on] clarity and closure in configurations and patterns that results in a standardization of spiritual values as well as of many other values. The French take forms very seriously; although they emphasize grace and ease they don't want things to go casually or informally, [and they have little interest in] spick-and-span American efficiency. The philosophy of standardization to an ideal [is a pervading theme in many areas of life, such as] the regularization of language [decreed by] the French Academy, the devotion to clear and lucid expression (*le mot juste*), and [the operation of] the French bureaucracy. [Notice, however, that this is not at all the same thing as] industrial standardization, [which is resisted in France,] especially if it [comes into] conflict with family traditions [of business management, as occurred] for instance in the linen trade and in bookbinding.

In French culture self-expression, [too, should display] taste, restraint, and discretion. There is a distrust of fundamental drives unless they are checked by discretion and convention. For [the French,] beauty [lies in] reason, not in some Faustian spirit of exhilaration in self-expression. So cooking and eating are arts, a sublimation of bodily needs — and the French think it is barbaric not to sublimate thus. The real French artist would never be lacking in good taste. There is no abundance of emotion and nothing which is not precise, clear, and measured, be it music or literature. Voltaire and Debussy caught the French spirit, where there can be profound thought but it is covered with a certain airiness, an exact casualness.[14] Wagner, [on the other hand,] was not accepted in France — he is too stirring, [too expressive of] revolt; and the French dislike Shakespeare because of the lack of emotional measure and [classical] form. Robinson Jeffers would be impossible in French literature. [Of course, not every French author perfectly represents the ideal.] Victor Hugo cannot be classic and chaste although he is impressionistic in technique.

[Another aspect of the French spirit] is their supreme indifference to other cultures or to what others think of them. [But perhaps what] this satisfaction with one's own culture [most represents is not something peculiar to the French but] what I would consider a criterion of the perfect development of a culture.[15] It is because they are so secure in their own values that [people] are uninterested in foreign influences. They live so well in their own culture that they are indifferent to [outsiders.]

This analysis of a people's *geist* could be done for other cultures too. In the culture (in the sense of *kultur*) of pre-war Russia, in the eighteenth and nineteenth centuries that is, [we see a spirit] very different [from the French.] Music and literature (for example Tchaikovsky, Dostoyevsky, and so on) were characterized by an overflowing of emotions, openness, and outspokenness — [even a] brutal emotional completeness. In a spiritual sense, it [was] easy for the Russian to overthrow any embodiment of the spirit of institutionalism; his real loyalties [were] elsewhere,[16] preoccupied with [an elemental humanity and an intense] spirituality. [It is a spirituality] with a double face — as close to Satan as to God. Perhaps the quintessential [work of this culture's literature is the] play *The Lower Depths*, with its faith in human nature at its worst. In the pages of Tolstoy, Dostoyevsky, Turgenev, Gorky, and Chekhov personality runs riot in its morbid moments of play with crime, in its depressions and apathies, in its generous enthusiasms and idealisms.[17] Russian writers seem to be [immersed] in raw human experience; [despite a certain French influence] they never surrendered to that [French] artificiality. Their music, too, has a stark quality, a more elemental, simpler emotional character. [All this is before the War and the Revolution of 1917, however.] It would be interesting to know if Russia has really changed emotionally, or whether this [cultural spirit we have just described] is not still the case.

What about the *kultur* of the Germans [themselves? This presents] a curious paradox. On the one hand there is a remarkable exactness and thoroughness, an extraordinary care and skill [with detail]; and with it, on the other hand, is a rather wishy-washy romanticism [exalting] the shadowy and the mystical. Really, [the Germans are] a very romantic people. Goethe [is a supreme example of] mystic romanticism with an occasional return to supreme brusqueness.[18]

The contemporary American, however, feels the overpowering necessity to utilize all possibilities or capabilities. If having a fortune is important to the French, making one is important to Americans; it is imperative to make as much money as possible. American culture is autobiographical in character, and its ideal is adventurous, with a certain tumultuousness of spirit always present that does not regard tradition too highly. [In a way there is] something of the mystic in the typical American, with his belief in answers, [especially as deriving from] education. [It is for this reason that he insists on] exactness, and on making evaluations in finite terms, with definite figures. Only in American culture could the phrase "fifty-fifty" have evolved, [for only here do we find such] willingness to measure intangibles; expression must be quantitative. There is a pretense of extreme objectivity, of objective control of situations which cannot be [tangibly measured]. To make of society a machine, understand it, and then control it — this is the American idea. Yet, the individual's life reveals a relative fragmentariness and contradiction.

[For our final examples, let us compare] the classical Hindu culture of India [with the culture of Americans and of the Chinese]. The Hindu ideal is curiously individualized, [but in a manner very different from the American or Chinese.] The sense of time differs greatly, [amounting to a virtual] disregard of it, [from an American point of view. This disregard contrasts strikingly with the] obsessive time-consciousness of all Western cultures, where time is [constantly being] measured and there is a keen awareness of its passing, [along with a strong] interest in history. The Chinese, too, have a vivid time sense and interest in past history, with a keen understanding of the value of dating cultural events, although theirs is not the instrumental sense of time that ours is. Hindu culture, however, does not care for dates. There is little emphasis on time location in Indian history or literature, for the Indians do not assign value to [such specifics] but feel that fundamental, perduring values are timeless and placeless. Unconcerned with an immediate world of cause and effect, [they attend instead to] a precise modality of principle: the world is made up of eternal principles which are found through suffering — suffering that is sometimes mistaken for pleasure. [Hindu culture is] a strange mixture of immersion in the immediate world of sense and at the same time a complete withdrawal from it. Since the sensory life [entails] suffering, thoughts of future happiness [concern not this life but] new reincarnations, [leading, ultimately, to] absorption in God. This sort of life is a paradise of the introvert. While the Chinese cultural ideal [devotes more attention to] the commonplace, and to awareness of the present moment, the Indian seems apathetic and unaware. To him the present, and the world of sense, are a vain illusion.

[Our second conception of culture,] *kultur*, [thus defines culture in terms of a particular people's] preferred qualities and evaluations, and their loyalty to [certain central themes and] master ideas. [With our first conception it shares an emphasis on] a group's unconscious selection of values as intrinsically more [important,] more characteristic, more significant in a spiritual sense than the rest.[19] But just how valuable is this definition? The whole terrain through which we [have just been] struggling is a hotbed of subjectivism, a splendid field for the airing of national conceits. [Yet] there need be no special quarrel with this conception of a national genius so long as it is not worshiped as an irreducible psychological fetish.[20] The anthropologist does not like this generalized view of culture, however. Ethnologists fight shy of broad generalizations and hastily defined concepts. They are therefore rather timid about operating with national spirits and geniuses. The chauvinism of national apologists, which sees in the spirits of their own peoples peculiar excellences utterly denied to less blessed denizens of the globe, largely justifies this timidity of the scientific students of civilization. Yet here, as so often, the precise knowledge of the scientist lags somewhat behind the more naive but more powerful insights of nonprofessional experience and impression. To deny to the genius of a people an ultimate psychological significance and to refer it to the specific historical development of that people is not, after all is said and done, to analyze it out of existence.[21] [It must, instead, even help to illuminate such ethnological problems of historical development as the selective "borrowing" of cultural traits, because it calls attention to the fact that] while elements are borrowed, they are being snugly fitted into a definite framework of values. ([Actually, there is some] danger in using the term "borrowing" for [this process, since the] traits are fitted into a pattern of values quite other [than that in which they originated].)

[In short,] the above two ideas of culture [share] an emphasis on [selectivity and] a sense of value. [Shorn of their more mystical and chauvinistic elements they are not unworthy of the anthropologist's attention. From the idea of *kultur* we may accept culture as signifying the characteristic mold of a civilization, while from the [first] conception of culture, that of a traditional type of individual refinement, we will borrow the notion of ideal form.[22] [From both we may adopt the emphasis on value.]

3. The Anthropological Idea of Culture

[While the first two definitions of "culture" are based, in their different ways, on concepts of selection and value, the anthropological idea of culture — supposedly, at least — is not. It concerns, instead,] all those aspects of human life that are socially inherited, as contrasted with those types of behavior that are biologically inherited and with those that [represent] individual reactions lacking historical continuity. [Perhaps the best-known anthropological definition is the one proposed by Tylor in 1871:] "Culture or civilization, taken in its wide ethnographic sense, is that complex whole which includes knowledge, belief, art, morals, law, custom, and any other capabilities and habits acquired by man as a member of society".[23]

[But although Tylor's definition is often cited,] it is illusory to think culture is clearly defined. [Only a slight alteration of Tylor's statement yields the following:] The evaluation or reaction of an individual to (1) patterns of behavior, (2) habits of mind, (3) traditions, (4) customs − which he learns as a member of society − is his culture. [But is it not the case that as soon as we have emphasized the individual's evaluations or reactions, our definition] equals personality [as much as, or rather than, culture? [Yet, we shall need to make a distinction between the two, since] this [individual] reaction may, in certain cases, influence the content of the culture. [Even] Rémy de Gourmont, who spent most of his time in an attic, [had his effect on the culture of his time.]

[Suppose, then, that we try to evade this difficulty by emphasizing the social and excluding that which is individual. But were we to] confuse the social with the cultural [we would only be exchanging one problem for another, for] "society" and "social" are ill-defined (and much fine literature [in the social sciences] is vitiated by this). "Social" as a term points in two directions: there is "social" in the sense of "acting in concert", or gregariousness; and there is "social" in the sense of falling back on the sanctions of the group − on the understanding of the group. [The first sense is not particularly helpful for an understanding of culture, since] the interactions of individuals as such may extend to enormous numbers of people and yet not be cultural. [It is true that] in normal situations culture is carried by collectivities − hence the ready confusion. But collective yawning, for example, may not be cultural. [In the company of others] an individual may react as an individual, or he may duplicate reflexes, [and neither of these, presumably, is quite what we thought we meant by "culture".]

[Indeed,] not enough attention has been paid to individual activity which is collective [but not cultural, perhaps because of the aforementioned confusion about the term "social". And perhaps we have also failed to recognize the extent to which an individual's behavior is culturally formed even when he lives alone. Even] the anchorite must rationalize [his actions] or connect himself in some way to a body of culture.

[The second meaning of "social", that is as involving] consensus and, [especially,] sanction, is better [suited to our purpose, since it draws our attention beyond behavioral acts.] Behavior, [no matter how collective, at most] illustrates culture but is not culture. It must always have meaning in terms of the opinion of a collectivity, ideal or actual, before it is culture. There is something of social evaluation in anything that is cultural; [certainly] it enters into every definition of culture I have made. Culture is not mere behavior, but *significant* behavior. A particular word in a given language is a good example: thus [the expression] "damn you", uttered ([let us suppose]) as a release of tension, is just as much at the mercy of society as any cultural trait [ordinarily found on an ethnologist's list]. Being the data of culture it cannot be merely haphazard syllables, for the choice of sounds is fixed by an unconscious trend of opinion. [No matter that our example is humble. Even if a conversation is utterly banal,] just to talk is of the highest cultural relevance, while running out of a theater in a fire scare may not be cultural at all. [It may be more important, certainly, but] importance has really nothing to do with a concept of culture. Sanction, [instead,] is significant, for the meanings of behavior rest on historical sanction and selection.

[We might even say that] the test of [whether a type of behavior is part of] culture is the ability to historicize it. [That is to say,] some types of behavior [are historically sanctioned in that they] have been selected as meaningful. As an illustration, we need not hesitate to call gesture a culturalized field, because it is subject to history and change. Neapolitan gestures, for example, are culturally determined [and locally specific; they are] not Latin or Mediterranean or racial. To be sure, behavior looked at as a purely physiological function — and all behavior is physiological [at some level, where it might be analyzed as involving] reflexes, relief activities, [and the like] — looked at as such it is not culture. [But to look at gesture only as physiology would be an error. As with so many other behaviors, in gesture] there are two fields of activity, the physiological and the psychological. [Developmentally][24] speaking, I think that culture is built on individual impulse, but we know very little about how individual behavior is actually [given psychological significance in the child's experience;] nor do we know very much about how social transmission [actually works.] In the world of significant activity — culture — we are never in the position to spot the psychobiological genesis of any one trait.

[Nevertheless, it is still perfectly possible to say that] gesture is cultural in that it is historically determined, changing from time to time. It is full of meaning, not on the level of the individual's reflex, but within a framework of conventions in a particular society. [Doubtless, the very fact of its conventionality contributes to gesture's social function, for a distinctive system of gestures helps to establish what we might call a] "community of motion". [The gestures] have a significance for society in that they give it a comfortable feeling of social relationship. We must not try to be too functional in our explanation [of such behaviors, however, for their] functionality is not all-important. Gestures cannot and should not always be interpreted from the original significance of a particular action. [It is more fruitful to consider their role as social symbols. But] even where there is no specific symbolism to apply to a particular [form of behavior or] social phenomenon, we should not press functionalism too far, or try to be too logical about the meanings of culture. The habit of being too functional is a paranoid mechanism, basically! The paranoid type of personality is logical to the nth degree, always looking for ad hoc explanations of everything, [and overestimating] the value of self-reference.[25] We cannot inquire too closely into the real relevance of cultural traits.

[Now, where might gesture fit into Tylor's definition of culture? Should it be listed as another item in the contents of culture, in addition to] knowledge, beliefs and morals, law and custom, and habits? [Does it not partake of all of these in some way?] The actual content of culture is enormous, [and we shall not capture its essence by itemizing. It seems to me, therefore, that] Tylor's definition of culture has outlived its usefulness. It merely helps to orient you, and does not go very deep. Tylor's definition is inadequate because it makes too much of those particular types of behavior that seem most important in a political sense, and of highly evaluative cultural elements such as religion. He is not wrong, but he prevents us from thinking clearly through to such cultural facts as gesture, whistling, speech, attitudes, or other elements which are unnoticed yet definitely cultural.

[Let me suggest a somewhat different] definition, then.[26] Any form of behavior, either explicit or implicit, overt or covert, which cannot be directly explained as physiologically necessary but can be interpreted in terms of the totality of meanings of a specific group, and which can be shown to be the result of a strictly historical process, is likely to be cultural in essence. "Historical process" means the conveyance of forms of behavior through social processes, either by suggestion or by direct instruction to the young.

This last [part of the definition] is needed because of the possibility that innate biological motor patterns [contribute or point] toward the symbolism [maintained by a group without actually being part of that symbolism.] History and consensus are the important [things, therefore]; [even] habit may be [cultural] if it is historically determined. Culture demands a historical continuum, implicitly or explicitly conveyed to the young by their elders, [though in general] unconscious assimilation plays a greater part than conscious learning, and implicit forms are more significant than explicit ones.

"Culture" in this third sense shares with our [second, Germanic] conception an emphasis on the spiritual possessions of the group rather than of the individual.[27] With our [first] conception it shares an emphasis on [historical tradition. And as modified, our definition shares with other conceptions a notion of form and selective valuation: there is a selection of behavioral forms that are meaningful to a group, that it recognizes as belonging to its world of significant acts. So perhaps there is more that is useful in these two first conceptions of "culture", and more that they have in common with our technical definition, than anthropologists are accustomed to admit. We shall have to look at our "true" definition of culture more closely.][28]

Notes

1. The preceding paragraph is quoted from Sapir (1924a), "Culture, genuine and spurious". Sapir's discussion of the term "culture" in this chapter clearly resembles a portion of his argument in the 1924 paper. I have drawn on a few passages from the 1924 text, therefore, in reconstructing this opening lecture of his course.
2. The preceding passage, from "when the question arises ...", is quoted from Sapir (1924a).
3. Here Sapir uses the term "civilization" rather than "culture" in the anthropological sense. See Sapir (1924a): "To avoid confusion with other uses of the word 'culture', uses which emphatically involve the application of a scale of values, I shall, where necessary, use 'civilization' in lieu of the ethnologist's 'culture'".
4. The preceding sentence is quoted from Sapir (1924a).
5. In 1933 Sapir seems to have called this a "caste system".
6. This statement, from one notetaker, seems somewhat to contradict other notetakers' reference to a "caste system" and noble endogamy. Sapir's 1915 paper, "The social organization of the West Coast tribes", indicates that intermarriage between nobles and other ranks was impossible in theory and rare in practice. If the note is accurate,

perhaps in this passage Sapir was alluding to those "cases in which men of lower rank have by dint of reckless potlatching gained the ascendancy over their betters, gradually displacing them in one or more of the privileges belonging to their rank" (Sapir 1915c).

7. W. Taylor's notes have a fuller statement: "But Northwest Coast Indians have a hierarchy and strong class distinction which depends on the doings of ancestors who established the family, the value lies in the right to sing, play, lay claim to ancestors and legends which is real and authoritative".

8. The notetaker adds: "(Visual memory keen as it is not obscured by substitutive symbol, memory, reading)".

9. The notetaker actually has "kudos".

10. The wording of the bracketed passage derives in part from Sapir (1924a).

11. The preceding passage, from "perhaps the most extraordinary thing...", is quoted from Sapir (1924a).

12. See H. Rickert (1899), *Kulturwissenschaft und Naturwissenschaft: Ein Vortrag*. This work was published in several editions. The fifth edition (1925) is probably the one most relevant to Sapir's lectures.

13. See Sapir (1924a): "A genuine culture is perfectly conceivable in any type or stage of civilization, in the mold of any national genius...".

14. The notetaker (W. Taylor) also has: "'French measure' in music is not really emotional but rather a limited, classical ecstasy (ballets). Exponents are Voltaire and Debussy".

15. See Sapir (1924a) for a similar notion, there termed cultural "genuineness".

16. The preceding passage, from "In a spiritual sense...", is quoted from Sapir (1924a).

17. The preceding sentence is quoted from Sapir (1924a).

18. In 1933 Sapir did not discuss German culture but instead mentioned the Pueblo Indians. Beaglehole's notes have: "The *geist* of a Pueblo people is quite another pattern — subdued sobriety, introversion, restraint, being the characteristics".

19. The preceding passage, from "as intrinsically...", is quoted from Sapir (1924a).

20. The preceding two sentences are each quoted from Sapir (1924a), where they occur in reverse order.

21. The preceding passage, from "Ethnologists fight shy...", is quoted from Sapir (1924a).

22. The preceding sentence is drawn from Sapir (1924a).

23. Although none of the notetakers quote Tylor's definition exactly, Mandelbaum gives a close paraphrase.

24. The notetaker source actually has "genetically", a word Sapir almost always uses in the developmental sense rather than in the biological sense. To avoid confusion for the modern reader I substitute "developmental" for "genetic" here and in many other passages.

25. A notetaker (W. Hill) adds: "To wit, Brown, & Mead, and Malinowski".

26. The notetaker has "Sapir's definition". Notice that Sapir shifts his definition away from the noun "culture" to the adjective "cultural" — from whole to attribute.

27. The preceding sentence is drawn from Sapir (1924a).

28. The wording of the bracketed passage comes partly from Sapir (1924a) and partly from notetaker passages already drawn upon.

Chapter Two

The Concept of Culture in the Social Sciences

1. [Methodological Problems in Anthropology]

[In the preceding lecture we began to consider] the anthropological sense of the term "culture" as embracing all those human reactions which are socially inherited, as contrasted with those lacking historical continuity or those based on biological heredity. [You will recall, however, that our] attempt at a closer definition [than Tylor's] led to [a glimpse of some] unexpected difficulties. [Let us examine some of these more carefully now.]

[Whatever else culture may be, the anthropologist insists that it is] a continued thing, [transcending the vagaries of] individual experience. For example, although the Minnesota accent [of a Mid-Western schoolboy from a rural background may] change naturally to an Oxford accent [if he should happen to cross the ocean for his university education, this change is merely a personal matter that has little to do with the gradual shifts of pronunciation that take place over the years in the language as a whole.][1] The English language goes on, with a continuity [of its own that does not depend on the particular events of an individual's personal history. Nor is] the biological sequence [by which our schoolboy passes from] birth to adulthood and [eventual] death [a cultural matter, even though cultural transmission involves the sequence of generations. We must therefore distinguish among at least] three fields of behavior or kinds of continuities: those continuities that are biologically necessary; those that are accidental or contingent; and those that are socialized. [It is the last that represents the] cultural continuities, for culture is in no regard accidental, [insofar as this characterizes that which is] individual and personal, nor does culture concern itself with that which is biologically necessary.

[What are the phenomena] belonging to culture, [then? Perhaps it seems obvious enough that] language, religion, monetary systems, polit-

ical [patterns such as] methods of voting, social organization, and literature all are in the continuity of culture. [But what do these grand rubrics
represent, in terms of behaviors the anthropologist might observe?] Is
culture an objectively [observable phenomenon] after all? It really is
extremely difficult and perhaps impossible to [identify what is cultural
with complete] objectivity. There seem to be certain things we [as indi-
viduals] cannot change, [and we call these] culture. [But, as I suggested
in last week's lecture, some activities] may [appear to partake of that
grand cultural] pageant just because they exercise many adherents. So
although my definition has emphasized the historical and social as apart
from the individual, it may be [that this distinction is largely] metaphorical
and that [the "social" in the sense we intend it here] cannot be isolated.

[We shall return to the problems inherent in the term "social" at some
length later on. For the moment, let us try another approach to the
problem of identifying what is cultural. We agree that we have excluded
the accidental from the realm of the cultural, as well as physiological
necessities as such. Yet, all behavior has a physiological dimension; so
how are we to isolate that which is cultural in it? Though we referred to
biological "necessity" earlier on, it is doubtful that we can solve our
dilemma by supposing that all necessity is biological. Even physiological]
necessity [is subject to cultural evaluation, entering the cultural dimension
as it] takes on a psychological character. The *locus* of this necessity is
important then; yet it can be [physiological or psychological,] individual
or general.

[Thus we have run into two kinds of difficulties. First,] no human
behavior can be discovered which is intrinsically or purely cultural.
[Second,] we have not been patient [in our thinking about] the actual
locus of culture, [for as soon as we] knew it was not in the individual [as
such we] jumped to the social uncritically. [And as if two difficulties were
not enough, there is yet a third, for we anthropologists have somehow
to infer the] continuity [between behavioral events, the continuity we are
going to attribute to socialization], if we are then to say we have culture.
That is, we claim that wherever this *pattern* [of behavior occurs we have
identified something cultural, since we know that the pattern's actual
manifestations may differ in irrelevant ways. But how do we get from
the behavior to the pattern?] It is illusory to think culture is clearly
defined. Its content is shaky, not fixed; the confines of the realm are not
given but have to be created.

[In practice,] "culture" is an ad hoc term for [those aspects of] experience that do in a sense transcend the individual and [to which we can

attribute] an historical and geographical continuity. The anthropologist slices culture out of behavior, [as it were −] that is, we abstract culture from behavior and label it with symbols − [not] objectively, [for objectivity in this realm] is not possible, but rather ad hoc, based on our experience of elements [of behavior] which are referred to by certain terms [in our language. We] discover a thing because, in a sense, we already know it. [Our "slicing" is done] through words, [and because we did not personally invent these terms we suppose that they] carve with objectivity.

Just as it is illusory to think culture is clearly defined, then, so it may be an illusion [to assume that the anthropologist can objectively describe and study] the totality of culture. [I suspect that what I am saying here will not please those anthropologists who like to think of themselves as properly] brought up in the austerities of a well-defined science of man.[2] The ideal of most anthropologists is [to proceed] like the chemist − to describe and classify objectively, not to value; personal factors should be absent. [Difficulties in realizing this ideal arise immediately in ethnographic work, however.] You start out describing socialized patterns, and end up by being biographical. You don't know whether you are interested in what you are going to abstract from observation or in behavior patterns.[3] [And so on. If we are honest with ourselves we must recognize that no matter how careful and scientific one tries to be, the student of culture faces some serious methodological dilemmas.]

The difficulty lies in the process of abstraction [necessary to anthropological analysis, and to the fact that] the behavioral data [you can observe] are connected with less easily observed material, [without which they cannot be understood. It is usually supposed that], ideally, [the less directly observed material, and its connection with behavior, are to be discovered through immersion in the culture]; but the idea of immersion in a culture seems contradictory to that certain aloofness necessary to analyze the patterns of behavior. The more you immerse yourself in a culture, the less ability you have to analyze the culture according to the anthropological ideal, for just as the Indian is not aware of the patterns of his culture, [so will you be unaware of them the more you become like him]. The more you identify yourself with the people, the less you are being an anthropologist, [in that sense].

There is a conflict of interest, therefore, between the anthropologist's ideal of participating in the culture, and his technique of analyzing the culture. To participate would be to psychologize; and in participating, things become too vital for analysis. As an anthropologist you want to tear every fact of the culture out of its individualized context. It is more important for the anthropologist to abstract patterns than to give a wealth of biographical detail, [and yet in so abstracting you must inevitably tend to lose sight of the actual experience of living individuals, to whom such patterns have real value in their interrelationships with other human beings.] In a way, the psychologist is much closer to the Indian than is the anthropologist, because he does not tear the [personal] context up.

The task of the anthropologist, then, cannot be [simply] to gather all observations available. The ideal of describing what one sees and hears is not enough. [If the purpose of anthropological work] is the analysis of how culture is made up of a system of patterns, and to understand the relationship of these, then what the anthropologist studies is not behavior at all, in the ordinary sense. His interest is not in the facts of behavior but in its typical patterns — not in the individual's experience, but in the patterns of culture. The anthropologist is not interested in behavior, but in the field of behavioral forms. From the study of [behavioral] forms, anthropologists build up the patterns which [(they believe)] are transferred, socialized, and carried by the individual. But not everything we observe has anything to do with pattern.

For example, could we base the study of religion on watching people in church? [Not everything we could observe in their behavior concerns religion, and not everything concerning their religion would be directly observable in their behavior.] Dorsey's study of the Arapaho Sun Dance[4] is a mélange of all kinds of observations some of which have nothing to do with the Sun Dance. [If you propose instead to study the Sun Dance as a form of religious expression,] you must reassert your data in the terms of the pattern you have analyzed out. [The usual] advice is to note everything, but you don't — you note those things that have to do with the pattern you are observing. Actually, if we made a complete encyclopedic survey of all the facts connected with religion, we would find that very few of them are directly related to the anthropologist's pattern of religion. The anthropologist's pattern is based on words — "religion", "God", etc. — and on the assumption that certain details can be omitted because they are like our own culture.

You need to understand the general behavior of the Indian, then, in order to make your abstractions [from observation, and even to select which observations you will take note of]. There is no such thing as "religious behavior" — there is [only] behavior. [When you propose to study religious behavior,] you dissociate this segment from the whole of which it is part. Hence, although a study of cultural behavior is worthwhile, it is not a true study of culture patterns. Indeed, the concept of "cultural behavior" is a hybrid, even contradictory concept — a conflict in terms. There can be no such thing, for behavior cannot be equated with patterns. [Behavior is a property of the individual, and while] we need more study of the individual in primitive society, it is not in itself the equivalent of a purely cultural survey. [Moreover, behavior is physiological and for this reason too its observation is not the same thing as a study of culture, for] culture is not concerned with the physiological necessities as such. Culture deals with them, but it is not concerned with them. They are implied, even taken for granted, but they are not relevant for cultural analysis. You observe behavior, from which you abstract culture.

[In proposing] criteria for a concept of culture, [then, we shall clearly have to leave] Tylor's definition [rather far behind. And we shall not have resolved all problems as to the locus of culture, or its relationship to individual psychology. Anthropology's frequent assumption] that culture is a superorganic, impersonal whole is a useful enough methodological principle to begin with but becomes a serious deterrent in the long run to the more dynamic study of the genesis and development of cultural patterns because these cannot be realistically disconnected from those organizations of ideas and feelings which constitute the individual.[5] Where do socialized patterns leave off and the primordial human being begin? We do not know yet where culture ends, [or how it affects and alters the persons who live with its help and in its influence.] The rate of modifiability of human beings in regard to [cultural] patterns is an interesting question. But it is useless to the versatility of the culture which is carried by them.

2. [Distinguishing Between the "Cultural" and the "Social"]

In contrast to psychology, which has no difficulty in discovering its subject matter — for its interest is in the [individual] human being, his behavior and reactions — anthropology has difficulty on the theoretical side in defining its subject matter. [First of all] it does not know whether to ascribe certain aspects of behavior to culture or to biology. Gesture, for example, [has seemed ambiguous in this way, as we saw in the preceding lecture. Moreover, anthropology has] difficulty distinguishing between social phenomena and individual phenomena. These difficulties [are inherent in] the anthropological sense of [the term] "culture". [The contrast with psychology does not arise because anthropology concentrates on the totality of behavior or on some portion thereof that] is deemed "social", but because "culture" is abstracted from the totality of human behavior.

Although we [often] mix the term "cultural" with the term "social", they are really quite distinct, [even in a way] antithetical. [Actually, there are some dangerous] pitfalls in the use of the term "social", [for if we inquire as to] its meaning we must realize that there are various concepts or implications of the word, and we must decide which is [to be invoked. To start with, there is the basic distinction between] "social" as arising from the [sheer] coming together of people — physical togetherness — and social togetherness. The biologist [might be concerned with] the physical togetherness of people, and the psychologist [might be interested in] the reinforcing of individual actions [that such propinquity facilitates;] but the sociologist [emphasizes] the organized behavior and ordered life of a group, [whose members need not always be physically in the same place, their] togetherness being of a different kind.[6]

[Not only are these two senses of the term "social" different, but they may even come into conflict with one another. The first definition,] "social" in the sense of gregariousness, or of human beings herded together in a band, [might, for example, be used to describe] a gang in the city, or a crowd at the theater. "Social" in the second [sense would describe] a social dictum, for instance that you should not say the word "Swell!" because it is [supposed to be] bad [grammar]; yet, on the other hand, [in a way the dictum itself is] antisocial because it is referred to [a disapproved] group among whom "Swell!" is the [normal] usage. [What is "social" here — the actual] use [by a group, or the] idea[tional] construct ([condemning that use?])

[For an example of a similar] difficulty, [suppose we return to our theater crowd; and suppose someone in the crowd yells,] "Fire!" [From one standpoint this act is] social behavior, because "fire" is a socially understood word; yet [its utterance] lets loose antisocial behavior (in our first sense of the term) [when the theater crowd panics.] The socially understood word [("socially" in the second sense)] dissolves the group of the other social type. So the first sense of the term is not enough [for the social scientist's needs, while the second sense] is essentially [a matter of] ideas.

Thus there is a fallacy in ascribing the term "social behavior" to a collectivity as such. Group behavior in this literal sense [may be comfortingly observable and] real, but it is irrelevant [to our purpose.] "Social behavior", so called, is both individual and collective; [it is anchored in the realm of ideas and understandings. Now, where does culture enter in? It has more to do with the second sense of "social" than the first. But if we really want to answer this question we shall have to make even finer distinctions among the meanings of the term "social".[7] [There seem to be five possibilities:]

(1) Social in the sense of "gregarious," [or the simple assemblage of people in an aggregate. It is difficult to find examples of this simple situation — a group gathered together at one place, say our theater crowd waiting for the curtain [to rise, considered] from a purely biological [viewpoint] as an ecological group, apart from the reasons for being there. The example cited earlier, of this theater crowd in a panic when someone yells, "Fire!", [might better illustrate the point.]

(2) Social in the "gregarious" sense plus cultural connotation. Our theater [aggregate] is now an opera crowd, expecting [a performance and to some degree knowledgeable about] the history of music. That is, we have people plus motives plus patterns, and so on.

(3) Social in the sense of an individual [whose thoughts or actions have a] group implication: for example the actions of a small child whose play activities [are oriented so as to] avoid parental taboos.

(4) Social in the sense of an individual [whose activities have] cultural connotations, including ethical evaluations. President Roosevelt is alone in his study but he is writing a speech, or preparing a bill, with reforms of cultural import. Or, as another example, Chauncey Johnny John thinking what he will say at the Green Corn Festival the night before the third day.[8]

(5) Social with reference only to *organization*,[9] for example political or geographical organization. We need an adjective other than "social" for this last type; perhaps it should properly be called "societal". If we say "social" with reference to organization, and mean "societal" organization, it is a good term [for what is studied in a] Science of Society.[10]

[In these examples we have distinguished individual activities from collective activities, and we have seen that cultural connotations can attach to either kind, although they need not.] Another way to distinguish among the many uses of the term "social" is to compare the various disciplines [that employ it, but with different connotations. Thus we might consider:][11]

(1) The ethical usage ([as in the expressions] "social sympathy", "social integration", "unselfish social work"). Ethical considerations may come under any of several [of the senses of "social" mentioned above,] since ethics involves the content [of one's actions] as opposed to considering the pattern;

(2) The biological usage (i. e. "gregarious", like ants and bees;

(3) The sociological usage (concerning structure and organization);

(4) The anthropological usage (concerning the peculiar nexus of a culture, which is historically conditioned — speech, tabus, beliefs, arts, and so on);

(5) The psychological usage (concerning individual evaluation and criticism).

[In short, it is highly misleading simply to equate the terms "cultural" and "social", or to assume that one has accounted for what culture is by referring to "social behavior" without further qualification.] "Cultural" and "social" tend to be associated together, but they are really distinct.

3. [Distinguishing Between Culture and Behavioral Phenomena]

[One of the greatest pitfalls in the term "social" is that its ambiguities may allow social scientists to persuade themselves that they are objectively observing physical behavior, when in fact they are not.] The social scientist is perpetually talking of ideas, and is bound by ideas, although [he often believes] that physical phenomena are what he means. There is a notional conflict between "culture" and behavior deemed "social": it is the conflict between cultural phenomena and natural or physical phenomena, [and it is masked by the ambiguities in the term "social".

Let us consider another example of these ambiguities, this time drawn from] religion. Going to church is social in the [collective sense, because there are a] lot of people there. [It is also social] in the [consensual sense, because the people] participate in communal ideas, "sin" for example. Yet most people do not pay [a great deal of] attention to the ceremony. Suppose, for instance, a girl [in the assembly is present but] does not pay attention; yet she is part of the "social" [occasion. She is] classified as participating from the mere fact that she goes with her father and does not voice her thoughts, which may differ greatly from the attitudes of the various [other] individuals who are there. If we call this mélange of ideas "religious", [or so identify her participation,] we make her a victim of [our own] idea [of what religion is.] We are not [taking an objective,] behavioristic [approach — nor could we, in the study of religion, for] "religion" is not actually a naturally visible or a physical entity. It is, rather, a collectivity of thought. Mere numbers arc not necessary [for "religious" behavior,] so that the concept of "social" in sense (1) is invalidated; yet we are again wrong [if we go too far in the opposite direction and] think that the collectivity was not the necessity at all but that the idea was the thing.

In the social sciences we are always torn between two poles: the interest in individual behavior, and the interest in cultural patterning and social understanding. [The realm of social science is] therefore hard to define — its object of study is confusing. [In much the same way] the delimitation of culture itself is difficult — unlike the objective delimitation of [subject matter in] the natural sciences. [In the social sciences] uncertainty generally prevails as to whether a given study belongs to the field of "culture" or to the field of actual behavior, whereas in the natural sciences everybody knows exactly what is being referred to [(what the object of study is)]. The psychologists concerned only with behavior are pretty near [that certainty] too, [although their object of study] always relapses into [merely] a more complex physiology. But in the social sciences we are always talking about two things: what people are actually doing in reference to social situations and, on the other hand, [our concern] with the social pattern, at the ethnological [level.] Either point of view would be justifiable, [but not their confusion.] Much "social science" is a half-hearted study of certain modes of behavior that have been tacitly (and often unavowedly) selected on cultural, not behavioristic, lines.

If you were a strictly [objective] social scientist you would never use the word "religion", for that presupposes certain categories [into which your observations are to fall. But it is not possible to avoid making use of any categories in observing social situations and activities.] Any set of activities is pre-judged in advance by the culture of the observer. [As a social scientist you may wish to use the term "religion" because you are trying to get at some sort of] universal meaning — [whatever it is that is responsible for] the diffusion of Christianity, [for instance. But you should not confuse this with a behaviorist psychology.] Religion from the point of view of psychology is quite a useless concept, since the psychologist is told in advance what religion is and that bothers [any true behaviorist.] Religion is not a thing that is [physiologically or] emotionally there, but a historically determined series of patterns interacting in a certain situation and [in a certain] series. [It is a cultural concept, and] a simple application of cultural concepts in a psychological investigation is naive.

The only way out is to say that the patterns are never [directly present] in action. Religion never "occurs" — it is never performed. All you can study is the behavior of certain individuals in particular situations that already have a cultural label. The [observer][12] should never start with patterns but with the individual, [from whose perspective] in any case the actualization of a pattern is never more than marginal.[13] No two people participating in a service have the same motives, the same feelings, or the same reasons [for being there.] Each individual is differently "religious", and you cannot accurately talk about a generalized "religious [person]". In the actual religious situation, moreover, [as we said before, not all the behavior that occurs is relevant to religion; some of it is merely] head-scratching. [In fact] you have the whole of human conduct flowing in, [and what you select to observe] depends on what you want to look at. Thus this situation that we called religious is more of a fiction than we thought it was. It's all in the terminology — it is merely the use of terminology that makes patterns. [This is as true for the native as for the ethnologist, incidentally, so as a social scientist you can also turn it to your advantage.] There is nothing that helps us find out so much about behavior as terms and language.

The conflict of cultural phenomena with natural or physical phenomena [also arises with regard to so-called "religious objects", or "fetishes".] Objects are not religion; fetishism has no place in the idea of culture, for it is [merely] the misplacement of memory by outworn tokens. For example, a ceremonial dancing shirt belongs to [the realms of] religion, decorative arts, technology (the history of clothing) — and to none of the three. If it is culture, it does not completely belong to any one [classification; for] culture is an idea, but a shirt is a piece of material. [If you want to call it] a piece of "material culture" [you must bear in mind that] although the material articles give us the means of [deducing some aspects of] the culture, one cannot hang on to them alone, [and treat] the shirt as a deposit of behavior. [If you wanted to understand its connection with religion you need not necessarily have collected the shirt itself at all. Instead,] you should have found out the relevance of the shirt, [the meaning for its users and the psychological background that caused people to make it in this way.][14] To get its import one must analyze it out of existence.

[The tendency on the part of some anthropologists to fetishize the fetish, as it were, that is to overemphasize the importance of objects just as a neurotic might overvalue the hair of the beloved,[15] is only the most extreme example of the misplaced identification of the cultural with the physical which we have also discussed with respect to the "objective" study of behavior. The point I want to make here is that] the patterns [of culture] as given by ethnologists [in their analyses] are not real things — they are merely the normal methods of interpreting behavior.[16] The cultural mode of studying behavior is a highly abstractionist view that is not really interested in behavior at all. You can't ever see culture; you see people behaving, and you interpret [their behavior] in abstracted terms, by gathering data on [what you consider to be] typical forms of behavior, [as if the behavior were] a pattern exemplified. Then you form theories as to how the patterns operate. The ethnologist is never a simon pure [behavioral observer, since] anthropology's interest is in the pattern, par excellence.

The distinction between the study of culture patterns and the study of actual detailed behavior is absolutely fundamental to the point of view presented here. The first represents a configurative viewpoint and [consists in] the study of a series of abstracted forms or patterns, while the second concerns behavior — "social" behavior [in some sense, perhaps, but] actual behavior [nonetheless, and as distinguishable from the abstracted forms as is the province of] the behaviorist from that of the historian.

4. Criteria for Culture

[Our discussion has focused on a number of methodological and conceptual difficulties relating to the anthropological notion of culture and having considerable importance for the position of anthropology in the social sciences. But so far we have perhaps said less about] what culture is [than about] what it is not. [If we are to be able to consider] social science from the cultural angle, [how shall we recognize cultural phenomena? The preceding discussion has suggested various criteria, which may now be examined more closely.]

4.1. [Culture depends upon criteria of value.]

The cultural, in behavior, is the valued rather than the nonvalued. [Value criteria apply both to the people whose culture we study and to our own methods of analysis.] No matter how objective we try to be, we unconsciously apply criteria of value to our data, and make certain value judgements in the selection of the behavior patterns to be studied. [And so do the people we study. For this reason] all cultural concepts are relative, depending on the peculiar ideology and historical background of particular cultures.

4.2. [Culture is nonbiological.]

The cultural is also nonbiological — [not only in the sense that] it is not hereditary, but also in the sense that it is dependent upon equivalences of phenomena which can be biologically or physically described but whose locus of equivalence is not to be found in biological explanation so far as that can at present go. [That is, although behavior has a physical dimension, cultural patterns] are not physically definable; they are only definable through [a principle of] substitutions. Culture [represents] an arbitrary theory of equivalences, where one set of physical facts can be translated into another (its symbolic equivalent), as spoken words can be translated into written ones. There is no limit to this fictitious world of symbolic equivalences, but rather, [ever] new combinations [matching] the infinite variety of experience. The locus of the pattern is not in biology or physics, so the culturalist is never interested in the biological or physical world [as such]. Even [our patterns of] adjustment to primary biological needs are plastered over with secondary cultural meanings. And we have learned to get away from those partly biological experiences which were responsible for our knowledge in the first place. [Arithmetic,] for example, [may have arisen from] counting the fingers on the hand, yet the concept of "ten" can be projected even though [a particular] individual has only seven fingers.

[Despite an anthropological consensus that culture depends upon social tradition rather than biological inheritance, the difficulty of distinguishing the pattern from the expression of the pattern means that] the anthropologist does not always know whether to ascribe certain aspects of behavior to culture or biology. Because culture is not concerned with physiological necessity as such, the total pattern called culture must not be implicit in the fact that the object of study is an organism. Falling down the stairs is not cultural ([even if the stairs themselves are a product of cultural activity]). Walking, eating, and mating are not culture, as regards their physiological functionality, although these biological factors are governed by culture in that the methods of preparing food, of taking a mate, and so on are governed by habits [and customs that are] socially [acquired and sanctioned]. Another good example of this [problem] is gesture; [as we saw earlier,] we need not hesitate to call "gesture" a culturalized field, because, [among other things,] it is subject to history and change. However, [we must be cautious about inferring that something is cultural rather than biological just because it has changed.] The rate of modifiability [of a pattern is not in itself a simple matter or a clearcut way to distinguish the biological, the individual, and the cultural, for] the rate of modifiability varies from pattern to pattern, from society to society, and from individual to individual.

4.3. [Culture has a social reference.]

The cultural is also often distinguished as being societal,[17] i. e. going on in relation to other members of the group; it involves the recognition of other people more clearly than we ordinarily do. But it would be difficult to find any biological fact of human behavior that does not involve interorganic connectedness — that is, there is no biological experience which is not ultimately societal — so this is not a [sufficient] defining characteristic. [We have to exclude the biological first.]

[We have already discussed] the difficulty of distinguishing between social phenomena and individual phenomena, and [the difference] between the "social" and the "cultural" — [but it is probably useful to emphasize once again that the activities which are culturally patterned, or have cultural relevance, need not be collective.] Antisocial or unsocial persons may produce cultural [forms] or social assets, [as for instance when an artist's work, produced in isolation,] integrates social ideas that have been lying around. From the [observational][18] point of view [this activity] is not "social", but in a cultural sense it is "social" and may be the best type of object of study for the social scientist. [Similarly,] a hermit is antisocial in one way, yet through census-[taking, use of] money, taxes, and so on, [even in his rationalization of self-isolation,] he is a part [of a larger community.] He may be an unwilling or unwitting [part, but he is in a sense] a member of society and [a participant in] culture. You can escape the "social" [in the sense of social gatherings,] but you cannot escape culture.

For the anthropologist, [therefore, what is important in behavior is not whether people perform it in a group situation but] the pattern of their behavior, those phenomena for which a social tradition is respon-

sible. A pattern is an assemblage of significant things, with a terminological key.

[Presumably, then,] when you limit yourself to pattern awareness, this
is anthropology. But an individual's awareness of the patterns of experience is conditioned by his individual history and experience, [and this
is as true of ourselves as it is of anyone else we study.] Is [it not
conceivable, therefore, that] our conception of "society" itself is a cultural
construct? As a matter of fact, all our concepts are mere patterns of our
culture, and the term "society" [is no exception. It] is a cultural construct
which is employed by individuals who stand in significant relations to
each other in order to help them in the interpretation of certain aspects
of their behavior.[19]

4.4. [Culture is made up of patterns.]

Strictly [speaking, then,] the anthropologist is concerned with the location
of patterns in the cultural order, [including] their origins, history, diffus-
ability, etc. When the cultural is distinguished as not hereditary, this
anthropological dictum of course makes reference to the patterns of
culture as such, though they all have hereditary determinants in the
organs and predispositions [through which they are manifested]. Any
patterns of behavior that are conceived of as having perduring reference
to a group and are not carried by the biological mechanism of heredity
give us the matrix out of which we can abstract the things called "cultural
patterns". The anthropologist is trained to follow the patterns rather
than the social entities that carry the patterns, although the historical
[transmission] of patterning means that perfected patterns of behavior
are conveniently located in social groups.

[The process of discovering a pattern is not the same as its historical
genesis or its ontogeny, however.] A good example of cultural pattern
[illustrating this difference] is the English language, [although any language might serve just as well, since] language is the most massively
unconscious pattern in all cultures. For the child, words are fraught with
emotion, backed by expression; they have a definite value, [in the sense
of an] emotional color. [For children] language is not definable in its own
terms, without emotion. For the adult, words are symbols. By gradually
unloading emotional values from a word we acquire a rubber-stamp
attitude toward it. [From this standpoint the strong emotional attachment
to one's language which can characterize] ethnocentrism, in the adult, is

a kind of childhood nostalgia, a longing for a [remembered] feeling of security within the close little group.

For the linguist, [interested in] the form of the language, the process of discovering linguistic patterns and the location of patterns of speech differs from the psychological discovery of speech [— the discovery of the psychological significance of a particular utterance in a particular situation]. In language, [there is actually an inverse relationship between complexity of form and complexity of contextual implication, for it is the] limitation of form to a minimum that [allows it to bear] a maximum of implication. [The linguist derives] an analysis of complex patterns [only by abstracting away] from the concrete actions [of speech. Thus English is a hierarchy of simple patterns abstracted from concrete situations which grow in complexity. Patterns are abstracted from an event; they are not a record of an event. The event [itself, the actual] situation, is the meeting of many patterns, [not only the one you select for attention in your process of analysis.] To understand an actual situation you are building pattern on pattern and the further down you dig, the more useless your patterns are in understanding the real situation, [the "meaning" of the event to the people actually involved in it.] When one says a word, one is angry, tired, and so on as well as manifesting a [linguistic] pattern. So although one could describe the behavior in cultural terms, the linguistic psychologist [must also realize that] the actual fact of behavior [is not governed only by them.] Only the psychiatrist can tell you [about the rest of] what is actually there.

The anthropologist's "culture", then, is the hierarchy of abstracted patterns and their complex interrelationships. We draw these abstractions from the behavior of individuals in social settings, by agreeing on certain fictions such as social organization, religion, and so on, which we employ as hitching posts for certain behavior patterns.[20] The cultural [aspect] is the core of a behavior pattern when all the individual factors and differences have been taken away. A single occurrence or phenomenon may be the result of an unlimited number of culture patterns — that is, it may split up into complicated participations having no [obvious] link — and in taking true stock of this occurrence, to place [an action such as a glancing] look in the totality of the [individual's] behavior and his relation with others, all these [patterns] should be considered; but generally in ethnology this cannot be done and should not be [undertaken.]

[Now, if] culture cannot be seen in the abstract, but is given in the forms of behavior, the sum of which make culture, then the locus of these [cultural] patterns — where they reside — [is problematic:] you cannot actually locate a pattern in time or space. We shall take language as our example.[21] Language is a very peculiar,[22] even paradoxical, thing because, on the face of it, it is one of the most patterned, one of the most culturalized, of habits, yet that one, above all others, which is supposed capable of articulating our inmost feelings. The very idea of going to the dictionary in order to find out what we ought to say is a paradox. What we "ought" to say is how we spontaneously react, and how can a dictionary – a storehouse of prepared meanings – tell us how we are spontaneously reacting? Everyone senses the paradoxical about the situation, and of course the more of an individualist he is, the more he proclaims the fetish of "preservation of his personality", the less patience he has with the dictionary. The more conformist he is, the more he thinks that people should, by whatever ethical warrant you like, be what society wishes them to be, the more apt he is to consult the dictionary. Language, then, suggests both individual reality and culture; [so it would be absurd to say that language is located in the dictionary. The dictionary is merely an object, a thing that symbolizes language with respect to a certain value situation – in which the patterns of language intersect with the patterning of authority.][23] The dictionary is an example of the cultifying of a certain type of [linguistic] behavior; it takes a normative point of view, ascribing value [to certain linguistic acts. That is, the dictionary, as a concrete object, is not language, but merely an expression of the patterning of authority with respect to linguistic behavior.]

For the anthropologist, culture is a conception, not a reality. And it is not a closed field; there are always new patterns [intersecting whichever one we happen to have focused attention upon. Consider, for instance, the expression,] "thank you", [spoken at the end of a] dinner [party. Analysis of the patterns in which this expression takes part would not be limited to those represented in a dictionary of English, but would include the system of] sounds, the characteristic order of sounds, and the grammar; [the relation of "thank you" to other] symbols of politeness, [at dinners or elsewhere]; the [placement of these symbols in relation to] the dinner's symbolism of courses, their preparation, [and their sequence;] the type of meeting [the dinner party represents, as compared with other types of social gathering; and so forth]. Thus the realm of culture is always widening.

[In sum,] culture is not behavior; it cannot be seen. It is, rather, an abstraction of concepts gained from experience. Since the realm of "culture" so set forth is no naturally established division of [the phenomena occurring in the] world, it is useless to look for thoroughly efficient causes within this cultural universe. The causal point of view is helpful, of course, in finding fairly uniform [historical] sequences [in different civilizations], but it is impossible to speak of cosmic causes in the study of culture. Nothing in nature except culture itself is able to facilitate the definition of culture.

5. Difficulties of the Social Sciences

[The anthropologist's difficulties in defining the concept of culture, and in distinguishing the cultural from the social and biological, are representative of] the difficulties of the social sciences in general — [difficulties they encounter] because the concept of culture is necessary to them — as compared with psychology and the natural sciences. Why is social science such a difficult thing? The difficulties inhere in the attempt to understand behavior from the standpoint of social patterning. [They arise, as we have already begun to see, in part from problems of abstraction, and in part from] the essentially arbitrary differentia of the "social" in the realm of behavior. Attempts to fit a science of culture, concerning relations of human beings, into a tight scheme as in the biological and other sciences [run into trouble because] we do not have the neat, tight universe with certain basic postulations and clearly definable problems as they have in, say, physics. [Physicists] know what particular corner of the universe they are dealing with; [the culturalist does not. Instead,] the culturalist, trying to abstract those qualities of total human behavior which are perduring, cannot be absolutely sure of the limits or bounds of what he is dealing with. Because culture is a self-enlarging field, the culturalist is dealing with an expanding and contracting world.

[Some of the] difficulties of the social sciences, then, as compared with the physical, are intrinsic [to their subject matter. These include:]

(1) The extreme complexity and multiplicity of all behavioral phenomena, whether viewed from the social or the cultural [standpoint]. There are no single motivations; [instead,] we have to deal with multiple determinations of our phenomena. This is not true of the physical world, [and it is therefore not unreasonable] for physicists to be so interested in defining [an all-encompassing] pattern.

(2) The essential uniqueness of all cultural phenomena.[24] ([In comparison,] see Rickert's [discussion] on the limits of natural science.)[25] The physicist deals with a conceptual universe, not with the real world of

experience. He has little interest in the particular events, while the social scientist does deal with specific occurrences in the real world — with facts that are unique. The hurt done to our understanding of these phenomena in abstracting from their particularities is not, it seems, altogether analogous to the necessary simplification of experience in the natural sciences. We cannot have the hundred-percent exactness of the physical sciences, for we are never far removed from the accidents of history. [Instead of a conceptual universe,] we try to deal with the specific, viewed through a conceptual [lens.] The difference between the [subject matters of the] physicist and the historian or social scientist is the difference between all possible [phenomena] and all actual phenomena.

(3) [The facts that we deal with in the social sciences are also facts that require, for their interpretation,] the concept of "value". Social science has trouble because it has to attempt to make abstractions from unique phenomena, [selected for the purpose because they] are personally meaningful to the scientist and to science. For example, technology has great prestige now, [so it stands out to the social scientist as an important dimension of cultural achievement; yet it may not be the most important achievement of some other society, whose accomplishments may therefore be overlooked.] Every time you abstract from the cultural [setting toward a] general [statement] you sacrifice something.

[Our difficulty arises, however, not only when we try to make generalizations, but at that earlier point — the construction of comparisons — upon which the generalizations are based.] Owing to our interest in patterning, as well as to our study of particular cultures, a comparison can never be made except in an abstractionist sense. In consequence, all classifications in the cultural domain are inexact, [and they are necessarily relative.] Classifications such as religion, social organization, and so on [do not have precise counterparts] in the primitive mind. Informants do not see the validity of our convenient conventions for classifying their culture.

[Other] difficulties of the social sciences are extrinsic, [deriving from qualities of the observer and from the present inadequacies of pertinent data and explanatory tools]:

(1) Difficulties of observation. What behavior is to be observed, so that the cultural [pattern] can be abstracted from it? [For instance, one may observe someone making] involuntary sounds; these are behavior, but they are not [relevant to] cultural patterns. Now, since it is physically impossible to see everything, [we have to make our] observations with reference to [some] criteria, and the investigator [can rarely escape] the

preconceptions that are due to one's original conditioning and cultural bias. [Thus some] difficulties of observation are due to the investigator's unconscious projection of his own cultural patterns, with all attendant meanings. This is a psychiatric tendency, rooted in egocentrism and the tendency to read oneself into one's environment, for one [naturally takes] more interest in what pertains to oneself; so observations are distorted, tending to be colored by the observer's own ego and by what is to his own interest or advantage. When, for example, Mr Smith overhears "Mr Seers is a damn fool" as "Mr Smith is a damn fool", [he illustrates] the difficulties of observation that are due to the fact that we have an interest in seeing things differently.

[Projection comes from the simultaneous existence of] two tendencies in oneself: insecurity and doubt about one's own ability, yet [at the same time] a mad hope that one is able [after all. The result is] a tendency to read another society from one's own experience, in the light of its projection of one's favorite meanings onto society. Knowledge and reasoning [are simply] more readily applied to things with which the observer's culture makes him more or less familiar. The sheer difficulty of making observations [by any more objective procedure makes this process of projection all the more likely to occur].

(2) The difficulties of historical reconstruction and interpretation. [Our information concerning] social phenomena comes to us not all at one time but at different historical levels, as memories, documents, opinions, [and so on,] evidence that has to be sifted, for it is notoriously fallacious. [Besides the possibility that some of this "evidence" may have to be discarded altogether,] the historical reconstruction of cultural data involves a process of interpolation, of drawing connections; in historical reconstruction you are imagining nexuses and connecting them. [In this process] we are always dealing with interpretations, because it is hard to know what to do with our materials [otherwise]. Interpretation is difficult, however, because its criteria are unevaluated. Interpolation makes for a risky reconstruction, because of the subjectivity of the interpretations [necessary for it.][26]

(3) The chronic paucity of data at one's disposal, and those data not all of equal value. [One reason interpolation becomes necessary is the scarcity] of materials in both ethnology and history. Here anthropology has a special difficulty, [as compared with the other social sciences.] Our data are unequivalent; the materials are in fragmentary condition, and in unequal assemblages, [so that what material we have] is not all equally [useful or important. To try to infer pattern from a] paucity of facts [is

obviously risky, since] one [new] fact may overthrow the whole pattern. Many important generalizations [that have been made have been] based on very little material, by a [sort of] pyramiding of implications; but although far-reaching conclusions can be made in this way, they are not entirely satisfactory. [27]

(4) Uncertainty with regard to the interpretation of objective social data. Inadequacies in the data and in [our] objective judgement of them can be partly corrected by statistical methods, but these sometimes lead to a spurious accuracy. Because [we feel] we must be accurate, we limit ourselves to [considering] those phenomena which are capable of finite formulation and accuracy; and so the whole is colored by over-accuracy and thus overemphasis on certain phenomena, others being relegated to the background. Exact statistics on inexact subjects are misleading. If you do not have a correct pattern in mind, the results are of no use. Statistics are a way of manipulating figures; they are not a methodology, for you only get out of statistics what you put in. They can tell you a lot about the occurrences of a pattern without telling [you anything about] the meaning of the pattern. [Just as] a hammer is not architecture — it is a tool — [so statistics must not be expected to construct meanings on their own accord].

(5) The extreme uncertainty pervading the field of psychology, which would be such a great explanatory tool for social science. If we had a firm psychology which gave us some sort of views of general personality, we should see a much clearer [path] in the social sciences. At present psychology is only theory, and in its extreme uncertainty and insufficiency it fails us. It is difficult for psychology to treat the individual as a member of society, so it tries to handle problems [pertaining to] the isolated individual. [But between the individual and society] there is no such chasm.

[Lacking a sufficient contribution from the field of psychology itself, the various social sciences have resorted to psychological pictures of their own, since] every fragmentary science of man, such as economics or political science or aesthetics or linguistics, needs at least a minimum set of assumptions about the nature of man in order to house the particular propositions and records of events which belong to its selected domain. [28] [Without a solid set of generalizations about actual human beings, we describe their] equivalents, seeking to explain [human] behavior [in terms of the supposed psychological characteristics of] the "economic man", "the religious man", or "the golf-playing man". These are convenient fictions, [but they are only fictions and ought to be recognized as such.

There is no "economic man";] there are, rather, certain individuals performing these roles.

[In the construction of such fictional psychologies] the theology of economics or aesthetics or of any other ordered science of man weighs just as heavily on us, whether we know it or not, as the outmoded theologies of gods and their worshippers. Not for one single moment can we allow ourselves to forget the experienced unity of the individual.[29] The "common man" is a fiction, [and so is his relevance to cultural patterns; actually,] the more you try to understand individuals the more what you ruled out as irrelevant to the pattern becomes important. The work of the pure ethnologist is the study of patterns; [in our attempt to explain them,] the great danger is that we become quasi-psychologists.

[Now in lamenting the lack of a psychology truly worthy of the name, I do not wish to suggest that the study of culture can be reduced to individual psychology.] Cultural levels of discourse are not strictly congruous with psychological ones, [any more than with biological levels.] The psychological problem [of the locus of culture] is still there, but it is a fallacy to localize it in the individual mind. Indeed, it is a psychological fallacy to localize behavior in the individual alone, for behavior patterns always involve more than one [person. If we want to understand individual] psychology [from the pattern point of view we have to] enlarge the individual, [so to speak,] to meet the [others with whom he is in] contact. [Similarly, to understand the psychological dimension of culture patterns one must] prune the social toward the coalescence [of interacting] individuals [for whom behavior has meaning.][30] The actual locus of culture is to be found not in the whole nor in the individual.

[Incidentally, the problem of the locus of culture does not trouble an anthropologist like] Radcliffe-Brown who takes a functionalist approach, for the functionalist believes that the key to the understanding of behavior lies only in the study of the relations of patterns. But the patterns which the functionalist deals with are in themselves abstractions; [it is an error to confuse them with] the behavior of individuals. There is no philosophical justification for a study of behavior in reference to abstractions [which must depend on aprioristic conceptions. From this standpoint] Radcliffe-Brown is a conceptualist; and all strictly conceptual, [or aprioristic,] definitions of culture are fallacious.

[I do not think we can do without psychology in the study of culture, but it needs to be a social psychology, and of a special kind.] The psychology of the group cannot be fruitfully discussed except on the basis of a profounder understanding of the way in which different sorts of personalities enter into significant relations with each other and on the basis of a more complete knowledge of the importance to be attached to directly purposive, as contrasted with symbolic, motives in human inter-action.[31] A really fruitful social psychology [does not select patterns beforehand, on the basis of some preconception or conscious articulation of their purpose. Instead, it] throws all patterns into a common pool and discusses meaning — [their symbolism, and their significance for the individuals interacting by means of them] — and picks illustrations from the pool. In that sense the study of culture is more ramified and diverse [than the functionalist envisions.]

Now, the more you study meanings, the more you come back to individual meanings. [Ideally, the psychoanalyst should be able to help us understand what these might be about. But meanings are attached to behavioral forms, and] the psychoanalyst is in no position to tell us what is behind the *forms* of behavior. In reference to individual meanings, then, we are driven to study culture.[32]

[In short, being a social scientist is not an easy task.] Those who study socialized behavior [face some] obvious and unanswerable criticism which they must be hard-boiled enough to resist. [Rather than giving in to quasi-psychologizing or to misleading statistical exercises, they must keep their sights firmly focused on the need to] study the essential nature of human interrelations in evaluated situations, and the meanings — for the individual of course — of the patterns which culture recognizes. The field of understanding of sociological human behavior is difficult, and we must resist the objective of refinement of technique. We cannot use the refined methods of statistics because we don't know what to do with them. But we cannot wait until our data are so carefully sifted as to be all a hundred percent suitable [for statistical applications. Perfect objectivity would doubtless be a good thing, but we can't have it; and] if we can't have a good thing we'll have [to make do with] a bad one.

Since even natural science is only *ad hoc* and subject to change, anthropology should not be worried about whether it is an "exact" science; it is a discipline *sui generis*. We are interested in the meanings for the individual of the patterns which culture recognizes, and this is a bastard field.

Notes

1. See the discussion of "drift" in Sapir's *Language* (1921).
2. The preceding sentence derives from Sapir (1939a).
3. It is unclear why the notetaker contrasts "what you are going to abstract from observation" with "behavior patterns". Perhaps the contrast here should really be between *observation* and *pattern*, to be more consistent with the rest of the argument.
4. See Dorsey (1903).
5. The preceding sentence, starting with "that culture is a superorganic ...", comes from Sapir (1932a).
6. For a somewhat similar discussion see Sapir's (1932b) encyclopedia article on "Group", with its argument that "the difficulty of deciding whether the group or the individual is to be looked upon as the primary concept in a general theory of society is enhanced by fatal ambiguities in the meaning of the term 'group'." The article goes on to make a "distinction between physical proximity on the one hand and the adoption of a symbolic role on the other. Between the two extremes comes a large class of group forms in which the emphasis is on definite, realistic purpose rather than on symbolism. the three major classes of groups are therefore those physically defined, those defined by specific purposes and those symbolically defined."
7. The five-fold distinction made here occurs only in the 1933 notes. I find it to be not fully consistent with the 1935 and 1936 discussions, where Sapir seems to identify culture more clearly with his second sense of the term "social" (as involving social sanction and a social frame of reference; see the "criteria for culture" section in later pages).
8. The reference may be to a ceremony among certain Iroquoian peoples.
9. I.e., without implying awareness of that organization or ideas about it, on the part of the people so organized.
10. I.e., sociology.
11. The explanation of these rubrics is somewhat obscure. It is unlikely that Sapir meant to exclude the ethical, the sociological, and the psychological from his concept of culture or from the discipline of anthropology. What is more likely is the suggestion that each discipline has used the term "social" with a special emphasis.
12. The notetaker actually has "behaviorist". I have altered the text because Sapir's usage of the terms "behavior" and "behaviorist" seems to conform only in part to the usage a modern reader would identify with the behaviorist psychology of Watson and Skinner. Sapir's term "behaviorist" shares with the psychologists' an emphasis on what is empirically observable, but Sapir does not necessarily share their physiological explanation for it.
13. That is to say, the individual acts from personal motives, not in order to actualize a pattern.
14. The bracketed material comes from an analogous example in Setzler's notes: "Distinction between culture and actual behavior. A set of pueblo pots studied, if [one wants to] understand historical significance of these pots one must study similar wares from [the surrounding] neighborhood and thereby arrive at a sequence of culture. This method [of study] explains method used by Zuni to make these pots [i. e., it distinguishes their method from that of other pueblo peoples]. On the other [hand] one might study

the psychological behavior of maker, and understand the background which caused the man to work in this way."

15. This passage is based on a concluding note in B. Whiting's notes: "Fetishism — hair of beloved. Anthrop. emphasis. mistake."

16. The notetaker adds: "The psychologists may have to blow up these patterns because of symbolism."

17. It is not clear whether the word "societal" in the 1936 notes (drawn upon here) reflects the precise definition Sapir had given this term in 1933.

18. The notetaker text actually has "behavioristic". See note 12, this chapter, on this term.

19. The preceding passage, from "the term 'society'", comes from Sapir (1932a).

20. The notetaker adds here: "Objectivism at mercy of words. Must abstract core."

21. This sentence, and the subsequent passage down to "Language, then, suggests both individual reality and culture", are quoted from Sapir (n.d. [1930]).

22. The text — a transcript from an oral presentation — has: "Language is a very somewhat peculiar, even paradoxical, thing ...".

23. The bracketed passage, as well as the subsequent two sentences, come from the notes of M. Rouse and E. Siskin. Rouse has: "Locus of patterns — where do they reside authority — a pattern / dictionary — example of cultifying [?] of a certain type of behavior / normative point of view / ascription of value." Siskin, in a different lecture (from 1934), has: "Culture cannot be defined in terms of things ('lists') or overt patterns ... culture defined as valued kinds of activities. Value situations symbolized by objects, things. (You do not define culture by naming objects.)"

24. The notetaker adds: "This doesn't bother a functionalist."

25. See H. Rickert (1902), fifth edition 1929.

26. W. Taylor's notes add: "Relative stratigraphy is hard to obtain due to personal factor of examinee and his reinterpretation due to geographical distribution."

27. In 1935 Sapir apparently gave an illustration from the ethnographic study of North America, and its reliance on memory culture. The notetaker has: "Paucity of material — do they live up to culture? Did whites upset? Is it ideal?"

28. The preceding passage, from "every fragmentary science ...", is quoted from Sapir (1939a).

29. The preceding two sentences are quoted from Sapir (1939a).

30. For somewhat similar arguments see Sapir (n.d. [1930]) and (1932b).

31. The preceding sentence is quoted from Sapir (1932b). Notice, too, that elsewhere in his lectures Sapir again connects "functionalism" with too heavy an explanatory reliance on conscious purposivity. See chapter 4.

32. See Sapir (n.d. [1930]) for a similar argument.

Chapter Three

Causes of Culture

What causes culture? The question cannot be answered unless you accept Kroeber's concept of the Superorganic; [it does not make sense, at least as thus phrased, in the light of the view of culture presented here — that] culture is something we abstract from behavioral phenomena. [Moreover, to phrase the question in terms of multiple] determinants of culture, or criteria for the determination of culture, [will not solve our problem.] On examination, we shall find that what we consider to be criteria for the determination of culture are in themselves selectively cultural.

This [problem of criteria selection] at once arises when it is a question of comparing cultural elements of two different cultures. The very thing that you are comparing people for will not stay put — even your table of contents shifts and varies and metamorphoses with different cultures. The task seems easier than it is, because we have preferred values and project the importance of [those aspects of culture that are significant] for us, such as music, onto the Hottentot. For example, a high development of music in one culture may not be strictly comparable to music in another culture. A logical comparison should be with, say, a high development of etiquette in the second culture. Thus it might be possible in some cultures to be as etiquette-alive as we are music-alive, and a man might well be an artist in manners who might stress and nuance the factors of etiquette as nicely and as delicately as Kreisler manipulates the violin. Artistic accomplishments are possible in etiquette as in music, but we are not attuned to them.

The important thing is to beware of projecting personal evaluations based on one's own culture into the task of evaluating justly another culture. [We are too easily misled by] the fallacy of [taking as] absolute values our own preferred values, such as the preference of music over etiquette. Why [do we have this preference, anyway]? In our own culture music is highly valued because it is so very individualistic, [according] prestige to the individual performer, and our culture stresses individual differences. Yet, in another culture where music is a group possession and the locus of musical appreciation coincides with the total membership of the group, musical evaluation will inevitably be on a different plane of appreciation.[1]

[Criteria for culture are sometimes supposed to be justified on the basis of a notion of cultural progress, with our own culture representing a stage of advancement.] But there cannot be any absolute criteria of progress; to [compare cultures on such a scale] would be to assert that we have such objective, concrete criteria. Many questions we ask about culture thus are naive and blind in that we think we are connected to a definitely advancing pulse of onward change.

Nevertheless, what are the supposed determinants of culture, as they have been [proposed? Various factors external to culture have been proposed as possible determinants of its form, and it is worthwhile to examine the extent to which they do or do not have such influence.]

1. Race as a Supposed Determinant of Culture

[In previous lectures I have already commented on] the vanity of the usual attempts to understand culture as a biological concept. [To understand it] as a strictly racial expression [is therefore utterly fallacious. Still,] race is much heard of as a determinant of culture. [It is popularly presumed that] cultural achievement can be correlated with a specific racial stock because the relative ability of races determines [the forms of culture possible for them.[2] It is said, for example,] that the negro [has a special racial ability in] music. [But such statements ignore] factors of culture and setting, though they are the most important. Linguistic materials, too, cannot be correlated with a specific racial stock, for language does not exist apart from culture, that is, from the socially inherited assemblage of practices and beliefs that determines the texture of our lives.[3]

[Let us try to be clear, if brief, about why] race has no influence on culture, [starting with the assertion that a "superior race" will produce a higher record of cultural achievement.] So far as experience goes we have no knowledge of any race without culture, in the anthropological sense. [Even] the metaphor of the accumulation of culture patterns, [i. e. the notion that we have accumulated more culture than the primitives,] is not really true. The culture patterns of primitive groups are complex, and their behavior is just as conventional as ours. [Indeed, with regard to the force of convention one could even say that] primitive groups are much more bound by culture, and there is probably more fixity to that culture than in the culture of the "civilized". Much of the history of the world is a process of loosening up the feeling of cultural necessity. Eskimo grammar is much more complicated than ours, and Navajo religion is much more complicated than ours. But the difference in cultures is one of degree rather than kind.

As regards technology, we evidently have a greater fund of knowledge, but the average person in a primitive group is more in touch with the totality of technological knowledge of the group than we are. We share in many parts of culture [only] by having them available in the specialized technological knowledge of our various [sub]groups, in which we participate [not directly but] through symbols. So while our total accumulation of cultural goods may be greater than that of a primitive group, we as individuals are not in touch with a great portion of it. The actual cultural associations of an individual in our own culture are no more than those in a primitive culture. In the psychological sense all races of men are on the same cultural plane, and the primitive is no closer to nature than we are. [The reverse is nearer to the truth: although] the primitive doesn't have more culture, he is more cultured in the anthropological sense.

[The question of accumulation, therefore, is easily confused with a question of population size.] The [population] size of the race is determinant of many criteria [of its cultural achievement]: for example, if the United States had only half of its present population they could not carry on the present culture. We couldn't carry on our civilization without great numbers [of people. But those who assert that] cultural achievement can be correlated with a specific racial stock leave out numbers and then compare a small group with a very large group.

[If you are looking for] possible determinants of culture, the smaller group is the best field for study. [I say "group" here because we] should look to the community which carries the culture, not to the race at large. The community — the group which [we have identified as belonging to] a race — is responsible for culture, not race [itself;] and in measuring achievement one must always take into consideration the effective number [of people needed to bring about a particular result,] and what percentage [of the community's population is effectively [available for a particular project]. Building a house with five people, and building it with five thousand people, are not the same engineering project. You cannot jump from race to community and from community to culture.

Let us assume we have comparable units, however. Then the next difficulty is, what is the constitution — the makeup — of a race? [The concept of race is based on] a theory of racial homogeneity which is, actually, just a theory. No race can be called pure; therefore race is not definite enough to warrant study. [And although it is supposed to be biologically based, in practice the concept of] race is a blend of culture, nationality, and so on with the physical. Seizing on certain symbols to explain the differences between peoples, it [(the concept of race)] is biology-conscious,[4] although there is nothing to substantiate [the predominance of the physical over other factors. Indeed, other, nonmaterial factors once held more appeal as predominant symbols of differences between peoples. Today] the eugenicists' idealist biology and germ plasma have become what religion and soul were [to an earlier age. But] because of evolutionary theories [the religious explanations will not do for the eugenicists, who] feel nature is now going back on us and we must help nature [do its job].

[If the concept of race is so vague, why then the plethora of writings on the subject?] Our real interest in race, we must see, is not biological but emotional: it is emotional feeling that determines [what group is considered a] race, not biological homogeneity.[5] [This group, the "race",] is actually a culture unit, [to which feeling is attached. Now, racial] homogeneity is more determined by environment than biology anyway, because a change in environment [eventually leads to a] change in race, and [because the race may] develop homogeneity by [the very thoroughness of its] mixing. That is to say, when an intermixed group lives under certain conditions for a time, they will gain a certain degree of homogeneity; thus from the intermixing of two or more "races" will evolve another "race" — so where are you? [Another difficulty with the theory of racial homogeneity is the arbitrariness of the characteristics selected as racial markers and their non-congruence with other characteristics, for] groups which seem alike [in one respect] often have grave dissimilarities in another. You have to know what makes for homogeneity — [in what respect people are being judged as alike — before you can look for its consequences. Today] race is a symbol for homogeneity; [emotionally it seems to reflect] the extension of ego to your particular group. [The size and supposed homogeneity of this group thus depend on your point of view. Take,] for example the history of the English ["race" from] prehistoric to modern [times: it is a gradually wider extension, incorporating and mixing different groups —] Saxons, Jutes, Celtic [groups], and Normans (themselves mixed).

[But supposing that distinct races could be definitely identified,] could culture elements be explainable in terms of racially determined psychological determinants [such as intelligence]? And as a corollary: were this true, would it matter? If, for example, [you could demonstrate] the fact that a Zuni were more intelligent than a Navajo, would you have the right to explain the greater sophistication of Zuni clans and ceremonialism, [and other aspects of Zuni] culture, on this basis?

[The first problem is how we are to assess and compare] the intelligence of races, [to see how it might influence the level of their culture. Here we must not confuse the intelligence of persons with the characteristics of groups, for] there is no relation between personal intelligence and the status of culture. [Moreover, we shall have to beware of a serious methodological difficulty, for] you cannot test intelligence by means of tests which involve superiority for a person whose cultural experience makes him familiar with the subjects under consideration [in the test. His performance will] depend on his experience, [not only on his native intelligence.]

[We shall also have to distinguish] lack of intelligence from lack of emotional participation, [as for example if the test] stimulus is not relative to [a person's] experience, or if he has some negativism [about the test. Besides its connection with cultural experience, therefore,] the stimulus connects with a whole [emotional] field beyond [the realm of strictly] cultural values, and you have to get [some sense of] the symbols of participation for this person, to back up your understanding [of his behavior in the test. Actually, this problem points to the fact that our notion of "intelligence" is ill-defined and fails to recognize that] there are two types of intelligence, and they are quite different: the intelligence which insists on thinking things through for oneself, [which we may call] native intelligence; and social intelligence, which consists in adjusting to social and cultural patterns. [The difference is well illustrated by] the psychotic, who is often alarmingly intelligent but who applies his intelligence to problems that are not valid, usually those that have already been better solved. There is intelligence involved in using cultural forms, but [native] intelligence is not [what is necessarily] required.

Actually, to carry on a culture, both intelligence and stupidity are needed. Too much intelligence and initiative in a population would make the culture advance too fast, and go beyond the grasp of the majority or the median [individual] (in the normal curve of frequency). Look around you and see how little true thinking goes on — for example, when a person presses a button and watches a light go on. More intelligence is

required in using a [primitive] fire drill than in pressing a button to turn
on the lights. Turning on an electric light by means of pressing a button
is in our culture an act of faith. It does not require the intellect or
comprehension of forces involved that making fire by friction demands
of an individual living in an exotic culture. The so-called primitive will
have a great knowledge of the properties and qualities of woods and
techniques of manipulating them. We, [on the other hand,] may understand none of the complexities of electrical circuits, the property of a
sub-culture within our own — the electricians, analogous to the country
yokels and their knowledge of a [rural] environment unknown to us —
and in turn the electrician may not be able to explain electrical phenomena
to the satisfaction of the physicist. We as individuals are not more
intelligent than primitives because we make light by turning a switch
instead of by the use of a fire drill. That is group intelligence, based on
historical factors. It is not race that is evolving, but culture. The culture
shows "intelligence", not the individual.

[As the example of the light switch shows, it is important to] distinguish
between the [mental] life of a culture and its [technological] power.
Psychology [as such] doesn't help you to understand its life: here you
must get at historical factors. The intelligence of the people of a group
does not determine whether it has a high or a low culture; this is
historically determined. An individual Oklahoma Indian of low culture
may of course be much more intelligent than an Indian of a high culture
such as the Pueblo. Thus the business of trying to estimate the intelligence
of a group on the basis of its cultural artifacts is on a very shaky basis.
[And in any case,] the anthropologist thinks of the world of culture as
not racially defined.

[The notion of] "racial memory" [is another example of the confusion
of individual psychology with group affiliation, and of history with
biology.] "Racial memory" is not [racial at all; what is so labeled is, in]
reality, the memory of cultural forms in early childhood which are dear
to one. The fundamental truth [of the matter] is that it is not a matter
of the nervous system, but a matter of emotional significance.

[An attempt to argue that race influences culture through the operation
of differences in intelligence would run into several obstacles:] (1) [when
considering race, we must start by asking] what biological differences are
significant when it comes to the question of ability to adapt; (2) we know
very little as to what mental traits are associated with physical traits, or
about the [psychic] potentialities and abilities of a group [(as opposed to

an individual)]; and (3) the relation of intelligence to culture is by no means close — it is a fast and loose relationship.

[Yet, someone might contend,] the white race [has been responsible for] an accumulation of social goods of a high order. [If this is not due to] superior intelligence, then why is it so? [But — we must respond —] there is no stable relationship between physical nature, [including membership in the white] race as such, and the development of culture. There is tremendous cultural variation in the same race. You will find individuals in our midst who don't participate in "white" culture; you will find segments of the population (such as peasant farmers) who don't participate in it either; and you will find whole groups — white communities in the Caucasus — who don't participate in the traits ascribed to it. A degree of parallelism between the cultural and the racial [does exist, but it is] due [only] to geographical affinity. [Geographical connections are also important in understanding how it came about that the high development of western civilization was produced by members of the white race] — the strategic locality of the Mediterranean in relation to ancient culture centers, for example. Enough time has not elapsed for us to rule out the influence of the purely geographical factor in the accumulation of culture. We must not confuse history with appraisal.

There is no correlation, therefore, between race as such and the degree of development of culture — only a historically-determined association. Between race and culture there is really a psychological or emotional plane, and it is here that the [only] effect of race in culture [might lie].

[Now, I have already suggested that the group which is identified as a "race" is really a cultural unit, identified on the basis of its emotional significance. But is there, on the other hand, some racial determination of emotional tendencies?] If we assume that psychic qualities follow in the wake of physical qualities, [we should find] an association between race and mental characteristics [(as opposed to culture itself) — characteristics such as] temperamental differences. Are there certain expectations of temperament to be looked for in different races?

It is probable that certain physical characteristics imply certain mental characteristics.[6] Kretschmer's [studies of] physical types, [for example, try to give substance to] the intuitive feeling that there is a relation between physical constitution and mental set.[7] ["Mental sets" refer primarily to] divisions of an emotional order, made by psychiatrists, such as schizoid and manic-depressive — types of psychotic behavior. [The validity of the correlations] is as yet to be determined, but we must leave the door open for some theory of association or physical type and psychological difference.

[Can such correlations be linked with race?] Are there, then, racial differences in emotional characteristics, or psychic-emotional natures? Kretschmer's types are not races;[his subjects all came from the same local population.] We don't know whether the gross physical differences between races are of the same order as differences within a group. [Mental] tests in regard to differences between races have been of an intellectual, not an emotional, order. [Moreover,] temperamental phenomena and their various aspects are capable of only meager definition, [especially as applied to races]. That is, the Negro and American Indian are at the poles while the White race shows no uniform temperamental face but is individually heterogeneous. And as soon as a temperamental facet becomes an overt behavior trait, such as using the hand, then it becomes culture.

Thus temperament is highly culturalized; but it may also be racial. Personally,[8] I believe there is something to the "stolidity" of the American Indian — that the Indian has a basically different emotional makeup than the white man. (You must [at least] keep your mind open to possibilities. Liberalism with a closed mind is as bad as obscurantism.) Indians have more of a diffused than a concentrated emotionality, and they are less able to dissociate emotionality [from its object]. A purely rational appeal doesn't work [with them]; feelings must be involved. Perhaps they have the seeds of sentiment more than we have, and perhaps on this basis a more solid family life. But as to whether there is a physical basis for [these aspects of] emotional life [we cannot as yet say —] we can only make plausible guesses.

[Whatever their source,] emotional ties and personality differences are difficult to isolate within[9] the cultural pattern. We must deny the power of intelligence and temperament in shaping culture as a negative which we cannot explain, but admit the possibility of its existence to a degree. [That is, we must not discuss these factors] on a completely negative basis. [But as regards] cultural complexity, it would seem that historical antecedents are determinant. Culture is not the immediate expression of intelligence, race, or emotion, although these factors may enter into its growth. If there is a fundamental causality [in culture], it is history. [Any other] determinants of culture [can be only] secondary. All the cultures we have studied come to us with a rich environmental and cultural — in short, historical — background.

2. The Supposed Psychological Causation of Culture

[The question of racial causation of cultural form has led us to psychological causation, through consideration of intelligence and temperament. But] the sense in which psychology can be said to give us the causative factors of culture is strictly limited. The difficulty of applying psychological criteria to culture [is a topic to which we shall return at length, in later chapters.]

Anthropologists have [pointed out that] the trouble with the purely psychological interpretation of culture is that it ignores time and space. If psychologists have one factor in common, it is that they ignore history or have a sort of history *ad hoc*. [Thus even such radically different psychologists as] Watson and Freud often tend to disregard the time dimension and talk as if the individual were just about to create some cultural phenomenon *de novo*. [But any such individual has] a cultural heritage; and culture, [in turn], has absorbed the [creations of the] individual. The history of the culture is of great importance in interpreting cultural causation, although it can hardly be precisely placed in historical terms.

To understand [the individual's] relation to [his or her] environment you must study the whole mental background, and the potential energy of the psyche, not [just the] dynamic flow. The subject must be culturally defined to be psychologically treated — personality must be defined culturally before you talk about psychological causation.

[It is true that] in one sense all culture causality is psychological — [in that the individual is the effective carrier of tradition][10] — but because the culturalist abstracts his materials, he loses touch with the reality of basic psychological functioning. Then, these abstractions have sometimes been personalized as a psychologically-apposite datum: the group mind, or the group belief. When a pattern is abstracted and becomes [recast as] a [psychological] "problem", it is a bogus problem; for there is a tendency to treat abstract patterns as if they functioned as such, [i. e., psychologically]. For example, [in speaking of] the function of religion, abstract patterns are shuffled and one seeks to translate [these] patterns into a psychological situation — [supposedly the "cause" of religion, but really only] the social psychologists' after-the-event rationalization. There is always an enormous mass of purely historical material involved, [which they ignore].

In language, too, this has taken place. For example, the loss of English [inflectional] forms, etc., is blamed on Anglo-Saxon culture by psychologists of language [who speak of] the "English mind" and the "English language"; but it is to be truly blamed [only] on the usual [process of] simplification in language. [These processes] have no validity when applied specifically to persons. ([Consider] the verb system, with its [inflections expressing] time-sense and [the actions or states of] individuals, [such as the -*s* ending on the third person singular present tense. That our verbal inflections have simplified in these directions is not due to the "English mind",] but to historical growth. [The process is a formal one rather than a social-psychological one, as we can see when we observe the existence of forms violating the supposed psychology of time-sense and individualism:] "two plus two is four"; or, "she comes tomorrow".) The child seizes upon suggestions in language as absolutes; he has no alternative of his own. So we can't say that the individual necessarily participates psychologically in the extracted "psyche" of the language.[11]

Thus a psychological attack on the causative processes of culture is not in all cases justified. Every set of cultural patterns has its own psychological goal; and there are different levels and different denominators of the psychological aspect of culture. That is, [the psychological relevances of such different patterns as] the language, the parliament, and so on [cannot be the same]. The psychological disturbances [of patterning − individual variations and innovations −][12] do not define and cannot dictate absolutely the forms of culture, but rather are a conditioning factor or jumping-off place for the understandable and typical forms within a particular culture. The varying aspects of culture are subject to the impact of individual psychology in varying degree. There is a general similarity of the psychology of the individuals [in a particular community], and what we must notice[13] are these psychologic peculiarities which would not be allowed to affect the traits of a whole culture. [However, at the same time] there are probably forms of personality which do make for segregation of culture patterns. The problem to be solved is how much [this happens], and how.

[On the one hand,] there is a colossal resistance of the inherited [forms] to the psychological nuance of the moment. Cultural forms are rarely disturbed by psychological needs if they can be stretched or retained in any way − witness clumsy [systems of] orthography [retained from the past]. Institutions have a way of staying put out of all proportion to their real or supposed usefulness. [On the other hand,] culture is possessed of a great many disassociative forces, such as cultural specialization, which seems to be opposed to the integration of individuals or culture. Rectifying this disassociation is cultural inertia, a great factor in nullifying the impact of individual psychology. This is cultural conservatism, [in which we see that culture] is not totally and completely responsive to the psychological needs.

[We must therefore distinguish clearly between cultural form and psychological function. To see] form as function, as in Wundt's psychology, is naive. We can detect [large-scale] direction in language, but we can't correlate it with any large-scale psychological facts. Culture forms themselves are not directly explicable by psychological terms.

3. The [Supposed] Environmental Causation of Culture

Are environmental [factors] determinants [of cultural form?] Environmental considerations have some usefulness in the study of culture, but [as culture determinants] they are insufficient. The argument of environmental [determin]ists, like the cultural geographer Huntington,[14] is one huge fallacy. Though it is a culture on which [environmental] influences impinge, they forget this, [declaring instead that] America was destined to be agricultural — because of its alluvial plains. But [what about] the Amerindians, [who occupied this continent for millennia without farming those selfsame plains, even after agriculture was known to them? This interpretation of] history as [environmental destiny] is naive, [as is the view that] Canadian Indians must have less intelligence because they did not exploit the Saskatchewan plains [agriculturally], as opposed to the Anglo-Saxon [settlers] who almost immediately used them as wheatfields. [The reason this argument is naive is that] the mere presence of an economic stock in trade, [such as alluvial plains suitable for growing wheat], is not enough. You must have [the appropriate cultural] patterns.

We ourselves don't know the full possibilities of our environment, [nor can we see these independently of our culture.] Culture changes the environment; we have habits, not an inventoried knowledge of the cosmic possibilities. [And our habits may depend more on our history of contacts with other parts of the world than on the initial state of our own geographical setting. Our] use of coffee and tobacco, [for instance, is due to historical] accidents. We might have many [other] plants [in our environment that are] usable as stimulants and narcotics, [but we ignore them.] It is hard to see the environment except in terms of what you want.

The environment always has what you need if you are in a position to get what you need; unhappily, you are not always in a position to get it. We'd be sunk in the Eskimo's environment despite our fine technology, because the environment lacks the raw materials usable by our system; but an Eskimo would be equally helpless in our more "benevolent" environment, unequipped with our culture.

Thus there is more to the problem of environmental influence on culture than the simple example of the absence of snow houses in the Congo. [As with the psychological interpretation of culture, a strictly] environmental interpretation of culture ignores the interrelationships between cultural traits, and the history of the trait patterns. The great difficulty [with the notion of environmental causation] is that the cultural pattern determines the functional nature of the environment. The environment plus a datum of culture is a different thing from the environment alone. [In any case,] "environment" must include the cultural as well as the physical environment, for beyond the purely physical environment is an environment composed of the ideas of the people who live there. The real environment [includes] the cultural potentialities of these ideas, plus the basic [physical] environment.

Facts of environment are only important, then, if the natives think they are important. The cultural stock in trade means that you can redefine the environment in those terms. Culture insists on seeing things in its own terms; it defines what is beautiful and what is not. Environment as such is of no value to the culturalist. What is important is environment *as defined by culture* — what the natives have unconsciously culturally selected from the environment, and [their] cultural evaluation of it. [A people's] response to their environment is conditioned by their cultural heritage; it is not an immediate response. We see nothing beyond what we are trained to see.

The culturally interpreted environment, therefore, is just as important to a study of culture as a culturally interpreted psychology. Both the psychology and the environment have to be well activated in cultural understanding before being of much use [to the ethnologist. Before assuming any sort of] geographical determinism, one must consider the cultural urge. [Thus environment does indeed have an effect, but it is as] a culturally defined environment. Environment as defined by those participating in the culture is important [only] as a background factor in defining the direction of culture, [not as a significant cause. Indeed,] primitives often flout their environment because they are not culturally ready to take advantage of [the full potential of its] geography. They will go out of their way to secure things not in the immediate environment. [What is important are] the forms and attitudes already developed by culture; on these patterns environment has a facilitating effect.

[In other words, the main direction of influence is just the opposite of what the environmentalists would have it.] The environment is fitted to certain forms of culture patterns — or rather, environment is utilized and made relevant to a culture pattern (such as rice or wheat agriculture, etc.). Psychological demands ask for a cultural response, and cultural patterns, [in turn], demand solving; whereupon environment is required to fulfill these demands. Whether it does fulfill them is an environmental or geological or ecological problem. But environment does not dictate — culture pattern dictates. Environment is [only relevant in its] culturally weighted aspect, and one environment may be favorable or unfavorable according to the prevalent culture.

[An environment that does fulfill culturally dictated demands will not cause its inhabitants to look beyond their own cultural pattern, no matter how rich it may be from the point of view of an alien tradition.] So long as nature gives us some [sort of] food we don't go any further. [It does not seem as if human beings are impelled, because of some inherent drive toward the nutritionally perfect diet, to investigate and invent novel ways to exploit their particular locality.] Some bogus dieticians say we need such and such a diet; but isn't [the diet they recommend] a mere recording of the norms of [cultural] habit? [While dieticians claim we need a certain balance of meat and vegetables,] the Eskimo [get by] with all meat, and [large populations in] the Orient [survive on] all vegetables. Personally, I have faith that any people can work out its diet; we get too excited about it. [And we fail to notice that many of our dietary recommendations, and notions about the effects of food substances on our well-being, depend more upon food symbolism than on dietetic necessity. For the cultural aspect of diet also includes] food symbolism, as well as linguistic symbolism. [It is a system of rationalizations governing dietary habits.] You can rationalize the asparagus-eating habit once you have it, [while the effects of] coffee may be a collective illusion; and the dietetically perfect may lack a good symbolism [and therefore fail, as the malnourished do for physiological reasons, to enjoy a sense of well-being.]

[If the local geography should prove inadequate to a people's culturally defined needs (nutritional and otherwise), it is at least as likely, if not more likely, that people will try to secure those goods from elsewhere, than that they will reconsider their own locality and their accustomed ways of exploiting it. Indeed, in our own culture, however vaunted for its technological proficiency,] there is [a good deal of] ecologic ignorance. We import [certain materials], and wars are fought [to insure our ability to import them]; but why not turn back again to recheck the environment? In a siege we might be pressed to take inventory of our environment, [and we might find many possibilities not as yet tapped.]

[But it is not only in diet that environment supposedly influences cultural destiny.] It has been said that Greece was predestined to a high culture because of the happy blend in which it combined hilly with maritime country — the hilly [country fostering] individualism, and the [maritime providing] harbors for communication. [The futility of such statements should by now begin to be clear. We have only to remind ourselves that] Mesopotamia, [where a high culture emerged earlier than in Greece,] was a plain, [to begin to realize that] nothing in the environment as such is forcing [of particular cultural developments]. Environment is only favorable by and large. From Neanderthal man to today, not all [of cultural history] is to be credited to the specifically Greek environment. Our [present cultural] pattern, [deriving from] our Renaissance tradition, [places] perhaps relatively too much emphasis [on Greece as the source of all we see as lofty in our civilization, anyway.] We might just as well indict the Greek culture and environment for war and paranoia. To pick on the Nile valley, as does Elliot-Smith, is just as bad.[15]

[What can finally be said, then, about] environmental influence and its relation to culture? The environment is important as a detail, and as a negative factor by setting limits — it cannot give you what it does not possess, [regardless of your cultural pattern]. The relevance of the environment does have to be considered, for we live in it, and we are subject to its limitations. But our culture manages to transcend certain environmental limitations, as in the case of tea, which we [drink but] do not raise, and rice, which we [eat but] have not cultivated. Even among the most primitive people there is trade. No environment is self-declaratory. Thus environment can never be invoked as the primary cause [of a cultural pattern]. That it both positively and negatively sets limits, is the best we can say — and it is doubtful that we can approach both these limits at the same time or even, ordinarily, either. Environment is a modifier and refiner of culture, [not more.]

Where the ethnologist finds a relation between the environment and a culture trait, therefore, it is not a simple response-relation but a rather complex relation, the behavior showing relations to patterns arising in other areas. The tipi, for example, is not [best understood as] a response to the environment [in which it is found. In that environment,] timber is scarce, so that the [tipi] poles are cherished and have to be carried around with you. [The tipi] is largely an adaptation of a previous type of house, the semi-permanent bark house of the Eastern Woodlands, a conical type of bark lodge. The lodge was modified when people moved into an area where bark was not available. Carrying the poles of the tipi from time to time, the Plains Indians fought with the environment as much as working with it. Out of sheer conservatism you stick to the old pattern and apply it to an unfavorable environment.

The student of culture may tend to underestimate the environment's importance, but it is even more overwhelmingly true that anthropogeographers underestimate the culture impetus. They might say, [for example, given the combination of] rainfall, softwood cedars, and heraldry carving on the Northwest Coast, that this kind of country was predestined for heraldry − it could not but develop. [But we know, of course, that parts of the Northwest Coast are now shared by settler populations whose culture scarcely includes heraldry at all.] Every time you point to environmental determination you can point to similar people in a similar environment with different responses. [What is more determinative, therefore, is the specific cultural history, in which] − as with the Plains Indians − once a pattern is developed, people worry themselves into keeping it, [even if the environment changes, and trees are more, or less, abundant than before.] The eye that sees the occasional grove is the eye of culture, not of immediate perception.

4. Economic Determination of Culture

[The question of whether] economic factors determine or cause the form of culture is a difficult problem. [The greatest difficulty facing the economic determinist is to distinguish those economic causes from their cultural setting.] Any economic scheme of life is itself a highly cultural phenomenon; we cannot talk of a pattern of abstract economic needs apart from cultural needs. The stock elementals [of the economist] don't carry you very far [toward understanding human society and culture]. The economist constructs "economic man", with needs, and this man doesn't act as real men do psychologically and culturally. There is no universal pattern because the economic needs are always [conceived] in terms of the culture itself, and so they are always highly symbolic. For instance, we have needs such as an Easter bonnet that are hard to justify [in other than symbolic terms]. For the economist [this need] is as important as such as a morsel of bread (though not biologically). He never attempts to explain why Easter bonnets are valuable; he just accepts their value after the event, and studies their prices, etc., not the rich psychological problem [their value poses]. We can't say, then, that a scale of needs is primarily causal when the needs themselves are at least partially conditioned culturally.

The culturalist cannot place faith in any one aspect of culture as the sole influence [on the rest]. [How are we to be certain that] basic material, biological needs are more important than immaterial symbolic needs, or aesthetic needs? The concrete phenomenon involves any, some, or all of these [aspects of culture] in particular cases. Or [all these causes] may be always there. For example, once the church is established, there emerge vested interests [in the maintenance of its institutional structure and its officials, such as] the bishopric. Economic determinants may not be the root causes [of this phenomenon] — the tradition of Christianity as a cultural phenomenon may be much more important [in determining] the cultural or spiritual need for bishops (or, on the other hand, the tolerance of these economic parasites).

If you want to say that the final challenge and test of any social order is the economy, [in the sense of the biological maintenance of its members], you are right. But to what extent does this final test operate in the [daily] round of life? [It is true that] sooner or later [a social analysis must] get into the biological world's tyranny, and this gives economics some truth. But what of the symbolic, nonbiological tyrannies? Do religious needs take precedence over the material? Although, in our civilization, they don't now, they [once] did — and so [the question of precedence of needs is itself] a cultural matter. That is, we cannot say absolutely or a priori [that one or the other of these needs is more highly valued]. Such theorists [as do say so] are [themselves] immersed in culture. (We are victims of history too.) One can point to all sorts of evaluations in primitive societies, such as class distinction, ghost-fear, taboos, etc., [which may seem absolutely fundamental to their members]. Some societies have aesthetic motivations and determinants — for example the Japanese, as opposed to [American] pioneer society. The emphasis of value shifts indefinitely from society to society, and from time to time. There is a danger, therefore, in stressing the insistent values of one culture [as if they applied for all places and for] all time.

The question of economic value and needs thus goes far beyond the confines of economics, for the world of value of the economist is not the stark and real utilitarian world he wants but a conventionalized, symbolic world. Despite our pragmatism, our [economic] criteria are a post hoc interpretation. Before we can say what the causes [of cultural form] are we need to know some of the [cultural] picture itself, and the evaluations in it. Too many determinants are involved historically [for us to] pick out any grandiose one.

Significantly [for the question of economic determinism], material causes are not necessarily always present. For example, [the form of] Jewish late culture [cannot be explained] merely by the loss of the material elements of culture. [In this case as in any other,] the history behind [the form] is always involved; plenty of other peoples have lost political prestige, and so on. Human beings may be power driven, but it is culture that determines the patterns [of their behavior], and the environment [its] limits. You can't explain capitalism because of a supposed human nature or basic necessity — it may be due negatively to the loss of other values, [whose loss] may change the terrain entirely, so that the dominant individual may be forced into other patterns [if he is] to tower up [over others. Consider] the scientist, who today grubs unknown in a laboratory; or the banker, who, with the loss of prestige of bankers since the Crash, is not the patternable figure now, but a shabby one. Perhaps [there is now occurring] a shift to political leaders, [where towering individuals can now be found, such as] Roosevelt, Hitler, Mussolini, and Stalin.

[Indeed,] there may even be conflicts between cultural needs and material needs. For example, our cultural need for competition, individually and collectively, may be harmful — it may dwarf the human personality, driving to suicide and insanity, [by the way it both] encourages and discourages the individual. The symbolism of capitalism [would declare that it] is an ego-satisfying [form of] society, but statistically not even in that can it be universal for all individuals [(that is to say, not all individuals' egos would be satisfied in this manner)]. There is a cultural symbolism, a mythology — not a biological [necessity] — rationalizing [the supposed appropriateness of capitalism] for all societies. Where the Middle Ages [saw] a theocratic-Stoic structure of the Universe, Capitalism [sees] biological human nature.

[So all-encompassing is the evaluation of] economics [today] that modern literature is at its mercy. Whether it bolsters up these preferred ideas or attacks them, literature is a mirror of our ideas of economic dominance. Yet, it should be a function of literature and art, because they are wishful thinking (and should be so), to [offer] phantasy and suggest desires, [including] desirable alternatives [to our present society]. [Art should be] more than the servant of economic forces. [If it is only this, perhaps] artists may be too well regarded by the system, and cease to be artists. Or [else the artist] may be (and traditionally is) a perpetual revolutionist.

[The cultural theorist, too, must recognize that the emergence of economic questions to the foreground of cultural inquiry, as if they took precedence in determining other aspects of cultural form, is but a part of our present system of cultural conventions, with its insistence on a biologically rooted, materialistic human nature. If it is the task of theory to rise above mythology − to be more than] a legitimized collective lunacy − [then,] to find out what are the relative precedences of cultural values is one of the cultural theorist's grand problems.

4. [Summary]

Like racial and psychological "determinants", therefore, environment [and its exploitation in a material economy are] not fundamental as a defining cause of culture. The causes of culture cannot be determined. Culture is only a philosophically determined abstraction and cannot have a physical-like cause.

[There is something fundamentally misleading, therefore, about the search for] causative factors in general, [in the study of the social world]. Cause is a relative concept; it is not compelling, but in variable sequence. The causative relation expressed as A causes B is never experimentally borne out, for there are always extraneous effects and elements that make a pure cause and effect relation only the convenient fiction of mathematics and metaphysics. We never deal with real entities as such, [even] in the physical sciences − for science, [removed as it is from the particulars of real-world events,][16] is a pyramidal fiction, of which physics is the ultimate zenith. The [supposed] rigors of the social sciences, such as the clan, etc., are fictional constructs [too]. In human affairs it is just social convention that enables men to talk of equivalents at all.

We might better leave the pyramidal fictions to the philosophers. For our worlds of fictions are not congruent: to the social scientist, as to the artist, the world is defined by things which are *ad hoc*, as they seem on the surface, while [the world of] science is not. [That is to say, the world of science is defined by what supposedly lies under, or is abstracted from superficial appearances.] The world of the plastic artist is one where there are no accidents. For him things are what they seem to be.

Is [the scientist's world] our concern in ethnography? The persistence of entities in the [physical] world is a very different thing from the persistence of entities in the social world. There, it is the condition of the thing being received by the human intelligence, not what the thing really is, that is important. Social science operates in the world of relative fictions – the "world of meanings", as J. M. Mecklin [has put it.][17] It is a world of "as they say", dealing with "what a thing is said to be worth", not what it really is in the physical sense. [Our] causal relations, therefore, are of a derivative nature. Speech meanings are fictions, [though speech is] located in the physical world, as things of the artist are. But the facts of the physical world are of minor importance in the realm of social phenomena. In social phenomena, no matter how carefully you define your terms and set up your formulation there always must be a large amount of leakage [between definition and instances]. Thus in the social world the physicist's causal sequence is debarred because the social world is an artificially [constructed] world. We must [abandon the search for those causal sequences,] and restrict ourselves to typical sequences.

Notes

1. This discussion of music, which comes from the 1933 notes, is juxtaposed there with classroom exercises and discussions on the history and distribution of piano-playing. See Appendix 1 of the CWES edition of this work.
2. Many of the same arguments about race and culture appear in Sapir's published papers, (1925a) "Are the Nordics a Superior Race?" and (1924c) "Racial Superiority".
3. The preceding passage, from "language does not exist ...", is quoted from chapter 10 of Sapir's *Language* (1921).
4. I.e., focused on biological phenomena as symbolic of difference.
5. See Sapir's (1924c) article, "Racial superiority", which argues that claims about racial superiority rest on an emotional basis – the feeling of loyalty to one's ethnic group – rather than on any biological sense of the term "race".
6. This statement comes from 1936–7. In 1935–36, however, Sapir seems to have expressed considerable skepticism about any racial connection with psychology, including Kretschmer's types. B. Whiting has: "Assume are psychic types (this probably not true) / still not race / psychic as in race cult [?] all [?] physical types. Is a trait physical, psychic, or what. Cultural probably."
7. See Ernest Kretschmer (1925), *Physique and Character*.
8. Throughout this section Sapir seems to have emphasized that his statements suggesting

racial differences in temperament represent only personal opinions and guesses, not well- founded claims.

9. I.e., distinguish from.

10. See Sapir (1932a), "Cultural Anthropology and Psychiatry": "We are not, therefore, to begin with a simple contrast between social patterns and individual behavior, whether normal or abnormal, but we are, rather, to ask what is the meaning of culture in terms of individual behavior and whether the individual can, in a sense, be looked upon as the effective carrier of the culture of his group." See also Sapir (1934a), "The Emergence of the Concept of Personality in a Study of Cultures": "In spite of the often asserted impersonality of culture, the humble truth remains that vast reaches of culture, far from being in any real sense 'carried' by a community or a group as such, are discoverable only as the peculiar property of certain individuals, who cannot but give these cultural goods the impress of their own personality." (Note that this passage, as printed in Mandelbaum (1949: 594), seems to have a typographical error.)

11. LaBarre's notes add: "Language the official symbol of time sequence but not pragmatically (e.g., gesture, etc eke out); and many fossils, psychologically (gender) in European languages."

12. On psychological "disturbances", see Sapir (1921), *Language*, pp. 182−83, where "disturbance" refers to idiolectal variation: "The desire to hold on to a pattern, the tendency to 'correct' a disturbance by an elaborate chain of supplementary changes, often spread over centuries or even millennia − these psychic undercurrents of language are exceedingly difficult to understand in terms of individual psychology, though there can be no denial of their historical reality. What is the primary cause of the unsettling of a phonetic pattern and what is the cumulative force that selects these or those particular variations of the individual on which to float the pattern readjustments we hardly know." See also the discussion in Sapir (1938) on whether Two Crows could change the order of the letters of the alphabet, or the history of mathematics, by denying, respectively, that A is first and Z last, or that $2 + 2 = 4$.

13. I.e., what comes to our notice because it stands out as different from the community norm.

14. See Ellsworth Huntington (1915), *Civilization and Climate*, (third edition, revised, 1924); see also Huntington, Charles Clifford and Fred A. Carlson (1933), *The Geographic Basis of Society*, previously published in 1929 as *The Environmental Basis of Social Geography*.

15. See Grafton Elliot Smith (1915) and (1930). Elliot Smith's Egyptocentric view of human cultural history was much debated in anthropology in the 1920s, along with W. J. Perry's *Children of the Sun* (1923).

16. See discussion in chapter 2.

17. John Moffatt Mecklin, American historian. See Mecklin (1924), (1934).

Chapter Four

Elements of Culture

1. The Content of Culture

[To ask what] the determinants of culture are, [as we have done in the preceding lecture, is also to ask,] what is culture made up of? What does culture embrace? To ascertain this is by no means simple, because we have no *a priori* structure, or skeleton, of culture. Culture feeds upon itself, and the criteria of culture "stations" or focal points are in turn culturally determined. It is impossible to draw up in advance an intelligible table of contents or inventory of culture.

[As a starting point, however, we may say that] culture is defined in terms of forms of behavior, and the content of culture is made up of these forms, of which there are countless numbers. [The most diverse aspects of social life must be included.] Putting salt on meat is as much a cultural [form] as is worshiping God.

[Some writers, such as] Graebner, Foy, and Schmidt, [attempt to] inventory the contents of culture by making lists of culture traits [which prominently feature material objects —] food, clothing, etc.; [but their approach has major] deficiencies, for the listing of objects does not constitute culture. Indeed, the classification of material objects as such is not particularly useful. Objects are only the instrumentalities which are sign posts to culture. The most important thing about them is their utilization in patterns having meaning. Even a cathedral is not really a cultural object as such, while [so "natural" a thing as] a cliff may be made a cultural object used to cite boundaries of territory. To the archaeologist, [though he depends so largely on material objects as a source of evidence,] objects are of value only as inferential signposts to vanished cultural meanings. They only become objects of culture with reference to their use, when they are placed in a context of meaning. An object — whether it be cathedral, headland, paddle, arrow-point, or pot — is in fact only a cultural potential. Our cultural subject matter, therefore, is not objects at all, but patterns of behavior. [And these in turn must not be treated as if they were objects.] Modes of behavior are not objects, but culture.

The type of analysis [presented here, then, focuses upon] valued types of behavior patterns, of which material objects are [merely] signs and symbols. The object as such is nil — it only becomes a *thing* (as opposed to a nothing) as and if it is employed or interpreted. The "thing approach" is a fetishistic point of view that doesn't lead to the heart of culture. Culture cannot be defined in terms of things, or lists, or [even] overt patterns. [Instead,] culture must be defined as valued kinds of activities. You do not define culture by naming objects; rather, objects and things symbolize value situations.

How do the items of culture arrange themselves? — In a cultural pattern, [which we may define, for the moment, as] any clear, specific formal outline abstracted from the totality of behavior, [and involving] the [evaluative] judgements of a culture. As an example of a culture pattern, consider education. [In a sense the] ideal [of education] is the projection of the ego into the future by impressing our ideas on the young; it is the self-preservation technique of culture. The pattern of education [thus incorporates] all kinds of values. It also includes the set-up of institutions, administration, etc., with [official] degrees serving as symbols of advancement to a higher status. [A cultural pattern reaches into many realms of social life.]

[The view of cultural pattern and cultural contents that we will elaborate here is somewhat different from certain other uses of the term in anthropology today.] There seem to be two points of view as to culture patterns. One is a functional point of view: [assuming] a well thought-out scheme of fundamental [human] needs, the inclination of a type of behavior would depend on relativities of [its connection to] the basic needs. ([But, as we have pointed out in the preceding chapter,] when we try to classify patterns from the viewpoint of need, [we run into difficulty. How and] by whom are needs to be judged?) The second [approach to] culture patterns is an index, a series of headings ordering what are merely assemblages of cultural patterns. This is not a functional pattern, but a language list, merely language categories by means of which we artificially organize culture. In any index of a culture pattern, definitions of headings must be given to decide the presence or absence of a head, such as "war"; and so the question evolves into a more verbal argument. Moreover, various degrees of intensity within the heads [(i. e., relations among the headings)] call for thought and allow an additional margin of error. For example, [how would one index the headings involved in] education, [the culture pattern alluded to above?] And if we use a heading such as "religion", [thereby claiming there] are no peoples without religion, what do we mean?

[Here we must] emphasize the necessity for the anthropologist to study a culture in its own terms — to assemble cultural patterns through the terminology of the natives themselves. [Otherwise] we use only ad hoc schemes. Thus the point of view in Wissler's *Man and Culture*, which constructs such a scheme, cannot be utterly accepted.[1] [Nor can the work] of Roheim, whose attempt to interpret Australian society in terms of his own symbolism [must be considered a] failure.[2]

Such [a scheme as Wissler's, an ad hoc type of indexing] classification, is good only for ordering assemblages of cultural patterns — an index for convenience in comparing different [cultures]. But the levels of comparability of cultures vary greatly in different aspects, from language at the one end to religion at the other. Thus although language consists of articulate noises having symbolic value for some society, [and for it alone,] languages are convertible from one culture to another. Is this possible for other configurations of culture, when we compare dissociated elements in one society with those of another? [All too often,] in comparisons of cultures, use is made of patterns of fictionalized concepts and these concepts are compared. (Radcliffe-Brown, for example, is a conceptualist.)[3] This involves difficulties because (1) it is almost impossible to compare forms of behavior from patterns; (2) forms of behavior are unique to each culture and patterns are highly inexact classifications; (3) since cultural forms are historically determined, this increases the difficulty; and (4) there is uncertainty as to the interpretation of similar forms in different cultures. Who is to judge the use or value of a pattern — the native or the observer? The conformist or the rebel?

[Nevertheless, it is not impossible to classify culture patterns, as long as we focus on] form, rather than function. For despite our [supposed] pragmatism, our functional criteria are [only a] *post hoc* interpretation. This is why we can classify form so readily and [yet] baffle at classifying these experiences functionally. [Now,] what enables us to see culture objectively? There are three reasons — [or, in other words,] three criteria for discovering and classifying culture patterns:

(1) Human beings have the ability to [differentiate and] define some experiences as against others through the senses, and classify activities in physiological terms. That is, in a classification through the sheer testimony of the senses, the culture patterns have a very fundamental relation to physiological activities; they have a physiological validation. Paddling,

for example, impinges on the senses differently from making a word. [The two activities involve different] physiological movements.

(2) [There is already a] rough and ready theory of the classification of function, and the functioning of society, [constructed] by a society itself and later by the observer. The observer's theory may revise or even reverse [that which the society itself has]; [but for both, the presumption is that] everything is explainable.

(3) The third reason lies in the technique of reference which all societies develop through words. Words are very important instrumentalities in defining form and even function, of and by themselves. The ability to classify in advance comes from the use of words; e.g., having two words, religion and superstition, indicates two classifications. A society's classifications depend on the type of language used. You will see culture differently according to the symbolic implementation, the terminology, you work with.

These three items give a pretty firm feeling for form in culture — that is, they give cultural classifications in a strictly formal sense. Therefore it is easy to discover forms of culture, despite our relentless pragmatism. And form criteria are the most important in classifications. Functional definitions and criteria come later; they are of value only after the event. They are more difficult and more subtle; we don't know enough about society to get [to functional criteria] yet. The contents of culture [must take into account both] form and function, [but as yet we are on a firmer footing with the first of these than with the second, although] we may know more about functions in the future. Are the needs of man definitive and circumscribed, and thus easily satisfied, or are they an illusion? [If you simply assume they are definitive you will fail to recognize] the limitations and creative possibilities of culture.

Thus the functional point of view has its limitations. [In emphasizing form rather than function, at least for the time being, my approach differs from that (for example) of] Malinowski, who is an anti-formalist.

[But before leaving the question of classification behind, we may propose our] own classification of culture,[4] in terms of the classification of behavior patterns. Behavior patterns may be classified pragmatically or empirically, according to the way they are related to the following broad classes of activities:

(1) Patterns relating to economic life — the food quest, and the quest for shelter.

(2) Patterns relating to the production of material goods, of value *per se* or of instrumental value: manufactures, clothing, ornament.

(3) Patterns relating to individual development and mutual social interrelations as in kinship, marriage, war, etiquette, language.

(4) Patterns formulating the relations of man to supernatural or other-worldly powers: religious activities, sorcery, shamanism, death.

(5) Patterns formalizing the desire for aesthetic experience per se, or instrumental [in realizing it]: dance, graphic art, music.

(6) Patterns relating to the attitude of man to sustaining ideals: the vision quest, hunger strike, etc.

[It is important to emphasize that] this is not a hard and fast classification. It is impossible to draw up an intelligible table of contents or inventory of culture in advance. [The classification given here is only a convenience which must necessarily fail to capture the way in which] cultural elements [and patterns, in a given society,] aggregate themselves together, for this varies in different societies. You must try to visualize a kaleidoscopic variety of patterns caught up, in this way or that, by pattern configurations or ideas and taking color, habitation and name in terms of this ideal specific to a local time and space.

In a descriptive study, then, the author's task boils down to:

(1) Working out carefully the landscape of cultural forms as they naturally fall together.

(2) Starting out all over again as a psychological work on individuals as individuals in their own framework, and see how they work out their own needs.[5]

[A descriptive study should attempt, ultimately, to concern itself thus with both cultural form and function. For comparative purposes, however, a concern with function is problematic.] Again, it is important to realize the difficulties of comparing the contents of culture. Consider the difference between education in our culture and in, say, Eskimo culture. A prayer in Western society may equate with a primitive dance. Form is itself more important than function; in language the form remains the same but the function differs. E.g., the word *hussy* derives from *huswif* but with an entirely different meaning, while a new word, *madam*, takes the formal place of *huswif*. [And the concept of function is itself unclear.] If we take cultures as a whole it turns out to mean simply the cohesiveness of a group and the belonging of individuals to that group. But when we get down to specific things we've got to watch our step.

2. The Purpose of Culture

[Let us continue our discussion of form and function in culture with a broader consideration of cultural "purpose".][6] [Surely a great many of] the [supposedly] fundamental purposes of culture are really individual necessities and the rationalizations of those needs. "Preserving the heritage", "controlling aggression", and [accounts of] learning to smoke [are examples of such rationalizations in our own society].[7] [It would be a serious error to mistake our own society's rationalizations and conceptions of need for universal purposes.] Some purposes we want to hold on to — those which [really do represent] our biological needs we should keep because they are fundamental. But we can always reaffirm our biological purpose in such a way that [our other purposes will] seem right. [In other words, in keeping with the] pragmatism [of American society,] we will always try to find tangible purposes to any phase of our culture.

[Yet, from a cultural standpoint, even our most obviously biological purposes, such as eating, are expressed only indirectly.] Why was it necessary to culturize our needs such as food? Why this food and not that? Why prepare it this way and not that? In short, why did man have to evolve a more indirect method of satisfying his food needs instead of just going and getting it? [The challenge to the economic or biological determinist] is to try to prove the need for all this indirectness in regard to our purposes. For culture is not exactly squared to needs. Culture traits may at some point change their meaning. For example, [an income is necessary in our society for an individual to acquire food and other biological necessities; but, let the income grow large enough — say, to] an income of 75 million — and, [as so] often, [the "purpose" of the trait] changes into an expression of ego, or the assertion of it to gain kudos. Biological and psychological needs are satisfied by culture, but in addition, culture adds, through its own momentum, much more than these needs. [Indeed,] a potent social pattern may fly in the face of reason, of mutual advantage, and even of economic necessity.[8]

[What, then, is the relationship between cultural pattern and fundamental biological and psychological drives? Is it a mistake to suppose that such drives are related to culture at all? Here let us consider] art, [for the aesthetic is often said to lie at the opposite pole from biological necessity. It is sometimes even defined in this way. But this view is itself culturally determined, and should not prevent us from] assuming a psychological base for aesthetic expression. American culture is not [partic-ularly] conducive to the development of aesthetic expression. [A strong] convention inhibiting [the exploration of visual] form [is part of the American] religious [tradition, deriving from] the Puritans and from evangelical [movements in] England. Moreover, for great cultural devel-opment [in aesthetic forms] there is a need for a rich cultural background. From a cultural standpoint, it is possible to find [a society with] no artistic expression, due to lack of cultural background. There may also be some repressive mechanism of a cultural sort, such as militarism, and so on. From the viewpoint of instinct and innateness, therefore, I do not deny a physiological base or genetic[9] relation with cultural patterns, [even in the case of] art. It is fundamental. [But culture may inhibit drives as well as develop their expression.]

Indeed, any fundamental drive may be used by all manner of [cultural] purposes — [although the fact that cultural purposes cannot be specified in advance] does not mean there are not some typical purposes. Among the different purposes that may be given, some are functional: music, for example, may be [thought of] as a recreation. This "function" is only a secondary rationalization, however, [as we can see when] the form of aesthetic expression survives although its momentary purpose disappears. [So, for instance, musical works may be performed today for purposes entirely different from those which prevailed at their creation, as when sacred works are performed at concerts.] A second type of purpose concerns the association [of a cultural pattern] with other parts of culture. Really, music is simply a part of a total pattern which includes the kind of clothes worn [at musical occasions], the social status [of musicians and audiences], and so on. The purpose of music is so vast that it interpen-etrates all of culture. Music has every possible type of purpose.

[Similar considerations pertain to] religion. [What is its purpose? From one point of view,] religion is the ally of a symbolism of status. Although this may be a secondary factor, secondary factors are often very strong. From another, psychoanalytic point of view, [it may represent] wishful thinking, such as the desire for immortality, while the idea of the divine father [represents] the transfer of an attitudinal set from childhood. [The image of] childhood blessedness — of the child in a happy state — [is linked with] the father image and thus begins with heaven. [To choose among these viewpoints, or to infer some fundamental drive explaining religion, is impossible.] We can't say what drives are fundamental in religion. [Nor can we say that drives have altered, where the forms of religious activity have altered.] We can't say, for instance, that sadism [was responsible for] burning [people] at the stake and made it cruel, but that such sadism is lacking now. Psychological sadism is the same then and now; the important matter is [not a change in the nature of such motives, but in] how culture allows one's indulgence of sadism — [whether in realms] economic, religious, or intellectual). These causes may shift in importance in time and space, and in conceptual and actual [arenas]. Maybe religion feeds on basic ego and libidinal urges which may be redistributed.

The attempt to explain the purpose of any cultural manifestation [is vulnerable, therefore,] to a frontal attack, [which can show that there could] result any number of explanations for the actual content of the patterns. You cannot find a simple reason [for the form of a pattern] in the function of patterns — this is secondary. Any student who has worked through a considerable body of material [in comparative ethnology] is left with a very lively sense of the reality of types of organization to which no absolutely constant functions can be assigned. Moreover, the suspicion arises that many social units that now seem to be very clearly defined by their function may have had their origin in patterns which the lapse of time has reinterpreted beyond recognition. A very interesting problem arises — that of the possible transfer of a psychological attitude or mode of procedure which is proper to one type of social unit to another type of unit in which the attitude or procedure is not so clearly relevant. Undoubtedly such transfers have often taken place both on primitive and on sophisticated levels.[10]

[Still, even if] functional explanations [of particular cultural forms are] of limited usefulness because of the pitfalls they present, [one may nevertheless speak of cultural purpose in a more general sense. In this sense] there are two main purposes for culture. The first is a specific purpose: [to constrain the individual] to act in the same way as [is prescribed in] behavior patterns. The second is a general purpose: to actualize basic impulses in a harmonic fashion. Culture has the same purpose as [other forms of] adaptation to an environment — to actualize [(i. e., satisfy)] primary needs — [but it does so through a system of] mental substitutes. Culture may be a symbolic field, a fundamental system of indirections which [present] the possibility for a multiformity of expressions and allow the fundamental psychological drives of each individual to harmonize with each other, through secondary symbols of reference. The cultural pattern is a powerful system of channelized behavior[11] which actualizes certain basic impulses and gives the possibility for personal realization.

[From the point of view of individual psychology, you could say that] the purpose of culture is to serve as the total stock in trade for the realization and expression of the ego. But there is no genetic relation between certain impulses and certain [cultural] patterns.

3. Culture Traits and Complexes

Orthodox ethnology sees culture as the historical accumulation of culture traits. [The concept of] culture trait (or cultural element) [is a means by which] anthropologists study the movements of patterns without trying to evaluate them, or to determine their interrelationships with other parts of the culture. [By this means the anthropologist attends to] individual elements in the complexes of culture.

What are these elements of culture which the ethnologist talks about? [They include such phenomena as, e.g.,] cross-cousin marriage; dowry; buying ties for Christmas; chewing gum; writing on a blackboard with chalk; artificial heating; Saturday night baths; playing the piano. Culture is analyzed into thousands of elements, without limitation. The cultural universe is [also] an element; a type of behavior and [the culture's] philosophic explanation of it may be two traits, brought together.

What is a unitary cultural trait? Is it a unity depending on description or upon historical factors? Cultural traits can be of any size. However, when you make them universal you get into the psychological rather than the cultural world. Disintegrating a given element [into traits drawn from a universal set] leads to an implication of [common] humanity and [common] psychology. (Anthropologists [of this bent] find nothing unique in the cultural world.) You then explain things ([i. e., the occurrence of particular elements in particular places]) in terms of diffusion rather than in terms of parallelism. [Deciding on what is to be considered a unitary element is a loaded question, therefore.] Parallelism [as an explanation can be a useful] corrective note to the idea of universal traits [whose occurrence is always due to] cultural contact. Yet, these sorts of explanations after the fact must always be, in the absence of exact knowledge, a kind of "Just So" story.

Can traits be gathered together into complexes? There are two uses of the word "complex": (1) Traits which are functionally interrelated, e.g. the "horse complex". This is a natural complex, [since it reflects the] integration of traits naturally, [and the fact that an individual] trait [among them] never occurs alone. (2) Traits which are merely historically linked — e.g., Graebner's complexes, arbitrary associations of unrelated traits.[12] This conception of culture [imagines] an atomistic universe in which elements are grouped and regrouped according to fortuitous winds of history. [The focus is on] isolated histories of elements, fortuitous in their associations.

[This approach] will never lead to a true philosophy of culture because it neglects psychology. It does have its value in preventing thoughts of automatic associations, e.g. that cannibals have no music. Thus the term "complex" is useful when it is confined to meaning the togetherness of certain traits at a particular time and place, without any universal or necessary connection being assumed. But American anthropologists have tended to emphasize the fortuitousness of the coming together of the traits in a complex, [to the neglect of those intrinsic connections that might genuinely be sought. For example,] Christianity and its component parts, however small and seemingly insignificant, are a complex [in the functional sense] and divisible into traits which may lead far outside Christianity into irrelevant and contrasting fields. There is great resistance of [some] elements to analysis and separation, resistance offered by the emotional make-up of people. Some other associations are not resistant to separation, however they may seem to one outside the culture.

In history, trait analysis is very important because it shows the flexibility of culture (language, [for instance,] being forced to express what people desire to express and not remain so rigid as to prohibit communication of thought). The emphasis on diffusion as of really great importance was very surprising when first introduced. It had been supposed that each intelligent people would invent the things they needed. [But some ethnologists came to see trait diffusion as a kind of Darwinian] battle for the success or failure of ideas and culture elements, [whose] survival value was intrinsic. [The atomistic nature of the approach is what creates the problem, for the trait does not have an inherent value regardless of all other aspects of the culture.] One must have social sanctions before value may be attached to any individual creation. [That is to say,] the prestige-giving background of culture is imperative to the diffusion of culture and complicates a simple [picture of trait] diffusion. New ideas don't count — they don't "bite" — and traits do not diffuse, unless they are buttressed by symbols of prestige. The buttressed ideas and elements succeed; the others, [mere] phantasies, die.[13] The personality of the carrier is always a factor in diffusion, too, as with Chauncey Johnny John and his seed corn, or Alice Two Guns and the jumping style of women's dancing.[14] So is diffusion via [social principles such as] family removal or marriage, for people tend to keep up the old culture in their new surroundings. Thus the survival value of an element is both intrinsic and extrinsic.

[Having mapped the distribution of traits, the anthropologist is faced with the problem of discovering the point from which they diffused.] Wissler's centered system of diffusion [(which places the point of origin of a trait at the geographical center of its distribution)] may be criticized as simplistic, [as may any of those systems which insist on but a single point of origin.] There have probably been many tentative beginnings. The problem presented here by the cultural anthropologist is largely artificial; Old World and New World agriculture, for instance, are not really the same "trait". This tendency to deal with atomic culture-elements, in terms of isolable traits — as if there were no Lippertian *Lebensfürsorge* involved[15] — is antipsychological. Our terminology is our enemy too, for the mere use of the same term [(such as "agriculture")] prevents our seeing differences. ([This is a good reason to] use native names!)

The interest of anthropologists is fortunately gradually shifting from the trait analysis and description which was [once the be-all] and end-all of the discipline. For the trait point of view does not tell us much about culture. Consider, for example, the Plains [Indians'] arrangement of their camp in a circle, as compared with the smoothness of our table. Are these both traits of equal [significance]? The purposes for which we use tables might equally allow the use of a rough table. What about the bull-roarer of Australia, and the Nootka bull-roarer? (Bull-roarers have more prestige in anthropological circles than the polishedness of tables.) Are they the same trait?

We may well be made unhappy, when we deal with atomic elements, at the diffusion vs. independent development dilemma. [For the equation of the Australian and Nootka bull-roarers is] unfortunate. What work does the bull-roarer do, culturally? The Nootka bull-roarer is a game, owned by a certain lineage. It is only one game among many, played for prizes — prizes being the important part, a segment of the potlatch "trait". [Similarly,] it doesn't tell you anything about Plains Indians to know that they have their camp in a circle. To enumerate traits is of little [help], although our catalogue of traits gives us the illusion that something has been said.

[In sum,] it is useful to follow up the distribution of a trait but only as a preliminary study or point of departure, for a trait list provides only the signs of the presence of cultural dissimilarities (differences from our own [culture]). The isolation of these traits and the reconstruction of their history is important for the way it emphasizes the vagaries of historical accident in the processes of development. To give an example: historically our English language is a stranger to us. [By tracing the history of forms] the linguist can blow up our sentimental psychological configuration. [Thus the expression] "damn bitch" [unites forms derived from] Church Christianity and Norman hunting — strange bedfellows! Complexes don't necessarily belong together [just] because they do historically occur together. There are indeed some accidental complexes and configurations, [and trait histories can help reveal them.] But they can never take the place of the dynamic study of patterns. No culture consists of traits save in the atomistic sense.

The trait is really the enemy of the pattern — it is of no importance isolated from its configuration and too often has been elevated, as by Graebner, to fetishistic significance (fetishistic because attaching too much importance to the materiality of the thing pointed to). No trait belongs to any one culture. We can't claim any [particular] trait as ours — there is diffusion everywhere. To realize this breaks down some parochialism of thought (consider the connection of the Dakota corn farmer with Mesopotamia, or the history of the alphabet); but traits have no meaning. Some old-[fashioned] historians and anthropologists are still very much concerned as to who first cultivated wheat, who discovered barley, who invented the alphabet, etc. — but it doesn't matter. What matters is the meaning pattern [in which these elements occur]. It is after the event to say that the alphabet was an important invention; in the beginning it wasn't important at all. Shall we sing a hymn of praise to Irish monks, missionaries, Latins, Etruscans, West Greeks, Cadmus, or [to alphabet creators of] the East — Phoenicians? [The alphabet existed] before them, though. Columbus effectively "discovered" America to the European consciousness, though others preceded him. [Who is the great "discoverer", then?]

We don't know today what are the really great ideas. Nor did they in the past. We can't know what a culture-element can do cumulatively — hence many great men in history are great [only] retrospectively, merely in terms of their specific ancestry to modern man psychologically; and such evaluative history must be rewritten each generation. [In its early days the alphabet was] just a pattern, [deriving] from Egypt and with prestige value to the Semitic peoples, but not completely understood. [Only by the] accidents of history [have we acquired alphabetic writing rather than some other form, for it is] not the alphabet [as such] that does the work but the cumulative history. These few scratchings meant little to the Sinaitic people (like runes, [in a later age]). Ogham[16] likewise died, although as [a system] it was quite as spectacular or as dull as the Sinaitic alphabet — and yet few have ever heard of Ogham writing. Much of history, then, is invidious intellectual ancestor-hunting, reevaluative [according to the values of] the present time-level, not in terms of actual beginnings and contemporary importance. (Our elementary education [is full of such] systematized pabulum — "Eskimos live in snowhouses", "The Phoenicians invented the alphabet", "It gets colder as you go north".)

The order of the alphabet is traditional. Like a spell, [or the rhyme] "eeny meeny miney mo", [it has no intrinsic significance.] From the trait viewpoint it is right to connect [alphabetic order] with all these peoples, for it is a singularity, [a product of] historical continuity only. But from the cultural complex viewpoint [the connection would] not [be right.] Although you can't build a complete picture of culture without [any elements, or] traits, the alternative — to attach a once-for-all, [supposedly inherent] significance [to a trait] — is just as wrong. Traits are nothing in themselves, only fossils and habits full of irrationality and [laden with] prestige. The study of traits is valuable for distributive historical studies, but not for psychological synchronic explanations of culture. Notice, for example, the different horizons of u, v, w, x, q, and j historically. [They entered our alphabet at quite different times. But as regards our culture today,] we don't care about any of these things; we don't live under the dispensation of culture traits — nor do primitive people, probably. (Even Thor, [a trait now usually connected with Nordic peoples,] may be Ugro-Finnic [in origin]; and the pre-Indoeuropean people in England were Nordic [in many ways, though Nordic traits are often supposed to belong to the Indoeuropeans.])

While traits may be isolated from a purely descriptive or an historical standpoint, the latter is the real criterion for the culture trait. [In other words,] there is no real criterion for a culture trait save historical continuity. Description is suitable for large-scale, complicated traits [(showing the component parts),] but not for simple traits. For the trait *an sich* is nil. Its functions change from age to age, from people to people, and even, perhaps, from individual to individual. Contrast, for example, the historical study of the alphabet with its value as a symbol of education for the child of tender age: here the alphabet has dynamic value. Traits take on new significations from time to time, and hence it is impossible to construct history from them. [Trait analysis suggests] descriptive unity, as between Old and New World agricultural traits; historical unity, as in the relation between Christianity in New Haven and in Abyssinia; but cultural traits don't really exist. They are remade in each culture, according to its mythology and its rationalizations.

[As our discussion of culture elements illustrates, we] serve two masters, psychology and history — the meaning and the "how come" sides of anthropology. [From a cultural point of view,] the main purpose of studying traits is to give the necessary preliminary stock-taking of the culture; but the historical background [of culture] is not necessarily congruent with the situation today. Things mean what we think they mean, [not where they have come from.] Trait ethnology is really archaeology, [just] not of things dug from the ground. It is not cultural anthropology.

4. The Geography of Culture

The study of the diffusion of culture traits [has made much of] the logic of [their] spatial distribution. From the [geographical] extent of a trait, [one speculates as to whether the trait's occurrence is due to] old heritage or to secondary factors of distribution, [with most occurrences] probably due to distribution, in the last analysis. ([For a discussion of] diffusion, see Wissler's [1923] *Man and Culture*.)

[There has been much success in tracing the paths of diffusion by this means; yet the procedure has its limitations, especially for the more complex societies.] As civilized man transcends space as well as time, the [diffusional] picture is even less clear than in primitive societies. [Consider, for example, the spread of ideas through] university contacts: it is not topography, but the carriers [of the ideas] that are important [in determining their spread. Actually, this is true of any process of diffusion:] the distance as evaluated by the carriers is different from the actual location. We must *weight* geography, [measuring] not mileage but cultural-mileage.[17]

[This includes the fact that some ideas spread more easily than others.] There is little resistance to the spread of a myth — for instance, [we find] Grimm fairy stories in oriental settings — but not so with a kinship system. [But although a myth, or elements of a myth, may spread relatively easily,] the significance of the tale varies — not as part of the tale-trait, but subjective to the particular culture [in which the tale is found.] The Nootka suitor myths [can serve as an example. Among the Nootka,] the legend of the suitor winning a supernatural bride is embodied in the marriage ceremonial which symbolizes status. The legend [occurring] in the ceremonial is the same thing as a story in another locality, but the ceremonial one is a _topati_ ('privilege'), while the other tale is recreation. [So profoundly Nootka is the significance of the tale in its Nootka context, that it is] a disappointment to an informant with knowledge of its wider distribution as a literary product, [to learn that the tale does not belong to the Nootka alone.]

[Likewise,] the Star-husband myths of the Plains may be found among the Klamath;[18] and tales of magic flight occur in ancient Japan, in South America (Upper Amazon), and all over North America, as the same story but with different motives for the flight. This is no mere parallelism, [but a tale] adopted by different peoples and reinterpreted in local terms. The elements of these myth tales that are added or subtracted are as important as the common elements that are preserved throughout the myth as distributed. [A more complex,] large-scale example is the diffusion of Christianity. Documentary and terminological evidence are important in identifying the complex, with whose spread there are changes — [here and] there a different emphasis, and a modification.[19]

The interchange of traits does not require friendly relations between groups; even with a hostile relation there may be much borrowing. Diffusion is [perfectly] possible under conditions of war. But traits are never taken over exactly as they are received. Instead, borrowed elements must be assimilated to the already given background, and this assimilation is selective. Often, the subject culture picks up what may be considered very insignificant or trifling within the complex of the parent culture. This trifle or aspect may, however, be just what the subject culture is then in need of (or what it is entirely unconscious of). [The assimilation into our own culture] of jazz music from Africa, or of [elements of] southern speech from the Negro, are examples where it is just some aspect of a larger thing that is taken in. Probably any element might be assimilated, provided it may be reinterpreted. A culture may [even] adopt a trait the essence of which is antithetical to it, and refit [this element] to its general pattern.

The anthropologist has not done much work on the process of reinterpretation of traits by the receiving culture, [so we can make only a few general remarks about it]. Culture never somersaults: the process of reinterpretation is gradual. The technique of assimilation [must require a certain] preparedness, [on the part of] the receiving culture, to accept new things; selection [of the elements to be absorbed]; and integration [of the new traits] with something old and already ingrained. ([Here] the terminology is tremendously important. If you can call new customs by old names, they seem more acceptable.) In other words, there is not only a cosmos of reinterpretable traits; there are also communities of receptive peoples.

[Are nearby peoples most likely to be the receptive ones? Such receptivity is one way to think about] the concept of culture area, although the concept [first] arose from the need to arrange and systematically classify museum specimens for exhibition. [It represents a regional] clustering of characteristic culture traits and complexes. If traits were distributed only on the basis of chance, the distribution of any trait would be incongruent with that of other traits. [Where, however, we find an] amassing of traits by areas, [we speak of] "culture areas".

The English ethnologists have tended to neglect the [geographical] spread of culture traits. The idea of [cultural] evolution is more popular there. Frazer, for instance, was more interested in pointing out the typicality of the primitive reaction [than its regional differences].[20] The Americans, on the other hand, have sometimes attempted to mark off culture areas all over the map. Yet the reality of culture areas as clearcut entities seems to vary greatly. Though it has a didactic value, this type of classification can be — and too often is — overdone, for not all people can be fitted into such a scheme. Too much of a fetish has been made of the culture area concept. [It works] best for the Plains and the Northwest Coast; but elsewhere a passion for classification has run away with us, and one thinks other areas are of equal weight and cogency. As Boas [points out in] "American Myths",[21] the classificatory habits [deriving from] biological and zoological taxonomy have done anthropology a great deal of harm.

With regard to the mechanics of culture action, European [ethnologists have a somewhat similar] concept: the culture stratum. They are not so interested in area. But the "culture area" is a relatively simple concept in America as compared with the great complexity of [cultural] stratification in the Old World. [The European ethnologists] tried to work out the stratification of primitive cultures by describing distinct, disconnected cultural traits, naming the resulting pot-pourri of individual traits a "culture", and searching for other places with similar combinations. [A given locality may have many such "cultures", in stratified combination.] This is the Graebnerian point of view. As before, here we can talk of

[both] historical and psychological culture strata: [both points of view would apply.]

Is the culture area ([or stratum]) a mere description of culture flow, or is it, aside from that, a psychological unit? The latter! Although the culture area concept can be criticized [on the grounds] that there isn't the same degree of relation between [any] two traits [constituting it], there are, however, assemblages of people who understand each other's culture and feel themselves as a unity. [Our conception here represents] a sort of cross between political science and anthropology. This is the true psychological meaning of culture area: a nascent nationality. Under the dominating idea in an area there is a nascent feeling of unity; it is a potential nationality, in the sense that a nation represents a communality of understanding. For example, [consider] the Siouan and Cheyenne parfleche: what you say of the Sioux attitude you can say of a dozen other [peoples], and this is the psychological value of the culture area. A Sioux captured by a Blackfoot would feel at home in the culture even though [in the hands of] deadly enemies, whereas (say) a Pueblo [Indian] captured by a Plains tribe would not feel at home — he would not know what [his situation] is all about.

Some of our culture areas are very real things in the psychological sense; others are pretty weak in the knees. How many culture areas are psychological realities? On this basis, Plains culture, Southwest culture, and Northwest Coast culture are valid areas, but the others ([in North America]) do not have a sufficient psychological basis of unity. [As we have said,] the culture area really is a nascent nation, and many nations probably arose in just this way — [thus we may wish to] compare the different tribes in the Plains area with the different city states in Italy. But this notion of the culture area should never be confused with the notion of the state. The state is a method for compromising or solving antagonistic points of view; the Plains tribes, with their uniformity of [cultural] patterns, are a cultural unity, the psychological ground [for a state, if you will, but as yet lacking this method.]

What vital culture areas, [in this sense of the term,] could we recognize a hundred years ago in the civilized world, before modern industrialism set in? [A list might look as follows:]

(1) Occidental (Western European) culture, with its American derivatives.

(2) Saracenic (Islamic) culture in the Near East.

(3) The culture of India.

(4) East Asiatic culture — Chinese, with Japan as a derivative of that (also Korea).

(5) Possibly a Turkish-Altaic culture area (though probably not).

[At least the first] four of these are vital culture areas, cosmoses that in spite of tremendous diversities within them are psychological unities. In the course of time the cross-fertilization of traits has developed a common pattern of culture with a kind of commonality of feeling which transcends local and political differences. This is what anthropology should have meant by culture area.

Notes

1. The notetaker (I. Rouse) has: "Points out that this [Wissler's culture pattern] is not a functioning pattern, as his is." The reference is to Wissler (1923).
2. See Roheim (1932) and (1934), presumably the works Sapir might have had in mind.
3. Sapir apparently presented his views on Radcliffe-Brown's anthropology in various fora, though not in his published writings. See Benedict's comments, in a letter to Margaret Mead, on a paper Sapir gave at the 1932 meetings of the American Ethnological Society: "The speech was on Function and Pattern in modern anthropology, and it was aimed at Radcliffe-Brown..." (Mead 1959:325). Benedict's opinion of Sapir's paper was largely negative. The paper itself, if it ever existed in written form, is now lost.
4. It is not clear whether this classificatory scheme is Sapir's or Beaglehole's (in whose notes the scheme appears); I suspect the latter. Sapir may well have proposed that the students try to come up with a satisfactory classification so that, in comparing the proposals in class discussion, it could be shown that no one a priori scheme was preferable to another.
5. Beaglehole's notes have, in an apparently parallel passage, "Analyze the fundamental functions of society."
6. The notetaker (M. Rouse) links the heading, "Purpose of Culture", with "functions". See also the section entitled "Function and Form in Sociology" in Sapir's (1927a) "Anthropology and Sociology".
7. A notetaker (L. Taylor) adds: "Brill's explanation of smoking and his mental method of reaching that point, the shrinkage of space."
8. The preceding sentence is quoted from Sapir (1927a), "Anthropology and Sociology".
9. Recall that Sapir's use of the term "genetic" usually corresponds to what we would term "developmental" rather than "innately programmed". Since his sentence here does include a reference to innateness, however, I have retained the original term.
10. The preceding passage, from "Any student ...", is quoted from Sapir (1927a), "Anthropology and Sociology".
11. The notetaker has "possible behavior".
12. See, for example, Graebner (1911) and (1924).
13. Mandelbaum's notes add: "Here is the nuclear element, the spring board for your thesis on the economic determination of social status and prestige."

14. The notetaker (W. Hill) adds: "(Did Alice Two Guns live at Cattaraugus? Did the jumping style of dancing in Women's dance originate here at Coldspring or over there at Cattaraugus?)" The reference is to an Iroquoian group.
15. See Lippert (1886—87).
16. An early Irish system of writing using notches for vowels and lines for consonants to form an alphabet of 20 letters.
17. Similar wording, and many of the same ideas and examples, can be found in Sapir's (1916) *Time Perspective in Aboriginal American Culture: A Study in Method.* The view of culture is somewhat different, however.
18. See F. Boas (1891).
19. At this point LaBarre's notes have a long list of what are apparently further examples of ideas some of which have diffused and others have not; those that diffuse become rationalized according to the local cultural setting. Thus "the plank house [occurs] from the panhandle of Alaska to the Klamath River of northern California, [where the local culture] rationalizes [its construction from] redwood: you can make this self-evident (a soft wood, etc.) — but the Algonquians use birch bark [for a similar type of house]." Another example is "the medicine-bundle: the psychology of the present functioning element has nothing to do with its history." Other examples include the division of the Bible into sections, the history of Jewish law, the four (or sometimes six) cardinal points, the Navaho "unique origin-myth of the horse", short-story "plots" (Cinderella, Ulysses), and our "master formulae ... putting a value on services, attaching figures to intangibles (unintelligible in other societies)". The examples are not cited in enough detail to reveal what specific use Sapir made of them.
20. See Frazer (1917—20), *The Golden Bough.*
21. Boas (1916).

Chapter Five

The Patterning of Culture

1. The Configurative Point of View

[In the preceding lecture, I mentioned the concept of] culture stratum: the description of a pot-pourri of individual, distinct, disconnected cultural traits [that happen to occur at a particular historical period in a particular region]. This is the Graebnerian point of view, [among whose defects one might mention methodological problems; for although the stratum is supposedly defined in terms of historical combination,] without documentary evidence it is difficult to tell the age of traits.

[In contrast,] the point of view [put forward in this lecture] is configurational: the emphasis is not on the actuality of every bit of behavior, trait, or element, but on its position in relation to other elements. [That is to say, this point of view] emphasizes the placement of a cultural element rather than its content. Consider, for example, [the difference between] handing someone a nickel and handing him an unshaped bit of metal. [Though the substance of the two may be the same, the latter is not part of our system of coinage and has not the same meaning — a meaning in terms of which] a dime [(say) may be exchanged for] a bar of chocolate, or a doll. The dime, the chocolate bar, and the doll are [culturally] equated, [even though they are physically very different objects.] Such examples have a methodological significance: the principle of setting significant acts in a tight-fitting configurational scheme. The meaning of the act is not to be judged by its abstract content, but by its placement in the life of a people.

[With respect to trait analysis,] this symbolic or actual placement [of a cultural element] in a pattern of culture [— that is, the element's] psychological value — places a configuration upon a trait or complex. The logical analysis [of traits] can [otherwise] go too far and can [end up] being reckoned without cultural context. But [to remove a trait from its context is to strip] the trait of that latent or total cultural content that acts upon its meaning, response, and position.

[When viewed out of context, a trait's historical import may become severely distorted, for over time] the values and configuration [in which the trait occurs] may be completely transformed or reversed, due to changes in customs which may or may not be directly associated with the transformed trait or complex. When a pattern or complex begins or ends is uncertain; all that can be ascertained are the relationships among several of them. [The once] intrinsic value of coinage, for example, is a question of faith having arisen in deferred credit and thus has become another pattern. [More important than questions about the historical origins of patterns is] the question, what is the range of a pattern? What does it embrace in the psychological context of a culture?

[The importance of pattern, as compared with the overt content of an act of behavior, is illustrated by the possibility of] conflicts of classification ([i. e., behaviors that can be classified in terms of two conflicting patterns of meaning]). Biological and physical factors, [no matter how overt, are always susceptible to multiple interpretation as to how they are] classified and defined by cultural pattern, as when it is uncertain whether a man walking [in a particular way] is happy, drunk, physically disabled, on a slippery floor, etc. Hence the fallacy of judging the essential nature of a given culture [element] from external appearances.

[As compared with the culture stratum view] of Graebner, Father Schmidt, and others,[1] therefore, [we gain] a more intimate understanding of culture [when we turn our attention away from the spurious concreteness of individual elements (traits) and begin to view it in terms of] form. For behavior follows forms, [like a gesture following] a curve pattern that begins and comes definitely to a closure. The closure comes when all the elements contributing to the behavior are present and aid in the end of a set of responses. A behavior response gets its meaning in a setting of a behavior pattern. [For this reason there is a] feeling of uneasiness, incompleteness, and dissatisfaction when one or more of the elements in the behavior pattern is missing or replaced by an unexpected element. The lack of salt in a meal, a dignified friend calling you by your first name after [only] a short acquaintance, a man leaving the room during a lecture — [in such cases] we would feel uneasy until we could place the action [in an appropriate pattern]. (The walking out of the room is not [in itself] the significant part of the act. The important part of the act is the meaning — [why he walked out.]) Until we can interpret the act, we are in a non-closure state.

A glance at configurative (Gestalt) psychology [would confirm the importance of pattern in perception. One sees this in action also, as with the] lapse and closure of an action pattern.[2] People act with a feeling of closure in the future. Certain elements have great importance in the pattern. We reconstruct a plan of our action; each element has its relation to the pattern. The significance of each act depends upon its place in the pattern, and if we feel strongly the pattern in which the act belongs, our reaction to the act is "right". But patterns overlap: suppose we are discussing politics with a friend, when his child comes in[to the room]. How should we react to the child? [What pattern of conduct should now apply?] Intuition means the ability to see the map, the pattern of conduct, imaginatively. It is not the overt conduct that matters, but the arrangement.

Words tick off these configurations of conduct. Consider, for example, the words "tradesman" and "bandit" in relation to configurations of experience. "Tradesmen" refers to such people as Chicago business tradesmen, a [realm of] experience one is used to. [Suppose, however, that we encounter] businessmen [in a less familiar locale, as, perhaps,] in the bazaar trade in Asia, a trade based on bargaining; and [(the bargaining ending to our disadvantage) we call the bazaar men] "bandits". But they are not bandits — they are tradesmen; we call them bandits because we see their activity against the background of our configuration of behavior — [our expectations about how trade is carried out.] Thus words do not describe objective things as much as place objects in the behavior configuration.

[The point is that] we do not see things, we see significances. For instance, we may pretend these are all t's: t, T, +, [etc.],[3] yet they are all different.

[Let us consider a few more] examples of general patterns in behavior that are definable aside from content. To a painter, the whole world can be expressed in paints. Painting a rural barn, the artist does not paste pieces of wood on his canvas to get the texture more exact. [He relies, instead, on a pattern of visual relations that is definable quite apart from the actual substances of which the barn, on the one hand, and the medium of paint, on the other, are composed.] Or, [when I greet a child somewhat abruptly,] the child's mother pretends my brusque greeting [can be taken] as a nice one, and that that is the one I really meant. Interpretation [— placing a behavioral act in a pattern of significance — is what matters, not its physical content.] Conduct is seen not as what it is overtly, but in relation to a pattern, to a geometric plane [if you will, or a particular] context; [and contexts may overlap] or be switched, as in humor, [which we might think of as] an unconscious mathematics of changed contexts.

[The problem of locating the pattern in terms of which an element should be viewed is all the greater when we] observe cultural phenomena [deriving from a culture other than our own.] Inevitably, one places these "objective" phenomena according to one's own patterns – and [inevitably, too, one] experiences a shock on discovering the existence of entirely different patterns in a given culture from those that had obviously seemed to be present. Cultural phenomena are [always subject to] a double response, therefore. An ethnological specimen is viewed [quite differently] by an anthropologist [who sees it] in terms of a native culture, and a miner who, respectively, [sees it in terms of] his own. Cologne Cathedral, viewed as from the local or Catholic culture [of Cologne itself, will have a different significance] from the view of an anti-German Iowa farmer. When anything is viewed, one's own culture-confines are always present in varying degrees and aspects. ([This propensity to embrace new experiences or cultural elements within its framework is] what we might define as the carrying-power of a pattern.)

[In short,] a pattern is a theory of activity having meaning in terms of the typical event of a given society. (We may distinguish a pattern from the total configuration.) *A pattern is form, seen functionally.* Things which seem the same are not, unless they function similarly. [Indeed, in reviewing the problem of culture traits] my purpose is to show differences in seemingly similar objects – [functional differences that arise because the objects participate in different cultural configurations.]

2. The Patterning of Culture Exemplified: Speech

[Although we may define] cultural patterning [in terms of the relation between] form and function, [our cultural] analysis [is not thereby made simple.] The problem of form and the problem of function are very much more subtle than is generally envisaged. [To illustrate these problems, let us consider] speech; for language is a [particularly convenient] example of an elaborate [cultural] pattern that keeps itself going as a self-contained organism or system of behavior. [It is also a good illustration of the complexity of functions and of the inappropriateness of viewing pattern through an alien lens. For] linguistic analysis does not rest content with overhead functions; and pattern must be understood in terms of the ultimate analysis intuitively felt by any normal member of a given community.

Language is the supreme example of the fact that the total functioning of patterns is different from the functioning of a specific pattern. In two languages one may find the form (sound) and the function (meaning) of elements to be the same but the patterns totally different. It is the internal economy — the configurational analysis — that is completely different in all languages. Suppose, for example, that in language A, [the form] *wala* means 'house', and in language B there is also a form *wala* meaning 'house'. Yet although [the two forms] are linguistically and culturally the same they can still be [significantly] different. Why? Because there may still be a difference in the morphology or configuration of the languages. In language A, [*wala* consists of] *wa* + *la. wa* means 'to dwell', and *la* means 'that which is used'. In language B, however, *wala* [is composed from] *w-* + *ala* (where *ala* = 'house', and *w-* is a prefix marking neuter [gender]). [Thus the two forms are] functionally different in the two languages. [To put this point another way,] in language the same formal elements plus a different configurational union may equal two patterns, resulting in two separate languages.

[What, then, is the role of meaning, in language?[4] Does function, in this sense, determine form? Do meanings, as located in the world and its physical characteristics, explain the linguistic configurations in which people talk about them?] Although the exigencies of adjustment to the world are fairly uniform — hunger and [the search for] food, etc. — the languages about these [necessities] are very different. Meaning or reference are articulated by speech — we don't know the world before we have speech. If we don't have symbols, we don't have meanings.

By "speech" I mean the way in which groups symbolize thoughts and ideas, [in its totality, not just the individual word]. [Consider some expressions using the English word "drop":] you throw matches in the air, and they "drop"; but also one "drops" in attendance; and one "drops" out of sight. Now, there is a certain behavior to the word "drop", in that there is a uniformity to our conception of the word even if we use it in violent ways. Yet, you may also be able to express the same thing without using that word. In agreement, for instance, you can say "uh-huh" instead of "I agree". Thus the [wider] concept [you want to express] may be analyzed in another way. There are languages — Navajo, [again, for example] — that have no word [specifically] meaning "drop". Instead, in Navajo, analysis shows that [the expression we translate as] "drop" means the passing through space of stone, or mush, etc., showing that object as the main subject of thought. [The Navajo is] interested in the type of object which travels through space. This object is the nuclear idea, while the "dropping" idea comes in only as a prefixed element, adding an indication of a downward direction.[5] Thus [the Navajo] does not express "drop" in our sense.

"Give" is the same way. It is an illusion that languages express necessary fact instead of convenient expression for necessary fact — [an illusion] that makes us fallaciously believe that [the English sentence] "I will give it to you" is exactly equivalent to the Latin *id tibi dabo*, for example. Not only are the words not equivalent [in the English and the Latin,] but in the Navajo *nà•dè•c'a't* the idea of "giving" is not even [explicitly] expressed. [That is,] all languages do express the concept of giving but Navajo has no word for "give" though it expresses this through a specific arrangement of patterns. Indeed, there is an amazing variety of configurations [invoked] in expressing the sentence "I will give it to you" in different languages.[6]

[Thus there is no necessity that the meaning expressed by a particular word in English should be expressed in the form of a word in some other language.] A word is anything the language says is a word; and the overtones in words are irreplaceable, being incapable of synonyms. Actually, in language words as such do not have meaning without context. Even though a form may have a typical meaning usually associated with it, context can change this meaning entirely. Thus the form itself is not important — meaning is given by the context in which or to which it fits. Implication bears ninety percent of the work of language.[7]

[The same flexibility in the relation between form and meaning holds true for grammatical categories, as a means of expressing] a group of concepts, or one whole concept. For example, consider the use of the plural in English, [expressed with a grammatical tag.] Should we also have a tag denoting "brightness" vs. "dullness"? [Perhaps it seems more appropriate to have a grammatical expression for plurality because] plurality is more fundamental. Surely we know the difference between one and more than one, so we use plurals, while we don't use differences in color all the time. But it is a difference of degree, not of kind. Some languages do not allocate to plurality the same importance that we do [in English. Even in English,] we sometimes make a plural reference in the singular; plurals in English are used only spasmodically according to idiom. And some languages have no plurals — they only seem to. (In many American languages what seems at first sight to be a true plural of the noun turns out on closer analysis to be a distributive.[8]) We look for such things [as plurality] because they are a necessary concept to us: nouns must have number, [we assume].

[Similarly, we suppose] number is akin to gender; and we think of tense as being very important. But even tense forms are interchangeable under common usage; and there are languages, such as Yana, without tense tags. In Nootka, the first sentence of the story locates the time by denoting the tense. [After that, tense] is not referred to again. [The story] goes on in a general or present tense, and people know what's what. But they are very dogmatic on the aspect [of the verb]. Aspect is the geometric form of time: all events [can be conceived of as either] a point or a line, and this [distinction] is formalized by certain languages. "She burst into tears" is a point, while "she lived happily ever after" is a line; and this in Nootka is more important than tense. [Event shapes such as] (1) Momentary, (2) Durative, (3) Graduative, (4) Inceptive, (5) Pre-graduative, and (6) Iterative (based on 1, 2, and 4) are aspects found in Nootka and in some other languages, in varying combinations. Formally they are very clearly defined principles, whether [they are represented by] individually integrated symbols or not; that is, there is some flexibility in the content of the form. So the difference between what is formally necessary and what is logically necessary must be considered. Language is concerned with meaning, but it is also [— and more fundamentally —] concerned with form. [One might even say that] language is mainly concerned with form, with meanings a concern of psychology.

[There are many instances when the behavioral form provided by a pattern does not follow, or no longer follows, in any straightforward logical way from its content.] Consider, for example, verbs that are not entirely active [in their meaning but are treated as active in the linguistic structure:] in English the subject "I" is logically implied to be the active will in "I sleep" as well as "I run". [A sentence like] "I am hungry" might, [in terms of its content, be logically] better expressed with "hunger" as the active doer, as in [the German] *mich hungert* [or even the French] *j'ai faim*. In some languages, however, such as Sioux, a rigid distinction is made between truly active and static verbs. [In that case, pattern and content coincide more logically than in English.]

[It seems, then, that] when we get a pattern of behavior, we follow that [pattern] in spite of [being led, sometimes, into] illogical ideas or a feeling of inadequacy. We become used to it. We are comfortable in a groove of behavior. [Indeed,] it seems that no matter what [the] psychological origin may be, or complex of psychological origins, or a particular type of patterned conduct, the pattern itself will linger on by sheer inertia, which is a rather poor term for the accumulated force of social tradition, and entirely different principles of psychology come into play which may even cancel those which originally motivated the nucleus of the pattern of activity. Patterns of activity are continually getting away from their original psychological incitation.[9]

Thus a culture pattern does not present itself in a definite time frame — only as a relative point of completion. [To understand the operation of a pattern] one needs a long view, both backward and forward. In English, we have lost the feeling for gender in the noun; but, illogically, we [still] have genders in the pronoun — [reflecting] an archaic classification of the universe into masculine, feminine and neuter. ([Note that other classifications are perfectly possible, as for instance a classification into] big and little, as in some African languages, or animate and inanimate, as in Algonquin [languages].) Once a pattern of expression becomes solidified, we unconsciously run our behavior pattern into that mold.

[Many examples of the psychological force of pattern in behavior could be drawn, too, from the sound systems of languages.][10] [Consider the sounds] ŋ and *l* in Nootka: [if a speech sound were only a set of muscular movements of the vocal apparatus, then once you know how to make the sound you should be able to make it anywhere; but this is not so.] These sounds are used by the Nootka only in sacred chants and songs (where *l* is the ceremonial variant of *n*). Such special song-sounds are, at least so it would seem, pronounced with difficulty by Indians under ordinary circumstances, as in the handling of English words that contain them. The obvious inference is that one may react quite differently to the same speech-sound entering into dissimilar associations. This fact has, of course, a much wider psychological significance.[11]

[Similarly,] for English-speakers [attempting to speak German,] the sound *ts*, occurring as German *z* at the beginning of a word, is more difficult [to pronounce] than *zh* (French *j*), but not because we have never pronounced it. [In fact we have pronounced both of them. But only the French sound is provided for in the] configuration [of sound relations we already have in English]:

Between vowels:		At beginning of word:	
-zh-	-sh-	sh-	X
-z-	-s-	s-	z-
-v-	-f-	f-	v-
Table 1: Configuration [of some English Consonants]			

We have the feeling relations of X − [the configuration in which a sound of a particular sort, namely *zh*, could occur at the beginning of a word − while] *ts*, though expressed as German *z*, is thought of as two sounds, *t* + *s*, [a kind of combination forbidden, in our English sound pattern, from occurring at the beginning of a word. Consider too the English speech-sound] *wh* and [the sound one makes when] blowing out a candle. Behavioristically they are the same, but their contexts are different.[12]

[To understand the significance of an act of behavior, or even to be able to produce it at all, depends, therefore, on a pattern or context of its occurrence, which gives it meaning and possibility. And a given act (like the candle-blowing sound) may have more than one context, more than one pattern according to which it might be interpreted.] These choices of configuration are evaluations rather than measurements. [Measurements have to do with objective characteristics of an act or a thing; evaluations have to do with choosing the configuration within which it has meaning.]

Indeed, a configuration once understood can give meaning even if you don't know [exactly] what to do with [the details of] your structure. In language, the elements are discovered after the pattern is known, not vice versa. Once the form is satisfactory, configurational [relations] give the ability to make meanings ad hoc. Consider the following illustration, [concerning the parts of speech in] Yana. [The parts of speech are not somehow naturally given − as we can see by considering problems in their definition, history, and comparison. In the Indoeuropean languages, for example, the relations between nouns and adjectives have changed over time. In many languages, too, there may be so close a formal relationship between adjectives and verbs that it is not clear that they are really distinct categories.] If, in a language, verbs and adjectives have the same phrasing they must be the same. For Yana, compare [the "verbal" construction in (1)] with the "adjectival" [construction in (2)]:

(1) *ni-sa-* ‖ *si* │ *ndja*   present definite, 'I walk away', etc.
　　 ni-sa- ‖ *si* │ *numa*   present definite, 'you walk away'
　　 ni-sa- ‖ *ha* │ *ndja*   past definite, ['I ...']
　　 ni-sa- ‖ *ha* │ *numa*   past definite, ['you ...']
　　 ni-sa- ‖ *ti* │ *ndja*   indefinite, ['I ...']
　　 ni-sa- ‖ *ti* │ *numa*   indefinite, ['you ...']

(2) *dyul-* ‖ *si* │ *ndja,*   etc. 'I am long'

[In these two examples the glosses of morphemes are as follows:]

> *ni* — a single male being walks
> *sa* — off, away
> *si* — present tense
> *ndja* — first person singular
> *numa* — second person singular
> *ha* — past tense
> *ti* — indefinite [or quotative?]
> *djul* — long

[These examples show that] the paradigm for the adjective [in Yana] is the same as for the verb; all adjectival forms are classified as verbs. Nootka has the same, as do many other languages. Forms get established and become comfortable; they are then imposed on further experience. [We can see this in the] reduction and interchangeability of parts of speech.

[Whether in language or in other cultural domains, therefore, it is the configuration, not the content, that determines an element's meaning.] Just as you claim that giving a person a piece of paper is equivalent to giving him a fatted calf (and can prove this by the structure of the culture, [with its use of paper money or notes of credit]), so you can prove that every adjective is a verb by the structure of the language. [(I.e., in a particular language, with its particular configuration.)]

Thus we are very naive to look for exact equivalences in the patternings of language, or for that matter in all of culture. The complete meaning does not lie in the specific function of segmented bits of behavior but in functions of wider import. (To cite a [cultural] example: paying a visit may be due to [requirements of] reciprocity, not to immediate pleasure.) Simple necessary functions which can easily be linked with overt behavior are not the point of analysis — they do not necessarily constitute a pattern. [Only] a complete formal analysis — plus a complete understanding of the forms' functioning — will give us pattern.[13]

Language in its very nature is symbolic, and symbolic behavior lies more in the unconscious realm than does functional behavior, which is more in the conscious realm. [The stability of cultural pattern, and] society's unwillingness to change, are largely due to the symbolic texture of behavior, and [our] unconscious attachment to these modes of behavior that stand for larger contexts.

3. The *Topati* ('Privilege') Pattern among the Nootka[14]

The handy sociological terms we possess imply that the functional residues of behavior define logical and equivalent categories. This is obviously not so. All culture resolves itself into patterns but not in a departmental sense — rather in a terminological sense, [with its own terminology (i. e., the native term)] bearing a unifying concept. And the culture thus constituted is not an incremental, segregatable collection of patterns, but rather a manifold continuity of functions.

[To illustrate this point with another] example of cultural pattern, let us consider the concept of *topati*, 'privilege', among the Nootka Indians as a psychological aspect of culture, and the behavior in regard to this concept. This is not totemism, but an idea of privilege, status, or class, under which are grouped such diverse things as the right to use certain names, songs, fishing and hunting rites and ceremonies, etc. Among the Nootka there were nobles (chiefs), commoners who (like medieval villeins) were attached to noble households, and slaves.

How are you going to symbolize status in the society? *Topati*, literally 'black token' (probably originally a crest), is the name for certain privileges, ranging from the symbolic (such as names and songs) to the practical (rights to hunt and fish), that pass in the lineage and are the exclusive rights of that line.

The Nootka concept of privilege does not easily emerge from mere observation. Cultural data [are subject to] multiple interpretation, and objectively similar phenomena [may participate in] completely distinct patterns and orientations. Each *topati* activity has its counterpart in a [similar] activity that is not *topati*: there are *topati* songs, and also other songs; *topati* names, and other names; etc. [How, then, are we to locate the cultural pattern?] Vocabulary may be the key — a native term [such as *topati*] points to the reality of a culture pattern. The way to define the *topati* is to determine similar concepts which do not have the same value as *topati* concepts, e.g. nicknames, and songs of certain types. [By contrasting (say) songs that have a *topati* value with songs that do not, we can arrive at a pattern definition for *topati*. This coincides with the native's own interests, since] the native is interested in the *topati* aspect of a *topati* song, rather than in that song.

[We must consider, therefore, the realms of activity in which phenomena labeled as *topati* are found, in order to distinguish the *topati* aspects of the activity from other aspects. For, to define this cultural pattern, it would not suffice merely to describe our observations of events and add them up. As we have said,] the content of culture is not incremental. The meaning of an event in a society must be manifold, because the event is the crossroads of many cultural patterns. One behavior pattern is constellated in a group of patterns; thus behavior can be understood only in relation to these other patterns. Context is always needed to give the culture pattern.

[A kind of context especially] important in this area is the potlatch: every feast ceremony or public event is a potlatch — that is, at some point property is given away in a certain form. If you wish to affirm your status, you must give a ceremonial feast at which you distribute property. You don't merely give wealth; you are entitled to give a ceremony which is yours, and you must validate it by distribution [of gifts]. Giving a name to a daughter, for example, is an occasion for a feast, for the name belongs to the lineage — it has been owned by particular people in the past, and it is [therefore] valuable. The potlatch is the validation, or reaffirmation, of the privilege. [To put it another way,] the philosophy of the potlatch is the holding up of a privilege. It is not a simple economic system, but the affirmation of privilege and honoring people.

The subject of privileges is a vast one, and a complete enumeration of all the economic, ceremonial, and other privileges of one high in rank would take a long time.[15] [A few may be listed here to give an indication of the diversity of activities and realms of cultural life into which *topati* values enter.][16]

3.1. Legends

Legends act as the warrant for status. Mere precedent is not sufficient to establish status; the legend is also necessary. Thus a man's status is defined by the fact that he enters into the activities described in the legend. There is a feeling of participation in the deeds of ancient ancestors of the mythological past. Although many of the privileges [warranted] in legend are referred to only by implication, the legend is important both as a document [of privileged activities, names, and objects] and as a privilege [in itself], for the right to tell a certain *topati* legend with ceremonial properties, and to tell one for gain, is also a privilege. The legends belong to [particular] lineages, in which they are said to have been handed down from generation to generation. But there are also legends which are not *topati*.

3.2. Names

Hooked up with the *topati* legends are personal names, both of individuals and of objects. A child at five is given a name that doesn't have much connotation; later, he or she is given another name which has certain rights [attached to] it. Some names belong to first sons or daughters, some are for males [only] or females only, and some are for older people or for younger people. There are names for the sons of an older daughter and for sons of a younger daughter. (Everything that relates to war is associated with younger sons.) There are legends in the line of descent which use these names. There is a gradation of names, and the giving of names must be validated by the giving of property at a naming [ceremony]. Names are therefore changed from time to time, adding increased status. For example, a man can give certain names to his daughter as dowry on her marriage, and she can use these for her children. Names refer not only to persons, but also to things, e.g. canoes, houses, house posts etc., harpoons, caves, and rituals. However, there are also names which have no *topati* value, [such as] nicknames.

3.3. Ceremonial games

Ceremonial games for prizes are also recognized privileges, often dramatizing some incident in a legend. Given at potlatches, they also validate privilege and are often accompanied by a distribution of gifts. Songs introducing the games are part of the privilege.

3.4. Songs

[In addition to] the introductory song for a ceremonial game, there is a great variety of songs, [some of which are *topati* and some not]. Gambling songs, for example, are not *topati* — anyone is free to sing them. Club songs, love songs, etc. were also not privileged. The *topati* songs, however, were also many, and were named: for example, "Communicating with the spirit" songs, originally associated with whaling, are now used on many occasions. Originally they were intended to persuade the spirit in a whale to come toward the land rather than away. [Other examples of *topati* songs include]:

— Songs to announce important events, and secret announcement songs.

— Songs to demonstrate the possession of wealth, often in the context of a legend.

— Lullabies, which also connect with legends. You often put up a pole in the potlatch house, put the baby by it and sing a lullaby; then the host has to give away money.

— Woman-purchasing songs (beginning with the engagement, possibly a year before the marriage).

— Songs in connection with winter feasts, [especially] the wolf ritual. Only certain people can sing them, for acting as Wolf is *topati*. Many other varieties of songs are *topati*, as are dances of all sorts which go with the songs.

3.5. Ceremonial activities

Many particular ceremonial activities are *topati*: the lassoing of novices; the privilege of blackening the faces of those present at an exorcism; acting as Wolf; etc. Very often the privilege is owned by a woman, the oldest in the lineage. She can transfer the activity to a substitute and pay him for it — and this payment also enhances the *topati*.

3.6. Heraldry

The right to paint houseboards with certain paintings, and [indeed] all ceremonial features of the house, houseposts, and beams, are *topati*. For the [Nootka] house is a symbol as much as it is an instrument — it is something that symbolizes lineage and the status of the owner. The paintings on the outside of the house are likewise part of the house, as is the totem pole, which can only be understood in connection with the house structure. It is carved with symbolic animals and personages in myth. The carvings may represent several crests of different families —

[the representation constituting] more a social system, a crest armorial, than a totem proper. Originally [the totem pole was built] right up against the house; the door went through the pole, and the poles were merely a variation of the house posts. In order for the chiefs to exhibit all their crests they put them outside. Later variations put the posts away from the house (and [also gave rise to the] development of grave posts, which are probably similar symbolically to the house posts.

Behind the concept of crests is, [again,] the concept of privilege, *topati*. The crest [is itself] a privilege, as is the naming of houseposts, and the legends [represented on them]. [Illustrating these legends,] the totem pole figures are the pictures of an unwritten book.

3.7. Special ways of performing ceremonies

Special ways of performing ceremonies are also *topati*, and are often validated by family legends.

3.8. Chief's privileges

Certain symbols of status for the chief himself are considered to be *topati* — symbols of his office which are attached to it and inalienable. That is, they are not transferable from one situation to another as are these other privileges [we have mentioned]. For example, the way in which a whale is divided up among households is according to privilege, and the dorsal fin goes to the chief. So does the flotsam and jetsam, [for the chief has] the right to property that drifts up on the group's territory. [Similarly,] the privilege of taking the natural resources of a given type of land is such a *topati*. The boundaries of the tribe's territory, carefully guarded, may also be regarded as the *topati* of the chief.

It is also someone's special privilege to harpoon whales at the beaches where they burrow into the sand occasionally, though he may not otherwise own the land. This is illustrative of the [Nootka] conception of property, referring not to land as such (for land as such is not owned), but to the privilege of performing a certain activity there. The same [is true of] fishing places. [These privileges are] *topati*.

[Now, how shall we define the *topati* pattern underlying all these diverse activities?] One must not confuse the *topati* with the idea of value, for not all valuable things and activities are *topati*. One example is the secret way of preparing whale harpoons; these [preparations] are valuable, but they could not be *topati* since they are not made into public exhibitions. You cannot have a *topati* unless you are willing to show it in public; secret practices are not *topati*, because they do nothing to enhance your prestige or that of your ancestors. The *topati* is always public. It is a token, a crest of privilege — a matter of prestige. Therefore magic is not *topati*, although it is just as valuable. Rites and ceremonies to get power, which are secret and private, are not *topati*. *Topati* and [non-*topati* forms of] valuable knowledge are inherited differently. Moreover, power as such is not *topati*.

[We can now begin to identify the] things characteristic of *topati* — the pattern definition:

1. To be *topati* a thing must be public. It must be openly presented to people, known and talked about.

2. It cannot be exhibited without an expenditure of wealth, and having a feast.

3. It is the corporate right of a lineage, not of an individual; [it derives from one's] identification with a glorious ancestor.

4. There must be a tie-up with a legend, backing [the *topati*].

5. It must be localized. Every *topati* belongs to a place, and the legend refers to some place. (Localization is important [in general] on the North West Coast, and in California too, among the Hupa and Yurok.)

6. The individual's right to participate must be clear — you must have clear title to the privilege and be able to state your relationship to it. The normal way of gaining this right is by direct descent, in which both a rule of primogeniture and of male descent holds. Other ways to obtain a *topati* are by dowry, or by a ceremonial gift, in which you just hand over a right to someone; for example, a chief may give a *topati* to another chief, and this is expected to be returned later on. A *topati* can also be obtained by "hitting" — by force, [in other words, such as by] warfare or assassination. By this right of might, you just kill someone calmly and take his *topati*. [Or, you might] steal a box and mask from neighboring tribes, or conquer one of their fishing territories.

These samples [of Nootka life involving the *topati* system] suggest that [we should see] cultural pattern always as a configuration or aesthetic form rather than merely [as a set of] specific events. There is an analogy, therefore, between working out the grammar of a language and working out the pattern of the *topati*. The system of the *topati*, as a [cultural] pattern, is equivalent to a grammatical form, such as the system of the passive, [in the sense that] the form gives the background, pattern, or configuration to enable the hooking in of a type of behavior into a pattern or form of implications. [Thus, for instance,] all verbs have passives, although some, e.g. 'to go', are not logical; in the same way, many elements of culture are fitted into configurations merely by analogy, rather than by psychology.

[To reiterate:] this grammatical interpretation of a cultural pattern [is appropriate because] a cultural pattern is always a configuration − an aesthetic form into which a particular behavior, or event, may be fitted. To understand an event, you have to give it a locus, [and it is the configuration which] gives a locus for behavior. [However − as we have already pointed out −] the meaning of the event is manifold, because the event must be the crossroad of many patterns. Each culture "trait" fits into a number of different configurations. Perhaps even the simplest behavior pattern is complex because it fits in and intertwines with all kinds of others − [according to the] implications of the total cultural pattern. For example, the lullaby sung in a potlatch ties in with the whole pattern of *topati*. And it is the overhead meaning, rather than the simple function of a pattern, that helps explain the stability of the pattern in the face of culture contact. Because the event is the crossroad of many meanings, the immediate and simple function does not go very deep. What is needed [for our analysis, therefore,] is the meaning of the overhead valuation plus knowledge of the streams of meaning behind the configuration. We must know this before we have a functional analysis of any power.

We must therefore discover the leading motivations for these configurations − the master ideas of cultures. These leading motivations constitute the culture in an anthropological sense. They are the fundamental dynamic concepts involved in the notion of cultural patterns. Nothing in behavior, cultural or otherwise, can be understood except as seen in reference to configurations.

There has not been much analysis of culture from a configurational point of view so far. We see much more clearly individual psychology and [social] institutions; [yet a configurational analysis would be much more profound.] But culture is just as dynamic a thing as human behavior. Culture should be defined as a series of human activities in a configuration.

4. [Conclusion: Culture as Possible Events]

Culture, then, resolves itself into patterns, or configurations, not depart-
ments. The content of culture is not an incremental concept of the
Wisslerian type. The [configurational] point of view stands over against
an "objective" dichotomizing of data into cultural entities which are
[merely] the result of *a priori* prejudices. For instance, we have good
descriptive accounts of the Plains Indian cultures, but we lack a good
picture of our brackets — [our own cultural framework, from whose
vantage-point those descriptions were made.] An idea of relativity in
culture [is essential, therefore. What the Wisslerian type of analysis takes
as] absolute values are not valid. Their supposed objectivity represents,
instead, a projection of our own cultural system's emphasis on sensory
facts and things.]

[In our discussion of language, earlier in this lecture, we saw that for]
symbols such as words, [while there may be a] primary meaning implicit
in the form, there is also a derived meaning — which makes for glibness
of interpretation, on a personal scale. There is never a one-to-one relation
of symbol and referent, and this is because of the configurative richness
[of the system]. In the symbolic pyramid of a culture, very few bricks
touch the ground — there is a consecutive and endless passing of the
[referential] buck. Indeed, symbols become more meaningful as they
become dissociated from the actual experience. [Yet, the supposedly
objective types of analysis make] constant appeal to the senses. A sensory
fact has enormous potency for us — even though an object in itself has
no meaning, until it is related to something [else] in our experience. For
example, [even something so sensory as] odors are judged by their configurational setting. But because of this [potency] something like a sensation fetishism builds up [in our culture], where values are built up in
terms of the "thingness" of things. (The above blocked Thurstone's
response to the *wala* experiment.)[17]

[This kind of] projection [represents one of the] difficulties of social
science.[18] Thing fetishes are a danger. [We need to] get the definition [of
our observations not in terms of things, but] in terms of meaning. And,
in thinking configuratively, [culture] must not be [seen as] static — as a
structure — but as *possible events*. Cultural understandings are to be seen
in terms of possible behavior.

Thus it is absurd to enumerate a list of things as defining a culture.
Their participation in the culture, not the fetishistic thingness, is what

counts. You must put yourself in a behavioristic relation to a thing before it becomes an element of culture. What gives a thing its presentational value — makes it recognizable — is the multiplicity of behavioral situations of which it is a part. This is what defines a thing. If we are to understand it, we need to construct a typical picture of a series of behavioristic patterns, situations into which it (an object) may be placed. For things have no intrinsic values.

Any [putative] culture pattern must, [therefore,] be tested out as a behavior sequence. No pattern can be considered as peculiar, since each has its own behavior-value. Yet, we can never know all the behavioristic implications; and, to apply the behavioristic test requires a vast knowledge of the cultural background, which we don't have. [The point is that] the structure we call culture, or social understanding, is implicit in behavior itself. [So, in a way] it is not relevant to say we must test out culture in behavior. Instead, we must see culture as a behavior sequence. The test of a real grasp of understanding of culture is its interesting commonplaceness. That is what attests the reality of culture.

Notes

1. See Graebner (1911), (1924); Schmidt (1924), (1926−35); and other representatives of the *Kulturkreis* school of ethnology.
2. On Gestalt psychology, Sapir wrote to Benedict in 1925: "…I've been reading Koffka's 'Growth of the Mind' (Margaret's copy) and it's like some echo telling me what my intuition never quite had the courage to say out loud. It's the real book for background for a philosophy of culture, at least your/my philosophy, and I see the most fascinating and alarming possibilities of application of its principles, express and implied, mostly implied, to all behavior, art, music, culture, personality, and everything else. If somebody with an icy grin doesn't come around to temper my low fever, I'll soon be studying geometry over again in order to discover what really happens when a poem takes your breath away or you're at loggerheads with somebody. Nay more, unless a humanist like yourself stops me, I'll be drawing up plans for a generalized Geometry of Experience, in which each theorem will be casually illustrated from ordinary behavior, music, culture, and language. The idea, you perceive, is that all you really need to do to understand — anything, is to draw a figure in space (or time) and its relevance for any kind of interest can be discovered by just noting how it is cut by the plane (= context) of that interest…" (Mead 1959:177).
3. The notes show several different designs at this point, all interpretable as cursive shapes for the letter "t".
4. The discussion of words and grammatical categories embarked upon here seems to be meant to illustrate the following point: the relationship between form and function in language is complex because both form and function have several levels of organization.

Beaglehole's notes give a good summary: "Language is the supreme example of the fact that in two languages one may find the form (sound) and the function (Meaning) of elements to be the same but the patterns totally different. The total functioning of patterns is different from the functioning of a specific pattern. E.g., all languages express the concept of 'giving' but Navajo has no word for 'give' although it expresses this through a specific arrangement of patterns. The complete meaning does not lie in the specific function of segmented bits of behavior but in functions of wider import, e.g., paying a visit due to reciprocity and not to immediate pleasure. Simple functions linked with overt behavior are not the point of analysis." At the same time, Sapir also emphasizes the primacy, or analytic centrality, of form as compared with meaning or function.

5. At this point Sapir explained what he meant by "nuclear" concepts. One notetaker has: "Some word concepts are nuclear, such as 'plow'; some are derivative, such as 'plowman'."

6. See Sapir and Swadesh (1946), "American Indian Grammatical Categories", on the expression of the English sentence "He will give it to you" in six American Indian languages.

7. Here Sapir referred his audience to a work by Zona Gale (1928), *Portage, Wisconsin and Other Essays*.

8. The preceding sentence is quoted from Sapir and Swadesh (1946).

9. The preceding two sentences are quoted from Sapir (n.d. [1926]).

10. Here Sapir referred the students to his 1925 paper, "Sound Patterns in Language".

11. The preceding passage, from "Such special song-sounds", is quoted from Sapir (1915a), "Abnormal Types of Speech in Nootka".

12. See Sapir (1925b), "Sound Patterns in Language", for an extended development of this example.

13. By "complete" here Sapir seems to mean "multi-leveled".

14. Sapir's major published works on privilege, rank, and the potlatch in Northwest Coast societies are: "A Girls' Puberty Ceremony among the Nootka Indians" (1913); "The Social Organization of the West Coast Tribes" (1915); "A Sketch of the Social Organization of the Nass River Indians" (1915); and "Sayach'apis, a Nootka Trader" (1922). Although these works all date from the first half of his career, the topic continued to interest him in later years. In 1924 he gave a paper on "The Privilege Concept among the Nootka Indians" at the Toronto meeting of the British Association for the Advancement of Science (unfortunately, no manuscript or abstract of this paper has been found). In the late 1920's he gave a course at the University of Chicago on "The North West Coast Tribes", in which much of the material was organized around the concept of privilege. In 1927 he drew on the same subject matter as an example of cultural pattern, in "The Unconscious Patterning of Behavior in Society". The present chapter shows his reworking of the subject in the 1930's. See also the (1939b) "Songs for a Comox Dancing Mask" and the (1939c) *Nootka Texts*.

15. The preceding sentence is quoted from Sapir (1915c).

16. Sapir's published discussions of privilege and the potlatch, and the discussion in his course on "The North West Coast Tribes" (University of Chicago) are differently organized. The miscellaneous character of this list in the class notes, with the more organized analysis afterwards, seem to be related to the methodological points Sapir is making: that a culture pattern does not easily emerge from mere observation; that a pattern is embedded in a context of other patterns; and that the concept of privilege is

a "leading motivation" or "master idea" of Nootka culture, pervading many realms of social life.

17. Louis L. Thurstone (1887–1955), a psychologist at the University of Chicago.

18. See Chapter 2.

Chapter Six

The Development of Culture

1. The Concept of Development in Culture

[Our concepts of cultural dynamics, change, development, and progress are intimately related, but they have not always been distinguished from one another. In order to consider the concept of development in culture, we shall focus on the idea of] progress — a perilous subject, to be sure.

The idea of cultural progress is a relatively modern point of view. Indeed, it is a characteristic of modern man that even in our time, in spite of all, we must believe in progress. Even the most cynical person has a childlike faith in it. [Our forebears in] classical [antiquity] did not share this faith. On the contrary: for them the perfect time was in the past, and they were more likely [to emphasize] stories of deterioration, as with the [story of the] Garden of Eden, and the like. For the [early] Christians it was the same. [Later,] in the Middle Ages, [the characteristic view shifted toward a conception of] a very equilibrated world, neither improving nor decaying. All values were fixed; [they were expressed in] an international language [(Latin)]; and so on. ([In this respect] the world of today is a world of anxiety compared to the medieval world.)

Meanwhile, however, in the seventeenth century, science developed and colonization took place — [a change] that meant a complete breaking up of the old world. The notion of progress depends on this; it could no more be shaken off. It was founded on that [principle]: that on a basis of some new scientific discovery it was possible to measure progress, to prove that a generation was superior to the preceding generation, the immediate past. [Today] the idea of progress is a very strong element in culture — not only in our culture but, more and more, in other cultures too. The notion of indefinite perfectibility is taken for granted, [both] in its psychological aspect [(the perfectibility of the individual)] and in an outlook on culture [itself (the idea of cultural evolution)].

But what is the nature of progress? It was never proved that this progress, [the superiority of the modern scientific world,] was more than mechanical. Men were naturally tempted to think that this power could be applied to anything else. But there is something more.

[First of all, we should distinguish] "progress" from [mere] "development", even from "development with a tendency"; [for the concept of progress implies some evaluation of the tendency, namely that it represents an improvement. For example, a tendency to reduce the elaboration of some cultural form may be considered a] simplification, or a deterioration. It may be progress, [but whether it is or not depends on one's point of view. Most importantly, we must recognize that] the various levels of a whole cultural complex [may differ as to how a concept of] progress [applies to them.] For example, the individual's [cultural] stock-in-trade [may develop differently from that of the] culture [complex taken as a whole]. Paradoxically, then, as against growing complications [at one level we may need] the idea of compensatory simplifications [at another.] And where culture change [is seen as increased cultural] complexity, [we must make a distinction between] analyzing detail and finding a much more rich culture. For this we must know the meanings of objects in culture. The total complexity of the culture of a small hamlet may be higher than the splendid Greek cities.

[It now seems clear that] the earlier anthropologists oversimplified in emphasizing the progressive piling-up of power in the development of culture. But contemporary [anthropologists] go too far in the other direction by denying progress [altogether]. I am not wholly with those who would discard the concept. You have to be unreasonably broad-minded to feel we are no further along than Neanderthal Man. However, "progress" (at [whatever] level) [is so far only] an intuitive concept. Is there any one idea, or formula, [for what constitutes progress]?

The general concept of progress may be usefully split up into three conceptual strands: (1) technological progress or advance − the material, industrial, or power point of view; (2) spiritual progress − the moralistic point of view; and (3) the cyclical development of patterns − the aesthetic point of view.

1.1. Technological progress

Since the dawn of civilization there has been a progressive improvement in the amount of knowledge of the physical environment and an application of that knowledge to our use, the better to use and combat the physical elements. It is a long step from making a big fire with no matches or a fire board to central heating. [Similarly,] the fact that I can take a railway and travel quickly is progress, because I do that with a minimum of effort. (Let us take as given the reality of that kind of value.) In the field of power, then — that is to say, the ability to utilize the environment — human beings have lost essentially nothing since early times, but have, instead, conserved and added to [the technological repertoire]. This means progress implicitly. At least, it means mechanical progress. Although specific techniques have been lost, we have equivalents for every process ever developed, apparently; and we have greater technological power than ever before.

A good example of a great [technological] contribution is the tin can — a high point because it involves many technological processes and is of use to a great number [of people]. In terms of power, the tin can is more important than Etruscan vases. For the fact that objects are used in cultural sequences — their place in culture — is what makes them important, not the objects themselves. To set going a [cultural] current which means maximum utilization of the means at our disposal with a minimum of effort — this is progress.

This [definition of progress] is objective, not subjective. [Thus technological advances are easily recognized as such, despite other differences in cultural background.] Technological superiority is always copied by peoples with less superior knowledge who come in contact with superior technical knowledge. Either they learn how to handle advanced power devices or they are killed off; and besides, people continually hunt for ideas which give much with little effort. For example, the Eskimo woman readily takes over the sewing machine. [Moreover, on the level of] the individual there is a rapid self-orientation to a new cultural element (such as the tin can). As the knowledge of the use of power becomes common property, the accumulation of power cannot be stopped. ([Recall] Thurnwald's idea of the cumulative nature of material culture.)[1]

This concept of progress, of course, includes the development of ideas, since the ideas have at least the opportunity or potentiality of giving power. Increase of knowledge, then, is also an instrumental progress. Power and ideas are inextricably associated. [The ideas] enable us to anticipate the solution of possible future problems, they give us the ability to predict, and they pave the way for the ideas of the future. Mathematics, for example, [enables us to make] scientific projections [which, in turn, further our technological] power. [Even] pure mathematics [can be seen] as power — as an economical way of thinking — which may be applied to other problems. Mathematics enables one to go through the imaginary to the real; this is power. [The example of mathematics also illustrates how] the accumulated power of the past is used to build power for the future, because a certain system of mathematics was essential for Einstein's theory of relativity.

It is interesting that non-European groups very readily take up ideas that have technological power even if they are unfavorable about other ideas. Primitive man does not resist technological power [in the least; rather, he] is hospitable to it. [Yet, this ready acceptance suggests a] fatality about the use of power that is perhaps the most essential fact in culture.

[Thus] the increase of power in certain lines shows progress, [although there remains the question of] whether fast progress is at the expense of certain elements such as aesthetics, beauty, or peace. Actually, the occasional retrogression and loss of power only heightens the stature of the actual accumulation of progress in the long run. Despite occasional setbacks, the conservation of man's energy has constantly increased through technological inventions which increase our powers. There has been no loss of vital mechanical processes, but, instead, an adaptation of new methods, as in the sciences. Technological progress [involves a] growth in point of view as well as in technique, and [it results in] an ability to orient oneself in the world with increased efficiency (and success).

1.2. Spiritual progress

Now, about spiritual progress it is more difficult to be certain, for we are dealing with intangible values. Largely a question of opinions and ideas, this factor is under the influence of subjective impulses more [than technology is]. Culture is ghostly and full of fantasies — but nonetheless forcefully demanding and exacting. Moreover, spiritual progress is also conditioned by the culture itself. Each group has certain preferred modes of behavior [and considers certain moral] traits desirable, but these [preferences] contradict each other in different cultures. [They change according to] time and place.

Do there seem to be certain kinds of behavior, certain desirable traits or values, which people in general do tend to grope towards? Is there, for example, a general feeling of value in the immaterial world? It is certainly true that every people persists in thinking that some sorts of actions are better than others; and they place some special value on "high ideals". [It is true, too, that] the spiritual (or moral) includes the behavior traits by which people get into contact with other people. These are the behaviors which get a man called a "good fellow". [These generalities are rather vague, but we can still use them as a basis for asking whether] there is any development of consciousness — any means developed for the individual consciousness to survive. Has there been any progress in imagination?

What may be taken as the essential is the process of identification, and this means the question of [society] itself. [So we might rephrase our question about consciousness thus:] is there any tendency in the history of culture for a growth of imagination, [in the sense of] substitution of other egos for one's own consciousness? And has there been any widening of this tendency? I think we conserve our consciousness by identifying ourselves with the [social] group, for our consciousness survives with the group. Knowing you can't conserve your own consciousness [beyond] death you depute it to others, to the group as a whole. The wish to conserve the reality and permanence of your own consciousness is served by identifying it with a group.

Now, the idea of identifying oneself with members of one's own family is easy — [seeing] one's continuation in an identity with one's children. The idea of identifying oneself with people of another country is [more] difficult. [In fact, the psychological processes involved in identifying with one's own group may be precisely what makes it difficult.] The hostility toward other groups may be interpreted as due to the adjusting of control of impulses to one's own group. Thus the consciousness of different groups [entangles us in] the paradox of self-defense. Wanting to aggrandize one's own group, one belittles others.

[How far does the control of impulses go?] If I am a member of an Indian tribe I kill [other Indians, though] only for good reasons. If I am a citizen of the United States I don't kill [other citizens at all]. I have extended the range of my inhibitions. I cannot [even] kill a member of another nation if I am not protected by the ideology of war. Let us call this "spiritual progress". It is not disconnected from the first kind of progress, because a society is more efficient, if people do not kill one another.

In war, too, even if we do remain for the present as ruthless as ever, there seems to be progress in our attitude toward killing individuals not of our own group. [Unlike our ancestors of a few generations back,] we apologize for war, [and emphasize] the sanctity of human life, [preferring to] save a life rather than save Rheims Cathedral. [Compared with our forebears] we [have to] try harder to rationalize and justify war, because our feeling of responsibility for the lives of those not identified with us is greater. There were no pacifists in Greek times. [Today,] not only is there a pacifist movement but there is more real general conflict [(i. e., ambivalence)] in human beings than ever before, for there is more genuine awareness of others' [self-consciousness] and of the possibility of identification with those remote from us. The idealists who identify consciousness with humanity [as a whole, rather than with a particular individual or group may be seen, therefore,] as a step in the growth of imagination with reference to consciousness. Our realization of [the existence of] consciousness other than our own is here to stay.

Thus certain values have tended to take on increments from [one historical] period to another. The world of reference is larger than ever before. The growth of imagination [means] including more people in the group [with which one identifies.] (Christianity is the arch example.) The idea of cleanliness, [too, is an example of a] larger individual integration of the progressive tendency to include more people and to have more respect for the rights of others. In race prejudice, there seems to be real progress visible in the last generation, with a growth [in awareness] of consciousness of races other than our own. Education can be another example: the range of education is growing. It is [now] taken for granted that the crowd must be educated, because inasmuch as a man is respectable, we must develop his mind. This feeling is of the same nature as the feeling of the sanctity of human life.

So spiritual progress, in the sense of a willingness to give up a part of our own consciousness to help somebody else's consciousness, does occur, I think. Our feeling of responsibility for the life of those not identified with our group has increased greatly.

[There is an analogy between this process and the development of the individual, for] the growth of an individual's consciousness from childhood requires giving up a part of our own consciousness in order to give happiness to somebody else's consciousness. The perfect world of a small child is bought at a price of limitation of [its awareness of the] consciousness of the adults making its world. But as you grow up you resign part of your own consciousness so that others may have equal rights. We grow up in society and learn to resign or defer many of our satisfactions. [Similarly,] in the history of culture we seem to catch the growth of an ability to identify our consciousness with others. There is a growth of consciousness in people at large, as there is in the development of a child.

[Our assertion of spiritual progress in culture, and in the growth of imagination, is on a different footing from our discussion of technological progress, however. For, as we have said before,] there is danger in stressing the insistent values of one culture all the time. The emphasis of value shifts indefinitely from society to society, and from time to time. Spiritual progress is also conditioned by the culture itself. This progress is asserted and felt but it cannot be proved in the sense in which technological progress can.

Moreover, what our time views as progress may, viewed in perspective at a later date, appear to be a retrogression, for some things appear as great during their time but not so later. This gives rise to the concept of the cycle of cultural development. [We shall discuss this concept mainly with respect to aesthetic forms. But in spiritual] respects, too, there seems to be a cycle. As regards the growth of imaginative awareness, and greater concern for the value of human life and individual expression, we seem closer to the Greeks than to Medievals like the enthusiastic ecclesiastic in the heyday of the power of the Church.

1.3. Cyclical development of patterns

The aesthetic view of progress is not endlessly linear, but cyclical, [incorporating both] progress and decline. Perhaps this [cyclical development] is not progress, but it is often confused with it. If you study anything that has a form you see that in the beginning it is confused and imperfect; then gradually it develops and it arrives at a certain peak; but in complicating the form you become expressive by and by, [and this is not always an aesthetic advantage]. For instance, the Cathedral of Cologne is perhaps more magnificent but less beautiful than others that are more simple. The cycle of polyphonic music is the same. The peak has been reached by Palestrina; Bach is already a decay from the pure polyphonic point of view, [because the polyphony] is complicated with harmony. Haydn, [later,] abandons the polyphonic patterns [in favor of the harmonic ones].

Thus we find certain periods in music, for example, when the fundamental ideas are questioned, considered, and revised. Within those developments we are tempted to say that there is progress. But there is a confusion here between the aesthetic and the technological. [Cycles of change in the arts involve both.] For example, in a symphony, the elemental musical idea − the aesthetic [element] − is the simple tune, while the harmonization of the tune is technological, [a harnessing of] power. In jazz, the achievement is entirely technological, since the melodies and themes are threadbare; only their working has been emphasized. The technology [of jazz] is exciting but not creative — a mere bag of tricks. In modern music, Wagner is the great accelerator of technological advance. He set instrument makers specific problems, [and added] more horns for more power. But the excitement of technical advance [in the arts] does not endure. Honesty of impulse will outlast technical advance; aesthetics is more important than technique.

In modern instrumental music, [therefore, we have an illustration of how] things go through a cycle. [This form of] music developed out of polyphonic singing — a hint [(?)] in vocal music suggested a new type of music, the instrumental forms, with instruments being used instead of the human voice. Once a pattern of instrumental music is established, this is developed, and so there comes later a preoccupation with technique — more and more comes in the playing with technique. The cyclical climax of modern music is reached with Beethoven. This plateau is maintained for a time, but then people come in who [merely] carry out stunts. ([The case of] Wagner, [we might say,] is stunts plus genius.) Then things degenerate and drag on until, out of the confusion, a new idea comes in and a new cycle arises. We have passed the heyday of [the classical cycle in] music; now we are feeling for a new start.

[To recapitulate: when] form and technique are well fitted, the peak of development is soon reached. Then the epigones, trying to give a more personal meaning [to the forms], introduce tricks — modifications of technology rather than [changes of] idea — and somewhere along the way the cycle may begin again.

Within a given movement, or cycle, various samples of behavior may reasonably be compared, [and comparison is necessary, of course, for any assessment of progress. Across cycles this cannot be done.] It is impossible to compare a Chinese musical composition with our Beethoven symphonies because they come from different cultural patterns, and we don't know [the Chinese music's] cycle, its cultural pattern. A particular pattern, such as the classic musical tradition, [represents] the actualization of an idea in a [particular] group. Technological progress may be hitched to a cycle, [but across cultures we cannot reasonably assess how this has been done.]

The development of the English sonnet may also be used as an example [of cyclical development]. The first sonnets were crude copies of an Italian form; then came Shakespeare's sonnets. By now the sonnet has actualized itself, and it might be felt today that it has said all it has to say. Now it is more or less of a form, a stunt — it is difficult to find an authentic poet today who is doing his best work in the sonnet. So this is no longer the day of the authentic sonnet, though we have great technological expertness in the sonnet [form]. Although there is always a thrill in technical achievement, this is sometimes confused with aesthetic judgement.

Practically all aesthetic patterns run through such a gamut: a rise from humble beginnings, an authoritative pinnacle, a prestige hangover — then down! [The progress of an aesthetic cycle, then, means that] there is aesthetic development within an aesthetic idea. The work of art is an answer to a problem, and at certain stages that problem can be better solved.

Take, for example, the cyclical development of English drama. There are spurts of creativity, sometimes without any obvious continuity between them, in the Elizabethan, Restoration, late eighteenth century, and contemporary realistic [periods]. At the beginning, there were two relatively feeble strands: the miracle plays and the [classic] tradition. In a very short time the two strands are fused, quite unpretentiously. From this simple beginning, Elizabethan drama develops complexity. But after the rich productions of Marlowe, Shakespeare, and [their contemporaries], the development seems to wear itself out. The later dramatists after Shakespeare had a rich heritage, but they became preoccupied with technique, and we have a good deal of artificiality. Posterity is never much interested in purely technical problems. [In our eyes] the Elizabethan drama is still great; the writers after that were probably considered still greater during their own time, but they seem tawdry to us.

Thus the set of problems posed in a particular art form starts with fumbling, then moves forward to its peak with a few great exponents [of the form]. May this be because the set of problems arising out of a new form get an answer and reach a climax? Then technical problems begin to complicate [the idea], a slow decline sets in, and the movement [falls] down. [But despite the cyclical nature of the development,] there is a real progress in this sort of cycle, and of a sort which is to be found in many cultural phenomena — perhaps in the development of most cultural patterns.

We can talk of [all sorts of] problems in a cyclical sense. Ethnologists do concern themselves [with these matters] when they talk of pottery styles, types of house decoration, and the like. If we had sufficient evidence we could trace cycles in primitive art — Northwest Coast art, for example:

Haida and Tsimshian [art forms] are "classic", while Bella Coola [forms] are too baroque, fussy, and [formally] degenerate. [Our examples need not be drawn only from the arts.] The history of any religious movement, for instance, represents a cycle.

Even language forms have something like a cyclical development. Although the language's development is continuous, it is possible to define a certain set of linguistic forms — or point to a certain stage of development of a form — as classical. The classical stage would have a perfectly consistent and tightly-wrought use of forms. Now, people participating in an aesthetic cycle are not conscious of it, [so it may come as a bit of a surprise when I say that we are not in that kind of stage in modern English.] English today is in a kind of trough. It has not perfected its own possibilities, nor does it still do excellently what it did in the period of Gothic. Even Anglo-Saxon was a bit weaker, [in this respect,] than Gothic. For example, the weakness of gender in English today is not classical. If you call a ship "she" and the sun "he", then there should [(in a classical stage)] be a feeling of she-ness or he-ness about any noun; [but, as we know, in modern English there is not]. As another example, the suffix -*s* is used for three categories: [it marks] the possessive, the plural, and the third person singular in verbs; but in no case is it completely and consistently carried out. All are [only] weakly expressed. For the verb endings, the classical stage would have either *I go*, *you go*, *he go*, or [else something like] *I gon*, *you gom*, *he goes*, etc. There is some feeling in the verb as [the forms] merge toward obliterating the distinction between singular and plural altogether. But [English's] inconsistency with respect to case endings is also non-classical, and again there seems to be a tendency to cut these out altogether.[2] [A classical stage would] either carry these distinctions out consistently or do away with them.

[To the extent that English seems to show a tendency toward obliterating these kinds of affixes,] a movement toward a thoroughly analytic language may be in progress. Chinese has [already] gone through this cycle. A Scandinavian scholar found in the Confucian writings a case distinction in pronouns which was rather weak, a sort of echo of a formerly more synthetic language; but the Chinese has long ago become entirely analytic, depending entirely upon [separate words and word] order [to express grammatical relations,] instead of [word-]internal changes. Thus Chinese has anticipated us by discarding case and using a rule of order. The Chinese, [on the one hand, as an analytic language,] and the Sanskrit (or Greek and Latin), [on the other, as a synthetic language,] are both classical, then, even though of quite different form;

whereas the English is not a classical kind of language, because it is not thoroughly integrated.

[Incidentally,] there is no relation between [this concept of classical form in a] language and the literature which is expressed in it. Tibetan, for example, is a fine language from a linguistic point of view, but its literature is drivel.[3] [To say that the English language is not thoroughly integrated is to speak about something] quite different from the value of what is written with English.

This idea of cyclical [development] also applies in everyday life. [Not only can we trace] the rise and fall of [patterns in] drama, Gothic architecture, language forms, or Mohammedanism, but in the history of the railroad train or the automobile one may be able to trace a similar cycle of development. [Perhaps even in] democratic government [we can see] a drifting away [from an original idea]; or in science, where there has been a scrapping of traditional bundles [of knowledge, as with the decline of] alchemy and astrology. Certain questions have died out. ([But in science, perhaps] this is only change, [not decline; for] progress is not possible without destruction.)

The cycle is hard to define starkly, or to isolate. During its height, in the classic period, the cycle is so vital to the culture that it is unquestioned and taken for granted. There is a relation between form and need, such that at some point there is a complete equilibrium between them. But this balance does not remain. The questioning occurs and then comes a long period of weakening. As the cycle becomes less and less pure, it may be caught up with another meaning — but then it is really a new pattern.

There has been no evaluation of primitive culture on the basis of the cyclical idea. There are many dangers in this point of view, but [such evaluation] should be done if we are to understand primitive cultures. [For without some notion that] primitive culture [undergoes] climax and decay in its own terms, [we cannot usefully incorporate it in any conception of progress.] The primitive is not [just] a barbarian and a preliminary to "civilization". It is impossible to compare cultural details of one group with those of another unless there is a definite historical continuity. (In America, Walt Whitman [strikes a] primitive note; taken up by sophisticates in Europe and rephrased in French, he becomes a decadent.)

[In sum: we have distinguished] three kinds of progress, which get mixed up one with the other. [People of different times and places have not always accepted all three kinds,] but [(one might suspect)] each type of man will more or less believe in one of the three kinds of progress. As for mechanical progress, man has never lost anything in this realm; there has been an increase of power. Although the flow of consciousness has not [grown] in a steady line like power — there is an ebb and flow — on the whole there has been progress there too, in the gradual development of a consciousness transcending the self, or the ego. [As for the third kind:] for any complex pattern of expression you seem to have cycles of development.

[Perhaps the growth of cycles, with the possibility of a new pattern emerging out of an earlier one,] is the one vital idea worth saving out of the idea of progress. [It might be called an] epigonal view of progress. [As the pattern moves from a] primitive [stage] to a classical and then an epigonal one, there may be a rejuvenation so that the pattern doesn't die out. The epigonal period [involves] a realization of the potency of expressive forms — some progress in knowledge of psychic process, and a greater concern for the value of human life and individual expression.

2. [Coda: Symbols of Progress]

[Just as any idea has its symbolic expression, so it is with the idea of progress in our culture:] we have [our] preferred symbols of progress. [One of the most important realms for the expression of those symbols is education. But there can be a lag between what the culture has come to value most — what it sees as its signs of improvement over an earlier age — and what is enshrined in education, as the sign of an improved person.] For example, the prestige of knowing many languages has been carried over from the old Renaissance tradition. But, particularly in America, we no longer really believe in this. You cannot plan [school] curricula unless you know what symbols are authoritative, and have the greatest value. The symbols [of progress] are changing today; if the change isn't too fast, education may catch up.

[The relation of educational symbols to cultural ideas of progress can itself be seen as a cyclical pattern.] The English education of *Tom Brown's Schooldays* [illustrates] the classical part of a cycle, because those symbols were more authoritative in those days. Today no one is in a position to say what is a rational curriculum. We don't know what we have transcended, and what values are going to emerge as significant.[4]

Notes

1. Richard Thurnwald (1869–1954), German ethnologist/functionalist.
2. See the chapter on "Drift" in Sapir's (1921) *Language*.
3. Editorial apologies are hereby conveyed to Tibetans. Whether Sapir would have published a statement like this I do not know.
4. For other discussions of the dynamics of cultural and linguistic change see Sapir (1916), "Time Perspective", and (1921), *Language*. The present discussion is somewhat different from these earlier works, however.

Part II

The Individual's Place in Culture

Chapter Seven

Personality

1. The Relation of the Individual to Culture

[Although anthropologists sometimes entertain notions] to the contrary, anthropology is very much dependent on the individual, even necessitating rapport or good psychological relationships between two individuals. [This applies, in the first instance, to the anthropologist's relationships with individual informants, from whom so much of his information derives.] The fallacy, however important, [in anthropological method] is that the results [of those relationships with individuals] are considered — and definitely stated to be — culture, as a whole. [That is,] a person in the field presents the culture as a whole without realizing that the information depends upon the informant. [What is true for the anthropologist, moreover, is all the more compelling for the individual participating in society:] the individual has to conform and fit together the conflicting [versions] of culture [he encounters. Perhaps we see such a process most clearly when it concerns] a foreigner in this country [learning to conform,] or a southerner moving north. In the psychological sense, culture is not the thing that is given us. The culture of a group as a whole is not a true reality. What is given — what we do start with — is the individual and his behavior.

Analytically, the individual is the bearer of culture. Therefore, anthropologists' generalizations about the culture of a group are extremely theoretical. They depend upon his [sense of] sureness and [his] ability to extract significant uniformities from individuals' (separate) cultures and to generalize these into a pattern. Yet, it may turn out that his "culture", so extracted, is so formalized that it exists only as a mental construct and has no objective reality at all.

[In that case,] no individual [from the group whose culture it purported to be] would recognize it as his own culture — in many respects it would seem foreign to him. [But, if that were so, would there not be something questionable about the anthropologist's report? As we said before, pattern must be understood in terms of the ultimate analysis intuitively felt by any normal member of a given community.]¹ Remember, then, that the sole significance of a cultural pattern depends upon [its meaningfulness to the bearer:] the emotional reaction to it. This gives a test of the reality of cultural elements to individuals in the group.

[These considerations, however, while deriving from our concern with the supposedly impersonal forms of culture, also come within the framework of the individual's psychic constitution, or personality. As members of society,] we accept the forms of our culture; it is [imposed] upon us and then we consider it right. Even such things as the English plural, [a cultural form] thought to be individually passive, is — [by virtue of being a cultural form —] what the individual wants, what makes him feel easy, what has relevance for his specific personality. We identify ourselves with our cultural background, and this identification is quite as easy, and quite as possessed of relevance for the individual, as an association with any natural phenomena (associations which are often, along with other things, thought to hold validity for [the individual's] personality). There is really no part of culture which does not have some bearing on our personality. [That bearing need not be anything we are consciously aware of, for] we are often most biased when we are consciously most honest.

[Does this mean that the anthropologist's task simply resolves into that of the psychologist?] If the culture of a group is thus in a way impossible to formulate, what becomes of the anthropologist's calling, and how realistic can his approach be? [In falling back upon the individual, as the objectively given starting-point, we need not reject the concept of culture. On the contrary: we provide our formulations with better evidence.] Any statement, no matter how general, which can be made about culture needs the supporting testimony of a tangible person or persons, to whom such a statement is of real value in his system of interrelationships with other human beings. [But] if this is so, we shall, at last analysis, have to admit that any individual of a group has cultural definitions which do not apply to all the members of his group, which even, in specific instances, apply to him alone. Instead, therefore, of arguing from a supposed objectivity of culture to the problem of individual variation, we shall, for certain kinds of analysis, have to proceed in the opposite direction. We shall have to operate as though we knew nothing about culture but were interested in analyzing as well as we could what a given number of human beings accustomed to live with each other actually think and do in their day to day relationships. We shall then find that we are driven, willy-nilly, to the recognition of certain permanencies, in a relative sense, in these interrelationships, permanencies which can reasonably be counted on to perdure but which must also be recognized to be eternally subject to serious modification of form and meaning with the lapse of time and with those changes of personnel which are unavoidable in the history of any group of human beings.[2]

[Thus] it is not the concept of culture which is subtly misleading but the metaphysical locus to which culture is generally assigned. The true psychological locus of *a* culture is *the individual* or *a specifically enumerated list of individuals*.[3] [Notice, however, that we do not define] the individual [in the same way as would] the biologist. The biologist has no trouble in defining an individual, [but his definition is not ours.] "Individual", here, means not simply a biologically defined organism maintaining itself through physical impacts and symbolic substitutes of such impacts, but that total world of form, meaning, and implication of symbolic behavior which a given individual partly knows and directs, partly intuits and yields to, partly is ignorant of and is swayed by.[4]

[As anthropologists, then, we may — without too great a sense of contradictoriness —] believe in a world of discrete individuals but a oneness and continuity of culture. [The soundness of this belief rests on] our having a different view [of the individual] from [that of] the biologist. We have learned that the individual in isolation from society is a psychological fiction.[5] [For the same reasons, culture does not result from the juxtaposition of organisms.] We have discrete individuals, but — in the world of thought — could your individual plus another individual enable you to create American culture? [The answer must be an emphatic] no. You cannot dispense with any one individual; it is the total sum of individuals that makes up American culture. The culture historian must realize that every individual [who participates] in a culture[6] is necessary to its history.

[In relation to this totality we call culture,] individuality consists [not in the biological definition of organism but] in the recognition of the differences in the consciousnesses of the individuals [concerned — the recognition of] discrete personalities. [To the extent that we conceive of culture as a world of thought, we may believe in its oneness while also recognizing this differentiation. In fact,] we cannot get away from the individuality [inherent in] the concept of consciousness, or personality, since consciousness is the only approach we have to reality. Only by an act of faith can we transcend our own consciousness. The continuity of the individual stream of consciousness, which memory links together, causes the recognition of personality. [That is to say,] this connective memory [− rather than the boundary of the organism −] is our proof of individuality, our indication of the reality of the individual personality. [Memory is what gives it continuity, for] the biological organism is [always] changing.

2. [The Concept of Personality]

[Now, if our anthropological method obliges us to consider the individual and his personality, just what should we mean by "personality"?] Personality is a certain nuclear entity which is concerned [in all our activities] and objective in itself; [this is our starting point]. The exact definition is difficult, but it is significant that there is a problem posed. Although personality is hard to define, we act upon the concept just as a child works upon its concept of chairs and tables being a set as opposed to falling snow. He may not know the words for these things, [but he acts upon them as a set just the same. Let us attempt to be more articulate than this child, however, and consider how the term has been used in the past.]

[The term] "personality" derives from the Latin *persona*, a mask: a dramatic figure, transcending the petty, and given prestige − a person significant insofar as he is not himself. [In the ancient world] personality was artifice, the mask that society used to judge [a person by,] and so it was equivalent to status. [This definition,] equating a person's personality to his status, has a great tradition in literary [works, even if it has become uncongenial to us today. Thus we may feel] chilled by Homer's lack of interest in Ulysses's personality [in the psychological sense,] and by Shakespeare's Toryism, for even in Shakespeare personality is equivalent to status. Shakespeare's clowns, being lowly, are not psychologized. [Psychological depth is reserved for the higher statuses, as we see,] for example, in *Macbeth*.

It was Rousseau who started the vogue of the individual, with his *Confessions*, [a work] startlingly new in that he threw aside the mask and showed the personality beneath the status or role. [With a sort of] boasting about weaknesses, Rousseau took the back-stairs interest in gossip into the arena of literature, [where it was subsequently taken up by other writers −] Jane Austen, [for instance. Still more recent is the view of] personality as physiology, [a quite] modern [notion, as is the idea that] personality may be equivalent regardless of status. This is the coming view, [and it is virtually the opposite of what personality was to the Greeks].

[As this brief excursion into the history of the term indicates,] personality is an artificial concept having reality [only as we may choose to use it. Thus] the term "personality" is too variable in usage to be serviceable in scientific discussion unless its meaning is very carefully defined for a given context. There are several different ways of defining personality.

(1) The first definition of personality is a psychological one: the reification of the feeling of personal identity through continuous consciousness. [This definition takes an] introspective [approach, for] introspection presupposes the world of the individual consciousness. [It is a world where] there is a continuity of personality, it stays put — [and this is what gives it reality. Its] reality is in fact the mere phenomenon of continuity [of moments of consciousness which, if they have] no persistence, have little or no reality. The continuity of consciousness is, in an important [sense], all that I [really] know. That there is a buzzing external world is [a recognition] forced on me by society, [but it is not part of myself in the same way.] The personality is made up of the experiences it has had, and those things which it has not experienced cannot be said to exist in it. Personality defined in this way [is seen] in terms of the events that impinge upon the individual.

(2) As a purely physiological concept, the individual [may be considered] as a mechanism, and personality may be considered as the individual human organism with emphasis on those aspects of behavior which differentiate it from other organisms.[7] The biological definition of personality is a conception of organism, and the biologist is comfortable with this. He doesn't need [a notion of] consciousness — [or so he supposes.] But if it weren't for our consciousness, how could we recognize the identity of organisms? You get at the concept of organism through consciousness; could the concept of organism, [then, be merely] a projection of our own feeling of identity which surrounds our consciousness? This biological definition is not very helpful, therefore. We don't really know ourselves as individuals in the biological sense, but only as symbols of what we see around us.

(3) The sociological viewpoint today judges personality by the [social] role an individual plays. [In other words,] personality is defined in terms of a sociological abstraction and emphasis upon formal roles. [Other aspects of] personality, [such as the more psychological notion of] nuclear personality, are [treated as] an illusion which disappears when you abstract one's income, status, and so on, [and examine the general charac-

teristics of people filling these categories. By this means, for example, you can trace] the professional character of a businessman, and that of a bishop. Napoleon in the role of Emperor is his personality; individual X in the role of archbishop is his personality. But Napoleon as a reader of *The Sorrows of Werther*, weeping over what he read, was a personality in the psychiatric sense.

The sociological viewpoint defines personality as a series of roles, or [modes of] participation in society, which a person carves out for himself, or takes part in. A personality [in this sense], therefore, is the sum total of the individual's social participations. The individual [is seen] as the collectivity of behavior patterns. That is, all things called individuals are merely collocations of certain habits — a series of roles in a complex arrangement. [Now, as we have already indicated,] personality was first judged from the sociological point of view. Every man functioned in the part laid out for him by society. Thus Achilles and Ulysses were always heroes, and a slave was always a slave. Even if their acts were objectively similar they were treated differently — as arrogance or as impudence, as [an act of war] or a private [act of] murder. (Notice that this is true of the Bible and so through *Tom Jones* and the novel up to James Joyce). The Greeks were then primarily sociologists, [in their definition of personality.]

[But this definition is] fallacious, [or at least] not completely true, because it neglects the feeling of consciousness — the original intuitive sense of identity — which is implied in the psychological definition. It neglects our fantasies, for instance, and instead considers only our train of thoughts about the symbolization of the individual to the community. It is very easy to distinguish between the individual and his sociological role. [It is also necessary to do so. Otherwise you] confound the status of a person with himself.

[Moreover, these sociological abstractions] are not too valuable in tracing the genesis of personality. [For that we will need] a psychiatric viewpoint, where the basic principle is the priority of nuclear constellations in an infantile configuration. It is impossible to avoid the sociological viewpoint altogether, since it is economical at times to make status judgements and it is the very purpose of society to keep the basis of personality hidden. No one can afford to be too honest with himself. But the sociological viewpoint is incremental: personality is made up of [roles] $a + b + c + d$, where d is added last and is unaffected by what went before. The psychiatric viewpoint, [on the other hand,] is configurative, since the basic pattern a affects the total resulting set-up.

(4) Finally, there is the psychiatric definition of personality. This is the conception of nuclear personality, based on the sense of ourselves that we acquire in childhood. It has no connection with [the preceding definition] of personality. [Indeed, to distinguish these two definitions allows us to see the] independence of the individual in society from society's judgement of the individual. Consider aggression, for example, in [terms of this] contrast between the sociological and psychiatric viewpoints. Sociologically, aggression is defined in terms of behavior. Psychiatrically, however, aggression must be defined in personal symbolisms, hidden meanings, compensations, projections, and the like — so that one's actual behavior may show no signs at all of sociological aggression.

[The psychiatric] point of view [treats] personality as equivalent regardless of status. It levels down all personality — that is, it makes the data comparable — at the same general level of childhood, the infantile stage, when the patterns are just beginning to be fixed. Any particular set[-up] of personality at the starting point has a relative priority and will persist through the other [(later)] configurations. Thus the final actualization may be very different from the first innate bias, but the original ground plan may yet always be discerned. This is the kind of personality judgement that the psychiatrist uses. It [conceives of] personality as an integrative mechanism.[8] Overtly similar acts may be entirely different [in significance, therefore,] when fitted into the ground plan of personality. [An act of] theft, for example, may be heroism or criminality.

To know personality in this wise, a theory of personality today must really take into consideration two kinds of attitudes toward the individual: that which sees him as a mere culture carrier, or as the sociologically defined "man brought to trial" or "citizen of the state"; and that which sees him as an integrated entity in himself, a real persona, [starting from] the genetically[9] defined personality plus the accretions and changes wrought by the experience of years. [The first attitude sees] personality acts as the acts of a man of such and such a social status, while the second — the psychiatric approach — is rather a filling in of a personality on the basis of discovered nuclear characteristics. This is a Gestalt attack, a mode of observation that is aesthetic rather than teleological. [To put it another way, it is] an aesthetic interpretation of personality. My point of view, [then, is intended to combine] an aesthetic [mode of observation] with a Gestalt psychology of configuration and with the dynamism of the psychoanalyst.

The psychiatric point of view flows from within the intuitive consciousness — from the fact that we have a continuous consciousness which has not been disassociated since our childhood, [but instead] has been building up [from that nucleus]. I believe, therefore, in a concept of invariance of personality. It is possible for us to translate ourselves to our earlier personality without changing ourselves. [Our present experiences can be seen as the] equivalents of experiences [of the past, for we are continually] reliving old experiences [and feeling the] same feelings. It is the task of psychoanalysis to interlace present experiences with past ones. [The idea of] invariance [means that] one is never other than oneself.

Of course, the ability [for and propensity] towards introspection is different in different individuals, [and this affects what the psychiatrist actually does. In general, however, what the psychiatrist attempts to reveal is the process of] emotional transfer − [the process by which] our [present] experiences and contacts with people around us are to a large extent rephrasings or recallings of old attitudes, [deriving from] our infantile experience. [If some of these rephrasings seem to hinge on quite trivial aspects of an experience, it must be remembered that] the trivial may be just as [telling] a part of one's personality as the [more conspicuously] important.

What then are the determinants of personality − the things which fix this [sense of] primordial self? This is the weakest part of our approach, [because the determinants commonly suggested lie in realms poorly understood.] First are implications of biological structure − genetically determined heredity − of nervous characteristics, for example. Our ignorance of physiology, etc. [is such that] we don't know [much about this possibility.] Second are prenatal conditionings, experiences, experiences in the womb [that might also serve as personality] determinations. We don't know enough about [these conditionings] either. Third are early childhood experiences (up to the age of two or three), postnatal modifications [of the prenatally established self] − experiences of profound anxieties, for example − [to the extent that these represent] pre-cultural conditionings and determinations. These three factors, [it is generally assumed,] influence the basic personality [which, once] set up, [establishes a] permanent psychiatric ground plan for the individual at an early age.

The importance of the infantile configuration is shown in phenomena of regression to an earlier, easier plateau. As an analogy with a personality in the time dimension, consider a musical theme with variations where the theme is the basic configuration and the variations are more and more complex constructs using the fundamental pattern. This is an aesthetically constructive concept, whereas the personality building up is continuously adjustive. Yet, the form persists through all variations;

regression [just] means withdrawal to an earlier theme, to an earlier or simpler level of adjustment. In the persistence of childhood memories and infantile emotional tensions, discovered in regression, we see the persistence of the fundamental personality patterns throughout life. If you wish your adjustments to people to be real, you must get back to your primordial self.

[In later life there will always be] a tendency to lapse into the nuclear personality unless we can hitch on to a symbol [provided by] society. For example, acting as a student is a symbolization by which we come out of our nuclear personality. We keep on with certain studies, and so on, because of our symbolic feeling of oneness with society and gratitude to it, even though we have lost interest in their [subject matter]. The social process keeps us going – you need a social tradition to make you go on. Thus personalities are fitted into places [in society] in which they have no [intrinsic] interest. Their culture, and the people around them, throw them into a concept which they did not entertain about themselves. [The social process counters regression, then, for the very reason that social roles and their associated behavior are not based directly on the individual's personality in the psychiatric sense.][10]

[How might this disjunction come about? Why is it that, in our social encounters, we do not simply pursue an undifferentiated impulse to know one another's personalities as fully as possible? The answer, presumably, is that][11] A is not really interested in what B is, but what he can bear as symbol. We know each other only as roles. We take parts of personality from other people, but we can never entirely know another's personality. It is the very purpose of society to keep the basis of personality hidden, and no one can afford [to uncover everything.] There is something vague which cannot be delved into. Indeed, we don't need each other a hundred percent. What we need is an effective [but] partial participation. Many intelligent and worthy persons are uncomfortable in being admired, because people need to find in you those qualities they admire, [and you know that] sooner or later you are going to ruin their picture. Every human relationship is a temporary implicit contract, [not a total immersion].

To completely know another would mean sacrifice [of oneself, and] we don't want to be swallowed by another's personality. Even a child wants [sometimes] to feel a stranger to its mother – complete identification is resisted. Therefore we can never know or afford to know the whole truth about personality. [Instead, the] key persons [in our lives, much of the time, are] doing duty for what almost anyone else could give. [And just as we cannot afford to concern ourselves too deeply with another's personality, the same is true for our own.] Being concerned with oneself is a sign of insecurity and defiance. [Although we may often phrase that concern in terms of claims to our own uniqueness — for it is more acceptable to maintain that] "I am one of a million in this matter" [than that "I am interested in my own personality" — most of] us get sick and tired of the impulse to know ourselves. (But Proust did not!)

[There is a certain tension, then, in our feelings about personality, a] duality of interest in the facts of behavior [as to whether we see them in terms of personality or not.] In anthropology, [similarly,] there are two viewpoints: the psychological — "I wish to hold on to my personality", and the sociological — "I do not wish to hold onto my personality".

3. [The Uses of Psychiatric Theories in Anthropology]

[The approach to personality we will need in anthropology must resemble the psychiatrist's in its emphasis on configuration and genesis (i. e., personality development), but its need to incorporate the personality's social setting will distinguish it from any psychiatric theory presently established.] Psychoanalysis is valuable for its way of thinking, not for its present formulas. Let us understand first of all, [therefore,] that we take [the ideas of] Freud, Jung, etc. [only] as working principles subject to modification by further knowledge.

The most elaborate and far reaching hypotheses on the development of personality which have yet been proposed are those of Freud and his school. The Freudian psychoanalysts analyze the personality topographically into a primary id, the sum of inherited impulses or cravings[12] — the libidinal drive; the ego, which is thought of as being built upon the id through the progressive development of the sense of external reality; and the superego, the socially conditioned sum of forces which restrain the individual from the direct satisfaction of the id. The characteristic interplay of these personality zones, itself determined chiefly by the special pattern of family relationships into which the individual has had to fit himself in the earliest years of his life, is responsible for a variety of personality types.[13] [However,] although Freud is interested in typical dynamisms and mechanisms of personality formation, he does not construct a theory of personality types. [On this point and others the Freudian school of psychoanalysts are divided.] Jung, [for example,] is interested in types, [based on the idea that] not all people will develop in the same way under the same conditions. [We shall pursue this matter in a later chapter. But in many respects] Jung, Adler, and Rank, in revolt against Freud, overemphasized their points of difference [with him].

[For the anthropologist,] Freud's [work] is [useful as] a way of thinking, not as a body of doctrine. [Consider, for example, the famous] Oedipus complex, in our culture and others. The important thing is that certain nuclear situations inevitably affect the emotional and personality development of the child, whatever the type of society [he is born into.] Some type of family situation − some kind of human relationship − holds everywhere, whether [specifically] on the model of Oedipus or not. The child is not born in a cultural or social vacuum. [His personal] symbology is subjective to a [particular] culture, and it is a mistake to make a fetish of doctrines [of symbological development based only on European clinical material.] Thus the Oedipus Complex is simply a common sense human situation which may be found in the Trobriand Islands or anywhere − under differing conditions, true, but with the same simple human situation pattern. When Malinowski, in *Sex and Repression in Savage Society*, [presented certain] strictures on Freud by showing a new modification [of the Oedipus Complex] due to a different social context − [so that the Trobriand child's] transference of early bents or sets [tended] toward the maternal uncle instead of the mother − Freud's disciples reviled him. [To them, the essential thing about] Oedipus was the correlation of transference along sex lines. Yet the Freudians should welcome Malinowski's [work,] since although he shows that with a different familial set-up in the Trobriands the Oedipus complex [*per se*] does not hold, nevertheless he shows that even here there is an important conditioning of the child at an early age by family relationships. Thus he extends the basic Freudian concept, rather than upsetting it.

[For the uses of the anthropologist, therefore,] psychiatric analysis must be schematic, save in the actual case study. For example, there are many types and actual varieties of jealousy, though possibly the basis of all [of them] may be a negative reaction to interference by others with the libidinal fixation upon a certain individual. [Whether it is about jealousy or some other aspect of personality formation,] what the schematic view would show is the importance of nuclear home attitudes and situations for the child: the influence of the parents and their relations one to another; the effect upon the unclouded intuitive understanding of the child; the function of emotional attitudes; and the effect on [a person's] later life (at mating, [especially]) of prior nuclear symbolisms even though these are projected or transformed later in new situations.

[In summary, the anthropologist can find much of value in the psychiatric approach to personality, but in its outlines rather than its specific formulations. In favoring a psychiatric view I] do not for a moment mean to assert that any psychiatry that has as yet been evolved is in a position to do much more than to ask intelligent questions.[14] [The insights we seek are only beginning to emerge.] A vital understanding of personality depends upon the development of a powerful dynamic psychology — which will be a genetic[15] psychology in a social setting. Using Freudian concepts cast in a configurative Gestalt pattern, it will be interested solely in actual social settings and not in stimulus, response, and the rest [of the behaviorist's representation of them] — the whole view being influenced by aesthetic considerations, which will look for the fundamental theme and then for the recurring variations.

Notes

1. See the discussion of culture pattern in Chapter 5, and Sapir (1927c), "The Unconscious Patterning of Behavior in Society".
2. The preceding passage, beginning with "Any statement ...", is quoted from Sapir (1938), "Why Cultural Anthropology Needs the Psychiatrist".
3. The preceding two sentences are quoted from Sapir (1932a), "Cultural Anthropology and Psychiatry". Italics are original.
4. The preceding sentence is quoted from Sapir (1932a), "Cultural Anthropology and Psychiatry".
5. The preceding sentence is quoted from Sapir (1932a).
6. I insert "who participates" on the analogy of the statement in Sapir (1932a): "... the vast majority of participants in the total culture, if we may still speak in terms of a 'total culture'". Sapir's published writings of this period do not use the expression "individual in a culture", an expression that would treat "culture" as a synonym for "group" or "society".
7. A portion of the preceding sentence, starting with "and personality ...", is quoted from Sapir (1934), "Personality".
8. It is unclear from the class notes whether Sapir claimed that only the psychiatric view of personality sees it as an integrative mechanism, or whether the sociological view (personality as deriving from status) was also an integrative mechanism of a sort (presumably less coherently configured).
9. I.e., developmentally — not necessarily via biological heredity. But see Sapir's discussion on this point later in the chapter.
10. I insert the bracketed passage as a summary of the preceding paragraph, where Sapir argues again that personality (psychologically or psychiatrically defined) and social status are distinct. This does not mean, however, that he believed the two have no

influence on one another. For an argument that personality, or at least one's emotional state, is affected by an individual's social position, see Sapir's "Psychiatric and Cultural Pitfalls in the Business of Getting a Living" (1939a).

11. See Sapir (1934a), "The Emergence of the Concept of Personality in a Study of Cultures": "Why is it necessary to discover the contrast, real or fictitious, between culture and personality, or, to speak more accurately, between a segment of behavior seen as cultural pattern and a segment of behavior interpreted as having a person-defining value? Why cannot our interest in behavior maintain the undifferentiated character which it possessed in early childhood? The answer, presumably, is that each type of interest is necessary for the psychic preservation of the individual in an environment which experience makes increasingly complex and unassimilable on its own simple terms." Although Sapir's focus in the (1934a) paper is on the outside observer, he seems to suggest that the participant has the same duality of interest.

12. The preceding two sentences are quoted from Sapir (1934b), "Personality", although similar material is found in the class notes.

13. The preceding passage, from "the ego ...", is quoted from Sapir (1934b). Similar material is found in the class notes.

14. The preceding sentence is quoted from Sapir (1938).

15. I.e., developmental.

Chapter Eight

The Problem of Personality Types: A Review and Critique of Jung

1. The Type Point of View; Introvert and Extravert

[In the last lecture I mentioned that it is a matter of some disagreement within the Freudian school of psychoanalysis as to whether personalities can be classified into different types. This is not merely some trivial instance of internecine warfare. It concerns the very nature of personality integration, and it has many implications for a theory of personality formation, even if some of the most basic aspects of the problem have scarcely been addressed as yet by either side.]

Freud [himself] is more interested in typical mechanisms [of personality formation] than in types. He is not clear as to what the basic material of personality is; [instead, he seems to take the] attitude that the individual is indefinitely malleable, although the question of whether there are physiological types [remains open]. Jung, however, [proposes that there are] fundamental types over and above the mechanisms — that not all people will develop in the same way under the same environmental conditions. While Freud is [primarily] interested in individual cases, Jung goes in for the "racial mind" and believes in types given at birth (preformation, as opposed to epigenesis).

I believe Jung is fundamentally right [in proposing] a basic typology — various kinds of adjustment — in children, over and above the dynamic relations [with which Freud is concerned]. The importance of Jung's viewpoint [lies not in the specific causes he assumes, but in the idea that] childhood conditioning isn't everything. For example, one can't make a hysteric out of every child. With each child, his study shows, there is a varied type of adjustment depending upon the basic personality set-up. These varied differences of adjustment are something over and above the emotional conditioning that is due to specific familial [situations.]

Genetically determined predispositions[1] may be shown, for example, in [children's] varying sensitivity to loud noises, and their varying apperception — sensitivity to objects in the environment. In regard to this, [Jung's?] study shows that one child goes out readily to meet such objects. He identifies himself with them, explores them, handles and enjoys them. The other child hesitates, classifies them, and always seems to refer them to some evaluated past experience. Perhaps he values them in terms of some nostalgic feeling associated with the pleasure of suckling at the mother's breast. To identify objects around one with that feeling is the genesis of introverted behavior. The identifying type [of child] is the extravert, who participates fully in the world of sense, while the classifying type is the introvert, who holds back from the world of sense. (These types also [correspond] to Holt's "adience" and "abience".)

[But while one may describe these types as already existing among children,] Jung nowhere [really] discusses their genesis. Indeed, the genesis of [personality] types is a difficult [problem.] Are they to be explained in terms of hereditary dispositions given once and for all at conception, or is there some genetic explanation, such as that given above, [involving] empirical conditioning? [If the latter, should we seek its explanation, in turn,] in terms of Freudian mechanisms — or does the cultural configuration itself influence basic personality types? Jung gives no answer to these questions.

Is Jung's classification of personality types, then, genetic, post-genetic, or descriptive? I believe his classification to be mainly descriptive, not genetic or dynamic. [Presumably,] personality is [influenced by all these] factors — genetic, prenatal, and early conditioning — but Jung's study, [even though it purports] to be a causal one [and not only] a personal one, is not strictly scientific. ([Indeed, although his *Psychological Types*] is a fascinating and extraordinary book, it is never very closely reasoned.)[2] [About his notions of "racial mind" and "pre-formation" we should be particularly cautious.] It is not that the physical has nothing to do with psychology (and hence culture), but only that the definitions of physical phenomena are too naive and fallacious.

[Obviously, even a purely descriptive] classification of personality types has implications as to the formation of personality. [But personality is not simply a direct reflection of Jung's types.] A process of compensation [intervenes]. Society is not tolerant of extreme variations of personality, and because a person is always concerned with other people's opinion of him, with social pressure and potential praise or blame — [we might even say that] the potential judgement of society is the individual's main problem — he tries to compensate for those variations regarded as social defects, towards some [more approved] general type or behavior pattern. Hence, basic personality differences, if they exist, must be masked beneath the typical behavior. [Perhaps it is from one's own eyes that one's basic personality is most effectively hidden.] In our efforts to conform to a common ideal, we lose touch with our earlier selves. [The attempt to reach back to that nuclear constellation is the reason for] the psychiatric emphasis on the importance of the early years in the formation of personality, and for the attempt, in psychoanalysis, to determine personality types.

[Thus the relation between our basic orientation and our compensations does not easily rise into conscious awareness.] We have a persistent illusion of changing a great deal, but it seems likely that there really are perduring patterns in the individual's personality from early life. The basic pattern of the individual's behavior does not change — [even though] we like to feel we can change, probably for the better. [Now, when it concerns someone other than ourselves,] we are very quick to see incidents about a single individual as consistent and integrated, though this is of course inconsistent with the just-mentioned illusion. Various personal motives influence our belief about this question: we do not like to believe that we are ourselves not capable of great change in personality if we wish to change in any respect; and we also like to feel that we are influential in effecting changes in other people, by giving advice to those who look to us for guidance. [In a sense we are right in both our beliefs — that people are consistent and that people can change — insofar as the psychiatrist's concepts of basic adjustment and compensation correspond to them. And we are also not without support in our feeling that the influence people have on one another, in their advice and in their judgement, is important.] A sociological outlook and balancing are factors in personality, [because the identification with] sociological reality versus any other reality is essentially what extraversion and introversion are. The extravert [is the person] whose libido flows into those concerns which are connected with other people and the outside. The introvert, on the other hand, abstracts, consciously or unconsciously, his meanings from the outside world.

Jung claims that the difference between the extravert and the introvert is not merely a matter of interests. Compensation, for example, may make one's interests quite deceptive with respect to fundamental tendencies. [Moreover, interests could easily be confused with] the degree to which a personality is willing to unmask himself ([or is masked in the first place; consider the kind of person described by] the French word *simple* — an unrevised personality). [Instead, the difference between] extravert and introvert [concerns how one resolves the fundamental] conflict, [faced by] the child, between infantile fantasies and the external world. [It is the problem of helplessness] — your own weakness in attaining your infantile desires, [as compared with] the power about you, and the institutions and traditions [you encounter]. Man always knows he is a helpless being [in the face of his] environment and fellow beings, but he can't afford to admit it. You can't be healthy and yet realize this. Ways of adjusting, then, are ways of overcoming helplessness.

There are two ways of solving this problem of the conflict between the self and a powerful environment. You can blot out the one or the other — the external or the internal world. Realizing one's weakness in the midst of strong forces, one can either negate those forces, recognizing only those that one wishes to admit, or else deny the reality of one's weakness (in the extreme by denying the reality of oneself and identifying oneself with the environment, and other people, at every point). To blot out and deny all the external environment over which one has control [is the solution of] the introvert, the idealist who reinterprets the world in terms of something he has mentalized or verbalized. In its morbid extreme, this tendency becomes schizophrenia, *dementia praecox*; less extremely, it is seen in such organized movements as Christian Science and in the medieval mystic, who simplified the world around him through wishful thinking. This method is similar to the general problem of abstraction, which is the ability to ignore facts. Only certain things have value for the introvert; [beyond them, he has the] ability to deny the reality value of the external world. ([This propensity] is well exemplified by classical Hindu culture.)

The other method is to deny yourself, to deny the reality of your own weakness. The extravert identifies with the environment, the world of activity; [in effect,] he denies that there is anything to adjust. The world is what has value, in the face of this denudation of the personality. Words don't interest him save as symbols of adjustment to the world. He consciously denies the self as an entity. Instead, anything that happens in the world is the self. When this becomes morbid you have hysteria. In this case there is no introspection at all, and if the environment were taken away such a person would be lost.

The extravert is a mechanist; [the introvert, an] idealist. While the introvert [sees] — as in Descartes' thesis — an antagonism between the self and the world, the extravert identifies with the world and participates in it sympathetically and sensationalistically. He finds the environment friendly and swallows it in huge gob fulls. The introvert finds an unanalyzed value in intensity of experience, the extravert in extensity or numbers of experiences. ([By analogy with this pattern, then,] Christian theology is introverted, while the Mediterranean world is extraverted.) The extravert is an empiricist: [says he,] "A fact [is a fact], what more do you want?" The introvert, lacking the ability to value a thing as such, [instead] evaluates it subjectively: "A fact — what about it? So what? A fact of what order and meaning?"

The extravert is not necessarily [more] objective, [just] because his values lie in the immediate environment. Indeed, it may be questioned whether one is not here projecting oneself in order to identify [with the externalized projection,] and whether there is [actually] any more objectivity in extraversion than in introversion. Thoroughly extraverted people are unobjective, because they are the most bound up in the environment. The introvert, [on the other hand,] is a verbal realist, or objective subjectivist: the word is substituted for the world of internal reality. His sense of power comes from handling words and concepts in lieu of actual facts. Facts are not valued as such, but only in terms of personal evaluations.

These characterizations are polar extremes. [Actual analyses of real individuals would not usually show such stark contrasts. In fact,] actual analysis is difficult since there is a tendency for one type to compensate with the thinking of the opposite type. For example, Nietzsche was an introvert and a masochistic [personality,] but he hated this in himself and so invented the superman. [The inventor of the superman, then, was] not [exactly] a superman himself. Dewey was [personally] an introvert, but as a philosopher he writes with an extraverted ring, expressing the philosophy of the extravert in education by reason of an elaborate compensation mechanism. Thus introversion may be disguised by a pseudo-extraversion for reasons of personality adjustment. [We might also mention] Whitman in this respect, and note the paucity of hard images in his poetry. [Conversely,] a man may also be introverted in his intellectual life but extraverted in his personal relations. As an example, [one might compare] Coleridge's poetry with his relations with Wordsworth and his circle.

[Just as the personality types are not merely a matter of interests, so they do not directly link up with an individual's position in life. We can find examples of both types in all realms of activity.] It is an illusion [to think] that businessmen, for instance, are necessarily extraverted, for external activity may belie [the nature of] the ego. A mere description of behavior does not indicate the nature of the personality. [Instead, we] must interpret the flow of activity in terms of the mechanics of activities and thinking. In business, perhaps Carnegie is an example of the extravert, Ford of the introvert — the former enjoying the activity for its own sake, while Ford was somewhat discontented [with it and placed more importance on] idealistic principles ([as when sponsoring his] peace ship).

In religion, the early Christian movement seems to be an introverted one. Beginning at a time of great differences in wealth, its [introversion] was perhaps a social characteristic growing out of the extreme poverty of the people, as a denial of their external circumstances. [Later on] Luther seems to be a sample extravert, interested in his immediate environment and identifying himself with the masses (as, for example, in his colloquial translation of the Bible, and his realistic table talk). Calvin, with his interest in the "noble Bible" and so on as an ideal, seems rather more introverted. [Concerned with] rational respectability, he turned within himself, to emerge with a formula [for attaining it. Presumably] he would not have been sympathetic with evangelism.

[In politics,] Robespierre seems to have been an introvert, who swayed the masses by [the power of an] idea rather than for himself. President Wilson, too, was an introvert. [Thus at the close of the war, when the new boundaries of nations were to be decided,] an ethnological staff ([including] Dixon of Harvard)[3] was taken to Europe but not consulted. [Wilson's] interest was in ideological principles. The actual, picayune details of the distribution of peoples were of little interest to him.

In literature, [while we may tend to think of literary activity as typically introverted,] Dickens and Kipling come to mind as ready examples of extraversion. The essential thing, for example with the businessman, is not how busy a man keeps with external affairs but where he finds his maximum enjoyment.

In summary: the extravert identifies himself in his orientation with his environment, and feels no difference between himself and the thing out there. [To him] the principle must always be sacrificed for the facts. The introvert identifies himself with his own self-consciousness and abstracts from the environment that which he needs for the principles. The introvert overlooks the specific facts for the sake of selected general principles and control, while the extravert attends to the specific events in their sequence simply as events. Among scholarly pursuits, history tends toward the extremely extravert side; mathematics and conceptual science, toward the introvert. Thurstone's work in psychology seems extremely introverted, with its complete emphasis on method, precise definition, and complete lack of interest in practical problems or everyday values.

[As we pointed out earlier, however,] Jung's classification is descriptive, [not explanatory.] It cannot be used to explain behavior, as too many other factors, for example the symbolism of the situation, are also concerned. [The process of compensation, too, complicates any attempt to explain behavior as the direct result of personality type. For these reasons a strong note of] caution [must be sounded against overenthusiastic applications of Jung's classification.] Introversion and extraversion are to be evaluated not in terms of overt behavior, but in terms of subjective orientation — the personal subjective evaluations of meaning peculiar to the individual in question.[4] Failure to realize this leads to half-baked attempts to measure introversion and extraversion by means of psychological tests which are far too naive to be of value.

Actually, the whole concept of adjustment, as used by modern psychologists, is usually badly misunderstood, through a failure to realize the importance of subjective evaluations. [Moreover, adjustment is not just a matter of one's nature. One's] sociological outlook and balancing are [just as important] factors in the personality. [Thus we encounter the] pseudo-extravert: one who by circumstance is driven to extraverted behavior, though he should by nature be a well-adjusted introvert. [Similarly,] a-social behavior is needed by some who strive for external adjustment. [In short,] either "extravert" or "introvert" [as a personality classification] is devoid of value, except in terms of what culture demands. Jung makes the mistake of identifying [his types] with thought tendencies [alone, without reference to cultural form].

2. Jung's "Functional Types"

Jung also classifies [personality] according to "functional types", a term that is not actually very suitable for them. [He proposes four of these types:] the thinking, feeling, intuiting, and sensational, [grouped into] rational vs. irrational,[5] thus:

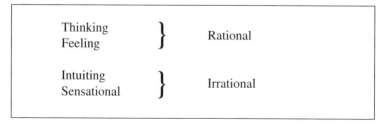

Figure 1: Jung's Psychological Types

[Like introversion and extraversion,] this personality classification is applicable at an early age.

These classifications are based not on the realm [of one's interests or activities,] but in the authoritative [psychological] function [governing their value]. Thought, feeling, sense, and intuition are concepts to indicate the type of [psychological] control, authority, or underpinning which is advanced for holding one's professed interests. For example, [one might compare] these four "authorities" as four different [reasons, or] desires, for learning a new language. One [person has a] love for play with words [(this is the sensational type)]; another desires to know about the life, material culture, and so on of the people [who speak the language]. One [person] learns languages which are symbols of authority for belonging to certain groups; [and another has] an intuitive sense of form as such, or an intuition that the language may later become important [to him. Each person engages in the same activity, but under the sway of a different authority.] Each authority derives its strength from compensated or sublimated libido impulses — [presumably] in a genetic fashion, [although we do not know exactly how this works.][6]

Jung's classification into functional types has been criticized, and justly so. [Taken] at face value the classification is absurd, because its criteria are not comparable. It is like [comparing] a red house and a gabled barn. But we should be charitable of the types nevertheless, for they are very valuable in that they emphasize the authoritative stamp in one's wish for the reality of an experience. Thus they stamp the kind of thing that gives things reality to people. In which kind of experience does value predominantly reside? This is what Jung really asks. Where Freud, moralistically, explains a maladjusted person by what has happened to him, Jung wishes to know how a person works.

[It should be noted from the start, however, that the classification] must be redefined and reinterpreted. Jung's distinction between rational and irrational certainly has to be redefined, [and we shall come to this shortly]. Putting the feeling and the thinking types together seems to be his most important contribution. The contrast between the sensational and the rational is also important, [with its corollary that] the rational (intellectual) and feeling concepts must be contrasted with the sensational concept. The intuitive concept, however, I believe is on a different plane from the other three, and needs to be seen as cross-cutting the other three classes. It applies to the rate of activity or adjustment rather than the kind of values.

[Even more than the introvert and extravert types,] these types are rarely found in their pristine purity. [Still, let us examine them more closely.]

(1) The sensory type is the person who places a great deal of emphasis on sensory experiences, and whose preferred values spring from experiences of a sensual order, such as eating and the palatal tastes, or the use of colors. The significances of sensation are very real, especially to children. Later in life, of course, sensation becomes symbolized; but when sensation [itself] becomes significant you have a peculiar type of person. From the Freudian standpoint the sensory type seems to be somewhat of an arrested type − that is, they do not show the normal sentiments. Freud would say that the sexual interests of these people are prematurely sublimated in sensory impressions, or on a sensory basis. [Thus the type is not based on learning.] A person from a very dull background might grow into a very sensation-[oriented] person, when the libido [is sublimated in this way] − when emotion enters into the sensational value, and it grows (as is possible) into a fetish. Jung believes that the sensational value might take the place of thought, if the person is given to sensing, not thinking.

When Jung says this type is irrational, he probably refers to disequilibrated action. I would say, rather, that it is disoriented − too greatly isolated from the totality of the problems of life. One cannot adjust well to life on the basis of these [sensory] values only. If you establish your values on a sensory basis you are dealing with a limited world. The organization of pure sensation is irrational because it does not connect you with the world − an emotional world disintegrates into the sensational. The reason why such a person can adjust and survive at all is that society has placed value on his values. It values [the sensory] to such an extent that, if he is good in his limited field, society will pay him for his product. If not he has a serious personal problem ([as we often see with the] artist or musician, for example).

Culture is selective as to [its emphasis on] sensory values. At some periods in some cultures, no value is given to them. [Usually, however,] some sensations have a social validation of their meaning, in terms of convention, tradition, or literature (e.g., the scent of the rose, which [combines] sensation plus a culturally left-over aura in Persian poetry and in the Romantic period). Other sensations, however, have only a private meaning, and the individual swayed by their authority is the [real exemplar of] the [sensory] type. The artist is typical. Thus there is a social side to sensations, a social history to them, while the callous person who yields to the authority of a collection of private sensations is self-indulgent, lacking social integration or social sympathy. Insofar as sensations are [only] privately validated, and because of the inherent disjunction of the various sense qualities, the sensational world is inherently an irrational or unordered one. As Jung says, this type can be intelligent. Its irrationality — and the sensory type always has some quality of fragmentariness and irrationality — [lies only in its preference for] sensory values instead of sentiments. These people follow their sensory values, which are not the same as the sentimental values. (Most human sentiments are really cultural artifacts, compulsions of a secondary nature.) [Yet, it might be worth remembering that what we often call] intelligence is really an after-the-event concept, a descriptive term applied after an individual has achieved a certain success.

(2) [In contrast to the sensory type, we have the] feeling type, which I believe to be the normal and most common type of adjustment. Jung calls this type "rational"; however, [these people] are actually in the grip of sentiment and feeling. They are "rational" only in that their thinking is tightly organized in the system of sentiments they have built up. Their whole world of experience is organized according to feeling, derived ultimately from love and hate, husbanded and organized. Everything is fitted into [this system of] evaluation — the person's feeling is completely implicative. Those who feel their way through experience, attaching a segment of love or hate to everything, cover the universe. There is nothing fragmentary about their attack. Where there is a high degree of organization, as for example in [the case of] Bismarck, this is probably traceable to a stable and satisfying emotional adjustment worked out in infancy.

The normal child lives in very much this kind of world, where everything has an aura of emotional value. [But most people do not retain this system in its entirety in adulthood.] In language, for example, every word has emotional values according to its associations, but children must divest themselves of emotion towards words as they grow up. Indeed, the whole of culture is pervaded by feeling [associations in this way.] Not all individuals are able to break up this organization — this highly organized feeling — that grows up in the mind of the individual. Thus, for example, if a person is brought up and is living in a certain cultural environment, his attitude toward other cultures and environments must necessarily be prejudiced and molded by the general ideas prevailing in his own culture. Hence the origin and use of such terms as "tricky Orient", "heathen Chinee".[7] He thinks he could not have got this without direct, sober experience, but as a matter of fact it is quite illogical.

[Actually, one's attitude toward other cultures might even make a suitable] test [distinguishing the feeling type of personality from the thinking type.] In response to a [request] to grade a list of nationalities in terms of likes, the feeling type usually does this easily, probably in terms of the emotional experiences of infancy and childhood. For example, the Hindu is disliked because of an association with unpleasant infantile experiences, and so on. The thinking type, however, seeing no reason for one preference rather than another, finds this [task] difficult.)

Jung's term "rational" [for this type], therefore, means "scaled according to emotions". These people have a complete attitude towards the world, but little to say about it, as they feel. [In fact, what they say may derive only from a superficial rationalization and not represent their fundamental attitude at all.] The declared opinions of intellectual people are not [to be] taken too seriously, except in a few rare cases. Sometimes such people are apparently quite radical, whereas in fact, they are conservative. The reality of the rational "feeling" life (as Jung expresses it) may be exemplified by [the case of] a friend of mine — a man who, for example, talks loud and long against private schools, yet he sends his son to one. [The other day] he spoke very vehemently against the proposal of dropping Latin as a graduation requirement, but when asked for the reason for his stand, said he did not know why he felt so. Dr. Samuel Johnson is [another] good example. Though his philosophy was [actually nonsense,] nevertheless by his dynamic personality he managed to magnetize his circle of admirers.

[In its purer forms this kind of adjustment is not untroubled. A complete] loyalty to feeling judgements [can be a] strain. The desire for travel and other escape mechanisms, for example, is due to the fatigue that comes with too great a load of feeling.

(3) The third type is the intellectual type, whose genesis is in the desire to solve problems. He finds unity and interest in verbalization — in conquering the world and winning admiration through the display of verbal facility, rationalizations, and command of the thought processes. [He tries to] understand the world in [purely] rational terms,[8] thinking the whole world will be righted if [its] illogical errors are only pointed out. He is the man who is calm in the face of disaster, [for the situation's] emotional charge is defused. He takes his father's funeral, for instance, as an opportunity to do scientific work. In his contacts with people, he divests the situation of its emotion, and thinks only of the actual situation. For example, he treats a shopkeeper only as a machine for solving a certain [problem, or carrying out a certain] function. If you go through

life thinking of people only in this instrumental sense, you have no free flow of feeling — only intellectual attitudes toward functions. The de-emotionalization of the objects in our environment is an intellectual act. You build up a rich world of observation and fact, with little investiture of feeling. But you cannot go about your daily business as though you were handling engineering problems.

In fact, a good deal of feeling is probably attached to these intellectual attitudes by a secondary process of rationalization. Perhaps [the whole intellectualizing process, and hence the personality type,] is secondary. Yet, many [people,] and not only intellectual giants, are of this type, divesting situations of their emotional [associations] and thinking of people in an instrumental [way]. Often what passes as feeling, [for them,] is only an intellectual attachment to known symbols of feeling. They have only an intellectual attitude toward functions, never [actual] feelings.

Rigorously thinking out [a problem,] and systematizing according to feeling, have the same organizing quality. [Perhaps we should say that] Jung's contribution [is to describe personality as] organization, [for the discussion of] these three types has stressed the organizational aspect. Each of them builds up a tight, complete attitude toward behavior and the universe. [In a sense] they try to be consistently reasonable. Actually, of course, type (2) and type (3) are interrelated. A child starts out with a feeling attitude toward life, and gradually takes over much of the intellectual attitude. From a dynamic standpoint, these two types stand together.

[In a sense, too,] the intelligence of the thinking type is derivative of fear. In essence, this intelligence is nothing more than the alert response to a danger stimulus — or, better put, it is a highly elaborated, exaggerated, sublimated response to anxiety situations, such as the anxiety to control the environment. Consider, for example, the person who sleeps little and wakes early, so as not to be caught napping: fear is the basis [of his behavioral pattern]. Consider also the fact that among the members of a secure social class like the English gentry, where there is no anxiety about position or future, there is to be found great stupidity. Intelligence, therefore, is a method of controlling one's environment, due to fear or anxiety motivations.

[It is not just that there is a "thinking type", then, but that] effective adjustment takes the form of thought. There are two approaches to the intellectual type: its rational adjustment, on the one hand (the well-adjusted aspect of this type), and the denudation of emotional content, on the other. Really they are both the same things, [but looking at the type in terms of emotional denudation shows us that you cannot be well adjusted if you carry this attitude to an extreme]. Feeling and thinking go together; [for the best adjustment, you] must get an equilibrium between them. Thus the feeling and thinking types are normally conjoined. Criminals, who are often found not to possess much feeling, are emotionally underdeveloped.

Generally one thinks and feels at the same time. You are unconscious of when you are doing the one and when the other, and you often do both together. But as thought has more prestige value than feeling, we call a lot of things thought that are really feeling. Thinking is often used to rationalize emotions, also. It is therefore the feeling type that tries to be most reasonable. That is, those who [most strongly] insist they are reasonable are often most bound by feeling. On the other hand, intellectuals often act casual because they are afraid of being too reasonable.

[Actually, our conception of "feeling" is perhaps itself ambiguous.] It isn't feeling that people differ in, but emotion, which is merely the use and expression of feeling in behavior.[9] Our capacity for emotion is physiologically the same, just as a man sitting on a chair all day has muscles though he does not use them. However, what a person does with emotion is a different thing. An emotional state is the mental correlate of [physical] activity; [thus he may make use of his capacity for emotion or not]. Many people tend to stifle emotion although they have a great amount of feeling. Yet, there are also those who may seem insincere because their [expression of] emotion seems excessive. [Paradoxically,] the point [at which we interpret an emotional state as] indifference is not far from [the point of greatest] expressiveness.

Actually there may be more emotion stored up in the unresponsive individual, because the expression of feeling probably releases emotion. Those who are wont to show feeling in the ordinary [course of their daily life] do not store up emotional energy. An ordinarily stolid person may suddenly "blow up", while those who express feeling a great deal may actually often be quite callous. We should not confuse emotion and feeling, therefore. Jung seems to make this distinction, but perhaps it is not very clear.

[Before continuing with Jung's fourth type, which I believe in any case is not on the same plane as the other three, let us reconsider his division of types into "rational" and "irrational". As I have suggested,] what he calls "rational" and "irrational" personalities could better be explained as "organized" and "unorganized", a more useful terminology which avoids the paradox detracting from Jung's. [Jung's terms are too easily confused with rationalization and reasoning, labels that apply primarily to his third type, yet] his "feeling type" being classified as "rational" is an important contribution that he has to make.

[Jung's] rational vs. irrational, [then, is not a question of intellectualism but] a question of organization and implications. Organization means harmony, the integration of a well-systematized universe, where taste and experience are blended through the intricacy and closeness of association. We [all] read order into experience, [and select certain events as our] points of reference [for that order, but the points of reference differ, as does the ultimate coherence and accessibility of the system built upon them.] For the mystic who craves a divine order, the buzzing of a bee mirrors the rhythm of the universe, [but other people will not evaluate the bee sound in the same way.] People, things, and events have implications, but not for everyone. If the sequences of events by which you establish order have only private meanings, and if you work on these implications instead of realities, you will be boring and you will hurt everyone's feelings. This is the "irrational" person, to Jung's way of thinking. He is often led by motives unknown to [the rest of] us, having a kind of necessity that leads him to do it. It has nothing to do with being right or wrong, it is [just] his preferred method of proceeding.

The thinking that insists on organization is rational, [whether or not it has anything to do with intellectual matters. Indeed, the success of our adaptation to society itself requires some measure of this kind of thinking.] The demands that society makes are highly organized, and it is hard for some people to keep track of this organization, although it is easy for others. (Take the example of giving parties and inviting people. [Knowing just what sort of party to give, and whom to invite, has actually quite a complicated social basis, and some people are much more attuned to these social intricacies.]

What Jung calls the "irrational" type, [then, as we have seen,] is not irrational [in the sense of] emotional [(as contrasted with reasoning)]. What Jung means is a kind of irrational that comes in the life of sensation and intuition. [It has to do with the completeness and coherence of the world one builds up.] One cannot build up an [unfragmented] world out of sensation, and hence [the sensational] type is irrational. [But Jung's assumption that he is dealing with basic types of thought tendencies presents some difficulties −] perhaps he has made too much of this thought business. [First of all,] it should be remembered that Jung's primary classification is on the conscious level. [Yet, much of our discussion of feeling, rationalizing, and so forth has concerned an unconscious level as well — and the possibility of a difference in the authorities governing the two. Moreover, Jung does not attend to the influence of the cultural configuration, and the sociological reality, to which the individual adapts.] In spite of his terminology and the great number of his categories, [this question of] social and cultural [adjustment] gives us some left-over unclassifiables. [To cite examples we gave earlier, there is a great difference between] the Persian poet, or poet of the [European] Romantic period, [whose valuing of sensations] is socially integrated and has a social history, and the callous, self-indulgent, [or more truly rebellious] person who yields to the authority [only of his] collection of private sensations. If the individual rests upon [private] sensational points of reference, he is a law unto himself, escaping socializing forces. Such people are irrational because they are injecting fresh valuations that are not accepted by the majority. [But Jung's classification does not leave room for considering social acceptability, or the ways] sensation becomes symbolized.

[Similar questions of acceptability arise elsewhere in the classification.] Reasoning is not far from — and might [even] be the same as — rationalization, the difference [lying only] in [our] acceptance of [their product: that is,] the acceptance of reasoning and non-acceptance of rationalization. Reasoning people rationalize everything. For example, we rationalize about the superiority of man over animals. A premise such as this is so universal that it is accepted by all, and as soon as someone questions it we rationalize it. [The contrast between the feeling type and the thinking type is therefore much less obvious, in practical terms, than Jung supposes.]

(4) [Jung's] fourth type is the intuitive type, not quite irrational (and unordered) as Jung would have it, but a new dimension — a difference of mode and rate of apprehension, as compared with ordinary comprehension; or, alert thinking, as opposed to laborious thinking. When we say a person is a good thinker, we [may] mean two contradictory things: one is alertness and rapid apprehension; the other is the rational configuration, the slow, plodding [process] of integrative thought. The fast kind is what Jung [calls] intuiting. According to him, it means a direct apprehension — without thought — of total relations, due to the operation within the individual of a primordial sense of integration. Animals are good examples: they often act intelligently without being intelligent.

The intuitive person is imaginative. He has a chronic inability to see things as they really are — that is, to see something and see nothing more; he sees ahead to potentialities. As an illustration, [suppose you] see two lines, thus:

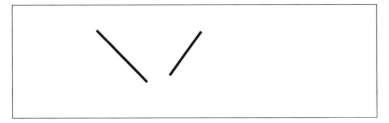

Figure 2: Imaginative Potentiality

If you imagine the point at which the two lines meet, you are using intuition. The mathematician [is an extreme of this type. When he suggests that] parallel lines meet in infinity, he sees the point rather than the lines — by mathematical intuition. [We might also say that] the intuitive mind is an historical mind, aware of all the relations that are locked up in the given configuration. Intuitive people look ahead, and foresee their actions, while non-intuitive people are afraid of implications, and stay with their sensations. Intuitives are symbolic, for they cannot see only the facts presented as such. For the intuitive type the awareness is of relations and not of entities so much.

The United States may be considered as having an intuitive culture, [at least] in the technical sense — always projecting a little more than can really be managed, taking a chance, and risking a lot in an attempt to realize some ideal. You take chances in order to "get in on the ground floor". A good politician must be intuitive. He is not interested in the *status quo* [for its own sake, but only in] using it as a starting point for changes hereafter. The successful businessman and the successful playwright must both be intuitive, seeing and displaying the implications [of a situation]. A great playwright has to be intuitive because he has such a short time to put over his ideas. A good actor, too, must be aware of the implications or he can spoil the playwright's play. Hence some great poets write poor plays, because they are too much intoxicated by the sensory elements [of the situation]. Some poets are intuitive, like Shelley and Blake — an intuitive person would like Shelley as a poet — while others are not, like the unintuitive Keats, who takes a sensory delight in words and confines himself to their sensory richness.

The intuitive person therefore must be defined not by the nature of his values, but by his degree of awareness of a situation's implications, and his rate of response [to them]. There is no content to intuition — it is, rather, a way of responding to a situation. Whatever its genesis, intuition is the direct awareness of relations.

Here, however, [we must propose] a modification of Jung's view. While Jung believes the intuitive type must be defined as a [separate] intellectual faculty, a more primordial kind of apperception, to me it is a phenomenon of rate of apprehension — shorthand thinking, in which minor elements merely don't appear explicitly in the consciousness. The intuitive mechanism [is rather like the intellectual equivalent of] getting on the night train at Washington and awaking to find yourself in New Haven, [without being conscious of the points in between.] I believe that intuition is better to be conceived as a matter of general awareness of implications and relations, which extends into all spheres of mental activity. It is a third dimension in individuals' cognitive feeling-life, [or perhaps] more a quantitative concept than a term to be applied to a special sphere of experience. You can have intuitives of all sorts, so this is [really] a criterion of a different kind.

Because intuition is [in large measure] merely a matter of rate, and the degree to which implications of form are made, I would not [consider] it as a special [personality] type. I would prefer Thinking Intuitive, Feeling Intuitive, Sensational Intuitive, etc., for one can well speak of intuition in sensation, in thought, or in feeling. Even within sensory experience there may be intuitive acts. An example of an intuitive sensationalist would be an expert cook who can project the result of combining [taste ingredients to create a new dish,] or a musical composer imaginatively reconstructing or planning ideal sensory experiences, like Beethoven's almost obsessive search for the perfect theme. (Much of life, however, is spent in inhibiting [this kind of] intuition.)

In just the same way there is emotional intuition, and intellectual intuition, [the latter sometimes in conflict with non-intuitive thinking.] The history of science is a [continual] battle between these two points of view, [which we may call] the observationist and the Einsteinian type (for Einstein is colossally intuitive, intellectually): [the type that] is interested in the unimaginative observation of facts, and [the type that] is interested in generalizations. The generalizations are derived from facts, but once a generalization is reached, the facts are disregarded and dismissed. The most obvious instance of intuitive study is in mathematics, which gives one structures in which to fit facts until finally one can practically neglect the facts altogether. Like great physicists who know the [results of the] critical tests [before making them,] great mathematicians know the answers before they are proven, [by a process of] projection. The geologist in the field [is another example of someone with an] awareness of total relations without all the data at his disposal.

Intuition, therefore, means an ability to respond to implications rather than to experiences, without [even] attending to all elements of the situation.[10] [But its results are not always pleasant or apt. The extreme intuitive,] Ibsen's Brand for example, has the cruelty and ruthlessness of the idealist, [always] substituting total implications for immediate experience. And because intuition is an inexplicit, unverbalized, immediate sense of relations, [it may also give rise to] idiotisms. [The intuitive's thought may show] a sort of dissociation, a schizoid quality.

[The question of social acceptability, too, is no less relevant to the intuitive than to other types in the classification. To people whose primary] loyalty is to experience, [intuitives] are disloyal Lloyd Georgers. [On the other hand, since society requires assumptions that are often counter to particular realities,] loyalty to reality can be anti-social, as opposed to a loyalty to the "rational" social [principles]. Samuel Butler's *The Way of All Flesh* [is an example of anti-social disloyalty, in its] protest against the bromidium that parents are kind to children.

3. Applications of the Types

[Let us consider (as Jung does)] some applications of the types in [philosophy and in] literary work. According to Jung, all philosophers try to interpret God and the universe according to the thoughts and ideals of their early training and view of life. Thus Bergsonism is the philosophy of the sensational, while Dewey and James are very thin philosophers who try to be hard-boiled. [The same process of personal interpretation applies in literature as well.] In [the work of] Anatole France, for example, the intellectual quality appears most conspicuously at the outset. The contemporary relevance of his emotional adjustment, his revolt, makes it more and more difficult to enjoy his works. There is too much emphasis on the intellectual machinery. The same is true of Shaw, who is primarily an intellectual artist, expressing no feeling; only, Shaw is still more private, and one cannot identify with his characters except as ideas, because Shaw himself does not identify with them — he simply invents them as ideas. His plays are a little hollow, for there is no emotional investment, no participation in universal feelings. ([A work that does so participate can therefore transcend its time and place.] Oedipus is still of great interest, because he deals with human feeling.)

Conrad, on the other hand, shows the opposite extreme of emphasis on the immediate reality of emotional experience. He is all feeling — he exhibits no intellect. He doesn't understand his own characters [in an intellectual sense,] but rather he is [just] actualizing himself, for he has not transcended his own personal problems. He over-feels his characters. He is obsessed with Lord Jim, because he can never get away from his own anxiety. [Perhaps] Conrad is mincing, for he triturates your feelings too much. Henry James, on the other hand, would like to feel a little more authentically than he really does.

In Keats we see a sensory poet, but one whose world of sensory experience is heavily laden with feeling. Coleridge, in contrast, though his "Rime of the Ancient Mariner" is classical for its evocative value, has less feeling attached to his sensory emphasis. And here is indicated the independence of this valuational classification from the extravert-introvert classification. For Kipling has perhaps equally a sensory emphasis, but it is quite extravert and objective, whereas Coleridge is an introvert, his images singularly devoid of realistic content or context, even though they are quite clear. Herein, perhaps, lies the difference between Coleridge and Kipling, or between Coleridge and Defoe, Stevenson, etc. as sensationalists. Let us take D'Annunzio and Coleridge: they are the arch-examples of extravert and introvert sensationalists respectively. In Coleridge's "Ancient Mariner" there is not an image that is not entirely vivid, and yet it is [somehow not quite real.] His sensations did not have to be real to be valid for him, but only the image of his sensations. D'Annunzio, on the other hand (or all extravert sensationalists), takes sensation as it is and identifies himself with it. Kipling would come under this class too.[11]

So it is possible to be maximally sensationalistic and yet introverted — in contradiction of Jung's early contention. As Lowes showed, Coleridge's images came almost entirely from his reading, not from his own imagination or his own sensory experiences. From the reading which satisfied his desire for exotic experience, he subjectively reassembled the imagery, but it remains literary, not re-evoking one's own sensations. Unlike Keats, Coleridge did not have a great wealth in his own experience of sensations that were interesting to him.

[Now, if we can apply Jung's classification to philosophers and literary figures, might we not also apply it to other writers, including Jung himself? Perhaps a] comparison of Jung and Freud, [on the basis of Jung's typology, might shed light on some of the comments that have been made about their work. Thus] Jung, being of an intuitive and not of the intellectual type, and also having difficulty in finding words, has a rather poor machinery [for presenting his ideas]. (Language, [we might say, supplies the] engines in the theory of human intercourse.) But he has at his back a large mass of rich clinical material and experience. The types are, [for him, a kind of] preservation of the ego; he places the personality in a world of values, each type being valuable in its own world.

Freud, [in comparison,] has a clearer idea of mechanisms. More schematic in feeling, he disregards the self-preservative organism in an individual personality − and so he kills the personality in dealing with it. Freud is a better theorist and scientist, Jung a better clinician. A criticism of Freud may be that he thinks of adjustment as a simple unilinear process, when in reality it is not so.[12]

[As regards the] opposition to Jung [within psychology − whether it comes from the Freudian school or elsewhere −] there is much to be said for some of Jung's opponents' conclusions, such as his inability to link up his theories with modern psychological terminologies. But he is, after all, a clinical physician untrained in the subtleties of academic psychology. In any case, the present task is to build up a powerful dynamic psychology that will function as an instrument of analysis. That will come from a blending of psychoanalysis with more formal psychological concepts.

4. [Summary and Implications]

Those who have read Dr. Jung's "Collected Papers on Analytical Psychology" may remember that in an earlier tentative classification of types he was disposed to identify the introverted with the thinking, the extraverted with the feeling type. These very dubious identifications have now been abandoned [in his more recent work, *Psychological Types*]. Dr. Jung is perfectly clear, and the reader will be with him, about the independence of a classification based on general attitude (extravert and introvert types) and one based on the specific functioning of the psyche. Whether Dr. Jung's theory of the existence of four distinct functional types of personality is correct it would be difficult to say. It may be that a given personality tends to find its way in the world chiefly by aid of the intellect, of emotion, of intuitive processes, or of sensation; [I would prefer to revise this scheme somewhat. But even if you accept it] it would be dangerous to erect the eight neatly sundered types that result from a crossing of the two points of view into a psychological dogma. We may be quite certain that such a classification is too scholastic to prove entirely sound and workable. [13]

[In their general outline, and without assuming they are exhaustive, Jung's distinctions among personality types organized on the basis of] sensation, thought, or feeling — [cross-cut by the dimension of] intuition — are all probable, it seems to me. [Just as with the introvert-extravert classification, however,] most of this [typology] is descriptive, not dynamic. [Were we to try to explore the genesis of the types, we would have some difficult questions to answer, including the relation between the two classifications.] Since there is no causal relation between Jung's functional types and the introvert-extravert types (value [types]), [do they have an entirely different genesis?]

Probably there is some biological, inherited basis for [at least some] of these types. They are not entirely caused by environment. The problem is, what values are to be attached to different kinds of phenomena, [and how does that association arise]? These values may be experiential, or they may be a product of one's nervous setup. The introvert-extravert [distinction] answers the question as to what sort of world you live in, based on [your] unconscious selection from the world of experience. [Perhaps this is] due to environmental determination, while the other types (feeling, thinking, etc.) compare more with the old idea of innate ability. These functional types [concern] preferred regions of experience, [based on] unconscious selections, [as opposed to the] value types.

As an example of [differences in] value types, [consider two possible approaches to the study of language. The first is interested in] language as an abstract [system of] meaning; [the second goes] beyond language [to what we experience directly, namely] speech. The emphasis on one or the other [is a difference] in content, not orientation as in the functional types. The field of speech [includes such matters as] speech melody ([i. e., is the melody someone uses] in a sentence when talking to you characteristic, [and if so, of what]?) and style ([i. e.,] to what [characteristics] are your [choices of] sentences or words attributed? To facility, to immaturity, or to what you have studied or imitated? [What about your] separation of words?) [What is of interest here is the totality of] the implications and significance of speech and gestures, and the enormous implicative power of individual experience.

[Although the two analyses seem to be distinct, the study of language cannot ultimately rely on only one of them. If] personality is largely reflected in the choice of words, here too we must distinguish carefully the social vocabulary norm from the more significantly personal choice of words. Individual variation exists, but it can be properly appraised only with reference to the social norm.[14] We human beings do not exist out of society. On the other hand, we can never have experience of social patterns as such, however greatly we may be interested in them. Society speaks through the individual.[15] [One or another approach may appeal to us depending on our own personality type, but neither has an absolute claim to the truth.]

[Insofar as we look for cultural patterns and attend top individual experience only to abstract from it,] we [anthropologists] are obtuse about the implications of personality data. [But are the psychologists really any better off? For all their attention to it,] the psychologists miss the vital problem of personality — the total value setup of the individual — since they persist in studying fragmentary psychological processes [and ignore the cultural forms in terms of which the personality meets the environment.] Perhaps we social scientists who are always asking psychologists to aid us can be of assistance to them in suggesting reformations of psychological problems. I don't think it is too supercilious to suggest that the borrowing need not be all on one side.[16]

Notes

1. Recall that Sapir does not necessarily mean "hereditary" when he speaks of the "genetically determined".
2. See Sapir (1923b), his published review of Jung's work: "Not until the last page is turned back does one fully realize how extraordinary a work one has been reading. It is often dry, it is sometimes impossible to follow, and it is never very closely reasoned, for Dr. Jung accepts intuitively as given, as elementary, concepts and psychological functions which others can get at only by the most painful of syntheses, if indeed they can find a way to some of them at all. But it is a fascinating book."
3. Roland B. Dixon (1875 – 1934).
4. In his 1926 presentation to the SSRC Hanover Conference, "Notes on Psychological Orientation in a Given Society", Sapir made a similar point: "[Compensation] means, then, you can't tell whether a person is extraverted or introverted by a simple study of overt behavior. That is where many make drastic mistakes. If your whole culture is extraverted, it has a bias. Any individual has to be very extraverted in order to count as extraverted. Kinds of compensations that are habitual will need to be of different types in different individuals. I have sometimes arrived at conclusions that are different

than those overtly suggested. I am thinking of a certain individual who would generally be considered introvert. I am convinced he is an extravert. He is playing up to an introverted society, to an introverted orientation familiar to him in childhood. His compensations are of a kind that need a certain kind of cultural knowledge to understand. If you carry these ideas to a logical conclusion, you will see, alarmingly enough, that psychology, psychiatry, all practical things we are interested in as to personality, are very much more involved with the problems of social science than we had thought."

5. In Table 1, next to the terms Rational and Irrational, the notetaker actually has "(organized)" and "(unorganized)", respectively. Since those parenthetical labels are Sapir's rather than Jung's, I omit them from this initial passage where Sapir is presenting Jung's own terms.

6. The notetaker has: " — in genetic fashion?" Again, Sapir probably means "developmental".

7. Here Sapir referred his audience to the writings of Bret Harte.

8. Here one notetaker (W. Hill) adds: "(A R Brown)".

9. It is clear that at this point Sapir distinguished between internal emotion and its expression, but the notes contradict each other as to which of these he called "emotion" and which "feeling".

10. At this point Sapir referred the 1933 class to his work on phonetic symbolism, Sapir (1929).

11. Here Sapir apparently referred the class to A. Machen's (1927) *The Hill of Dreams.*

12. The notes continue: "According to Jung, feeling is not emotion, but it is an effective manifestation of experience of the individual. For Jung, there is not much significant difference between the total emotional experience of different people." It is not clear whether this passage still represents a comparison with Freud.

13. The preceding paragraph is quoted from Sapir (1923b). The gist of the passage also appears in the class notes.

14. The preceding two sentences are quoted from Sapir (1927b), "Speech as a Personality Trait".

15. The preceding three sentences are each quoted from Sapir (1927b).

16. The preceding two sentences are quoted from Sapir (n.d.[1926]).

Chapter Nine

Psychological Aspects of Culture

1. [The Difficulty of Delimiting a Boundary Between Personality and Culture]

[If the psychologists' study of personality is deficient because] they persist in studying only fragmentary psychological processes, [omitting the cultural dimension,] the same is true in culture. There too we study fragmentary data. [As I have said,] we [anthropologists] are obtuse about the implications of data [that pertain to] personality. [The trouble is that both psychologists and anthropologists generally draw a sharp line between their disciplines and fail to recognize the overlap, even identity, of the problems they study.]

The failure of social science as a whole to relate the patterns of culture to germinal personality patterns is intelligible in view of the complexity of social phenomena and the recency of serious speculation on the relation of the individual to society. But there is growing recognition of the fact that the intimate study of personality is of fundamental concern to the social scientist.[1] [Indeed,] there is no reason why the culturalist should be afraid of the concept of personality, which must not, however, be thought of, as one inevitably does at the beginning of his thinking, as a mysterious entity resisting the historically given culture but rather as a distinctive configuration of experience which tends always to form a psychologically significant unit.[2]

[Thus the psychiatric view of personality as a configuration in which experience is organized in a system of psychological significance might also be applied to the problem of culture. So, for example, when we propose that] distinctions in nuclear attitudes are due to a difference in one's concept of a thing, [we might be speaking about personality or we might be speaking about culture. The attitude comprised in the individual's nuclear personality has an analogue in a cultural attitude, or what we might call] cultural loyalties − loyalties imbibed from your own culture which make you a little insensitive to the meanings in different cultures. You are obtuse to meanings that are not welcome, that do not fit into the old scheme of things

From the personalistic point of view, the whole field of culture can be regarded as a complex series of tests for personality — tests of ways in which the personality meets the environment. All cultures have the potentiality of psychological significance in personal terms. That is, the totality of culture offers endless opportunities for the construction and development of personality through the selection and reinterpretation of experience. [Conversely, too,] the totality of culture therefore is interpreted differently according to the kind of personality that the individual has. [Consider what happens to a person upon] entering a new cultural environment. The essential invariance of personality makes one alive and sensitive to some things and obtuse to others, [depending upon how the] new environment [matches up with] pivotal points from the old. [Your] awareness of certain things in a new cultural [setting] is a test of the old one, [a test of what the old one's pivotal points in fact were.]

The study of etiquette is [another] good way to [approach the relationship] between personality and culture, for it is a field that unites the field of culture and the field of personality. Its conventional forms [are clearly] goods of a highly cultural kind, [yet these forms are manipulated by individuals for the most personal purposes.] How should we delimit the boundary between personality and culture [here] — between the cultural form and the individual attitude? [When the same forms evince both] the permanence of cultural dogma, on the one hand, and the expressiveness of the individual, on the other, it is difficult to know just what you are dealing with. [The study of] family relations, or of clothing, [would be other good examples of fields with similar problems.] There is nothing vainer than to classify [such cultural] organizations unless you know their psychological correlates. Some organizations may divide up into quite different segments.

The relation between personality and culture — [that is, on the level of observable behavior, between] behavior [expressing the personal concerns of the] individual and behavior [expressing] cultural [forms — has become] my obsession.

2. [Attitudes, Values, and Symbolic Structures as Cultural Patterns]

[In order to approach the problem of culture and personality, then, let us begin with a] characterization of culture in psychological terms − [or, to put it another way, with an exploration of the] psychological aspects of culture. [Even the anthropologist who thinks of culture as an assemblage of traits might find something of the sort on his list, for] certain attitudes are definite traits of a culture. A distinguishing characteristic of American culture is our businesslike attitude − an insistence on clear business objectives and an efficient economic organization, and our consciousness of the blueprint and of the organization of time. [The concept of] self-help, and [the associated] tendency to action, [are similarly part of the] American [attitude.]

Can one go a little further in defining a culture from a quasi-psychological point of view? [Perhaps] a culture can be looked at as having a psychological imprint. [Just as] we can say that the member of a society belongs to a certain race, and the biological elements tend to express themselves in that way, we can also say that certain cultures have an ideal program that the participants tend to realize. They have a role, culturally imposed. [When I mention the expression of racial elements, however, I do not mean to suggest that a culture's psychological imprint has a biological basis, only a certain analogy between the two processes of program and expression. Whether] there can also be interaction between the two [kinds of] elements [is a problem to be investigated with careful study, not assumed from the start. For instance,] is the [relative] humorlessness[3] of the Indian [− at least from our point of view −] a racial characteristic or is it a cultural fact? [At this stage] I do not [think we can] know.

[Many aspects of individual experience that we are accustomed to thinking of as entirely personal must turn out, if this point of view is consistently adopted, to have a cultural basis. Even] dream formations are a cultural fact. We are ashamed to admit the obsessive value of a dream; primitive peoples are not. [For them] dreams are prognostic. [We need not take that evaluation of dreams literally in order to recognize that the content of dreams and the evaluation of their significance are culturally shaped. Similarly,] the motive of revenge is a cultural fact. In certain cultures you are expected to [take] revenge, more than in others. [We might even ask,] to what extent, [in a given culture,] is inhibition or sublimation possible? [This extent] will be different in different cultures. [For example, characteristics evaluated as] feminine are so resented in the male, in America, that the artist, who is [(in terms of such characteristics)] hermaphrodite, is blocked and has difficulty in developing himself.

[We must acknowledge, therefore, that many of the] motives and dynamic unconscious wishes[4] of the individual [derive from] cultural patterns [and reactions to them. How this works may be quite complex. Consider, for example,] the reactionary humanists' hatred for Rousseau — an opposition between pattern and protest. Thus we have the traditional man who is aesthetically comfortable in his vested psychological and cultural interests, as opposed to the trauma-driven innovator who meets life immediately, extra-culturally, and afresh. [But innovation is not always extra-cultural, however much the traditional man may see it that way.] Romantic [revolt becomes a pattern in its own right,] in opposition to the classical [scheme.]

This characterization of a culture [— in terms of patterned attitudes, motives, and values —] helps you to understand the lives of individuals and their relation to each other. For example, take a personal situation like two people [entering] a subway. Suppose each wants to pay his own way, his own carfare. Culture manifests itself in this situation, for there is a principle of economic independence and [of what constitutes a] debt relation [that is demonstrable] in the balance of how individuals spend money. In the countries of continental [Europe there would be] a different attitude. This is a system of value, and there are peculiar systems in each culture. In Italy, [for instance, we find a systematic value in] expressiveness; in Japan, in the evaluation of sensation; in China, in [the relatively] little solicitude toward salvation.

These are the patterns of culture, and they are at a different level from ordinary psychological behavior. [It is not that personality has no bearing upon them.] The solution of conflict, for example, is also affected by personality, [not only by cultural form. But it would be impossible in any case to assess personality utterly independently of culture.] Knowledge of the culture gives you a point of reference. You know what is the expected behavior; [only in relation to this can you interpret what the individual actually does.] [Consider, for example, a clinical case of neurosis: a girl patient engages in a ritual in which she throws shoes at a door. Now, if you are going to say that] the girl who threw shoes at the door [is "neurotic", you] have to know that throwing shoes isn't the culturally-patterned reaction to the situation — [that it involves, instead,] a refusal to accept culture, [and a creation of a] personal [system of] tabu and rituals. Neurosis is definable only in terms of a culture, which is implicitly present and acknowledged by the clinician. It is not explicit, [but it is crucial nonetheless.]

Anthropology has a great deal to teach psychiatry, therefore. The psychiatrists make the mistake of ignoring social factors, [especially] the different balances of values in different cultures. In fact, they are usually unaware of what the cultural values are. It is a fallacy [to conduct] a personality analysis without a sociological and cultural analysis first, for only after the cultural analysis can you really understand the personality. But psychiatrists set up a universal norm [of behavior] without considering this point.

[Of course, we can turn this argument around as well, for] there is never a simple dichotomy between individual personality and culture. [From the individual point of view,] actually, culture elements are merely symbols which enter into the total personality. Culture only takes account of the symbolism of behavior in the social sense. [There are other symbolisms, and (especially) attitudes toward symbolisms, which are personal.] Personality conflicts go beyond the plane of culture, [and we shall have a good deal more to say about this. For the time being, however, the point is that on the individual level] there never can be a mere expression of the cultural pattern. Personality always enters in. The dichotomy between culture and personality is not real, because they reinforce each other at all points.

In understanding culture [and its connection with the personality, however, it is not sufficient to consider only the particular symbols themselves.] The *placement*[5] of symbols is the important point of view. For example, [think of] a good singer [who performs] an operatic aria at an evening at the opera. [Now, the idea] that opera is a high form of culture is one of the values accepted by all. But if the singer, unasked, bursts into song at a tea party, the situation is different. [The aria] is the same cultural form, but in a different placement. At the tea, music exists only as something to be referred to, [not as behavior to be engaged in; and this distinction is often overlooked.] If you had asked any member of the party which they thought more important, a well sung aria or a tea, the answer would be the aria. But this is not taking cognizance of the placement of symbols. The question cannot be answered in the abstract, but must take into consideration time and place. The singer at a tea is not a singer [here and now]. She is a symbol of an important value outside, and is part of the ritual of the tea party. The singer as such is a point of reference in the formality of the tea ritual.

Absolutists, [attempting to determine the significance of a behavioral form like the operatic aria,] confuse contexts — they do not place symbols. Most of us are absolutists if caught off guard. But in that situation music did not exist, except as a symbol to be referred to. In that context it was [not appropriate as behavior, only as] a point of reference.

Most of our references are highly symbolic, [and the placement of these symbols in relation to one another is complex. This] structure of symbols makes it difficult for us to see the facts of our society and our cultural environment straight. Just as the configuration of elements in a spatial structure [may obscure our perception of any one of those elements individually, so] are we far from seeing our cultural environment [directly, except through this lens. In a sense it is a configuration of illusions:] it is the mapping of symbols that makes it possible for us to be mean to each other when we want to be nice — [that makes it possible for our behavior to be interpreted in some way other than what we intended — and creates a pyramid of misunderstandings that we hold about one another.][6] In a crisis, like the European war, such illusions are shattered and the pyramid of symbolisms falls.

[We are confronted by many contacts in ordinary life in which commonplace misunderstandings provide] examples of the placement of symbols. Suppose that A owes B, the head of a great business, twenty-five cents. A might want to pay B, but B says, "No, we will send you a bill." To him, taking the twenty-five cents would be misplacing symbols, because B at that moment was not B the [representative of the] business but Bill, a friend, and the idea of receiving the twenty-five cents out of context was upsetting. [In this incident A and B differ in their interpretation of the placement of the symbol, the twenty-five cents.] Not all people always interpret the placement of symbols in the same way.

[Perhaps it is not too fanciful to derive from our little tale of A and B some moral for those who like to think of] the "necessary history" of man [and his conflicts.] The needs of the biological organism are few, compared with the complications [introduced by] culture. But if culture complicates the satisfaction of biological needs too much, there comes resentment and anger, and the pyramid of cultural symbols crashes — [making way for] new cultural understandings, new complications, another crash, and so on. Conflicts [and crises, then,] may go beyond the plane of culture, [but they cannot be fully understood except in terms of the relations of individuals to one another through the medium of a structure of complicating, and sometimes misleading, cultural symbols. This is not, incidentally, the view taken by the authors of most ethnographic monographs.] The robots in ethnographic monographs don't care; they just do what they do, while culture, [by some mysterious means,] resolves the conflicts.

[It would be equally mistaken, however, to suppose that cultural symbols, even a lack of agreement on the placement of symbols, must necessarily lead to conflict any more than to its resolution.] Although people do not agree in their placement of symbols, two different people may live in harmony without really meaning the same things. They may even *do* the same things but have them *mean* entirely different things. What is necessary for them to share is only a minimal understanding, concerning the mechanics of the situation. [They may thus appear to agree quite profoundly, yet] their agreement is, [in a sense,] spurious, for it is without any analysis of the situation.

You get, therefore, two kinds of sliding scales:

(1) The sliding scale of the placement of symbolism within a cultural pattern — for the symbol may be of high value or low value, depending on its situation; and symbols are placed in different positions in different cultures.

(2) The sliding scale of the placement of symbolism according to personal (individual) values. [As we have said,] not all people interpret the placement of symbols in the same way. People make use of symbols in order to satisfy their own personal needs, [which may, of course, differ. Even] the same person can have different reactions to culture, according to [his or her] personal reactions to the placement of symbols. [And there are also differences in] the degree of personal participation, in an emotional sense, in the cultural situation.

Thus the placement of symbols in context [points up] the fallacy of [claiming to] observe the psychology of a culture, [as such.] The psychology of culture only arises in the relations of individuals; the psychology of *a* culture means nothing at all.

[If we take these discussions seriously we must conclude that] the implication of much of the social-psychological literature now being produced is a bit mischievous. [It confuses the two kinds of scales,] and their different strata of givens. This is what Mead and Benedict do — they confuse the individual psychology of all members of a society with the "as-if" psychology of a few. I use the term "as-if psychology" to describe the process of projection of personal values by the individual to evaluate cultural patterns, [so that a cultural standard of conduct is seen as if it represented the expression of a personality. This is a metaphorical identification,][7] not to be interpreted literally. The presumptive or "as if" psychological character of a culture is highly determinative, no doubt, of much in the externalized system of attitudes and habits which forms the visible personality of an individual.[8] It does not follow, however, that strictly social determinants, tending, as they do, to give visible form and meaning, in a cultural sense, to each of the thousands of modalities of experience which sum up the personality, can define the fundamental structure of such a personality.[9]

3. Culture as "As-If" Psychology

[Before we continue with our discussion of psychological aspects of culture, a note of caution must be sounded.] The term "cultural psychology" is ambiguous, and there has been much confusion between two types of psychological analysis of social behavior. The one is a statement of the general tendencies or traits characterizing a culture, such as the pattern of self-help in our culture; [as we have pointed out,] different cultures do have certain delineating factors, [including attitudes and] psychological standards about emotional expression. The other is a statement of certain kinds of actual behavior, [by actual individuals,] related to these cultural patterns. [In other words it is a statement of] the individual's psychology, and the problem of individual adjustment [to a cultural setting.] (This confusion is to be found, for instance, in the seven articles by psychiatrists about to be published in the *American Journal of Sociology*.[10] Alexander and Sullivan keep level-headed in their attempts to relate psychiatry and the social sciences, but some of the others are rather confused.)

These two kinds of psychology are not the same thing, but are in intimate relation with each other. [Moreover, the second kind has a further ambiguity, which perhaps we can see if we consider the notion of the individual's] integration. What do we mean by [this concept?] An adjustment to society, on the one hand − or the [coherence of the] thought, ideas, etc. of a man as seen by him, on the other hand? The same things can integrate or dis-integrate two different men.

[If the idea of a "cultural psychology" is so tangled, ought we to speak of such a thing at all? In a sense perhaps we ought not. Strictly speaking,] culture, in itself, has no psychology; only individuals [have a psychology. On the cultural plane] there is only [what I call] the "as-if psychology". That is to say, there is a psychological standard[11] in each culture as to how much emotion is to be expressed, and so on. This is the as-if psychology which belongs to the culture itself, not with the individual personality. [If we call this a psychology we are speaking] *as if* this scheme of life were the actual expression of individuality. The danger of [too literal an interpretation of this process] in the social formulations of the anthropologist and the sociologist is by no means an imaginary one. Certain recent attempts, in part brilliant and stimulating, to impose upon the actual psychologies of actual people, in continuous and tangible relations to each other, a generalized psychology based on the real or supposed psychological implications of cultural forms, show clearly what confusions in our thinking are likely to result when social science turns psychiatric without, in the process, allowing its own historically deter- mined concepts to dissolve into those larger ones which have meaning for psychology and psychiatry.[12]

Ruth Benedict's book, *Patterns of Culture*, is a brilliant exposition of as-if psychology, but with confusion about the distinction made here. She is not clear on the distinction between the as-if psychology she is dis- cussing and the psychology of the individual.[13] A culture cannot be paranoid. [To call it so suggests] the failure to distinguish between the as-if psychology and the actual psychology of the people participating in the culture.[14] The difficulty with *Patterns of Culture* is that certain objective facts of culture which are low toned are given huge significance. [I suspect that individual] Dobu and Kwakiutl are very like ourselves; they just are manipulating a different set of patterns. [We have no right to assume that a given pattern or ritual necessarily implies a certain emotional significance or personality adjustment in its practitioners, with- out demonstration at the level of the individual. Perhaps] the Navajo ritual can be considered as just their way of chewing gum. You have to know the individual before you know what the baggage of his culture means to him.

In itself, culture has no psychology. It is [just] a low-toned series of rituals, a rubber stamping waiting to be given meaning by you. The importance of cultural differences for individual adjustment [may well be] exaggerated, [therefore, for we may equally well suppose that culture means nothing until the individual, with his personality configuration, gives it meaning. In other words,] the apparent psychological differences of cultures are superficial — although they must be understood, of course, to know how to gauge the individual's expressions of his reactions.

[What I want] to bring out clearly [here is] the extreme methodological importance of distinguishing between actual psychological processes which are of individual location and presumptive or as-if psychological pictures which may be abstracted from cultural phenomena and which may give significant direction to individual development. To speak of a whole culture as having a personality configuration is, of course, a pleasing image, but I am afraid that it belongs more to the order of aesthetic or poetic constructs than of scientific ones.[15] [It is a useful metaphor for cultural patterning, but it loses its usefulness if it is taken literally.]

[For this very reason − that one is dealing with aesthetic constructs −] it is easier to apply a thing like Jung's [classification of] psychological types to cultures than to individuals. If you take the way of life of a community as a "psychology", it is easy to classify your cultures. On this basis, [one might speak of extraverted and introverted cultures: thus] American culture[16] of today on the whole is extraverted, recognizing no efficacy in unexpressed or only subtly expressed tendencies. We are willing to court private ill-will so long as it does not gain public expression. The Chinese and Japanese cultures seem definitely more introverted, [emphasizing] internal feeling (note, [for example, the Japanese custom of] hari-kiri, and the Chinese [type of] suicide [committed] so as to haunt one's enemy). But this [characterization of the culture] does not mean that the individual is extravert or introvert.

[If we consider] the possibility of constructing a typology of culture on the basis of a psychology of individual types, [then, we must not lose sight of the fact that] the social psychologies of such cultural types are not to be interpreted literally, but as as-if psychologies. Culture types are fictitious, but they are useful − [at least] until we have a more powerful knowledge of personality types − as a point of view regarding the relation of the individual to society. In the culture typology, culture is personalized, so that an individual acts extravertedly in adjusting to it.[17] Moreover, the typology is important for understanding cultural [integration.] The more fully one tries to understand a culture, the more it seems to take on the characteristics of a personality organization.[18]

In other words, we can look upon socialized behavior as *symbolic of psychological processes* not [necessarily] illustrated by the individuals themselves. ... So we can characterize whole cultures psychologically without predicating those particular psychological reactions of the individuals who carry on the culture. That is somewhat uncanny, but I think it is a reasonably correct view to take of society.[19]

[In this light let us consider some examples of what we might call strongly introverted cultures. In this sense of the term] some of the

Amerind tribes seem introverted, as Benedict shows. For instance, the Yuman culture of the lower Colorado, with its emphasis on dream experiences, is certainly an introverted type of culture. [To them] it is possible to annihilate time and space by dreams and get back to the beginnings of things and to the source of all potencies. If this kind of mechanism — the actualizing of power through wishes and dream creation — which is like the shrinking child's wish-phantasies, becomes habit, values may grow up around it and accumulate, [tending toward] that introverted cast of society (an extraverted society would kill the introverted meaning and recast it; or it may be loaded in another direction at a critical point). When the Yuman says, "I know that this is true because I saw it in a dream", he is in immediate touch with truth, and the symbolic triumph [gives him a] great kick. This society puts premiums on as-if introversion. There is a masking of true extraverts, then, for the extraverts are using the mechanisms provided by society, [including] a narcissistic libido expression — no color or glamour. The extreme romanticism of the early nineteenth century would probably be quite impossible in many of these societies.

Some of the [other] Amerind religions too, like the Mohave, seem almost neurotically introverted. In some Amerind religions this goes so far as a real denial of the evidential value of the external world in an annihilation of time, with the shaman going back to the creation and actually seeing standardized events there. This is an introvertedly evangelical religion, then. Mohave culture has a strange dreamlike character, an introverted [cast,] while the external culture is quite colorless. It is important to recognize that this is generally the case. Usually if the outer life is colorless one is apt to assume [a correspondingly] poor development of the inner life, when [actually] just the opposite is true. Introverted cultures are generally correlated with sober and drab material cultures, [because they place] less emphasis on external values.

It makes good sense, then, to talk about extraversion and introversion in culture as a helpful guard against undervaluation of the development of other peoples who have different values from those of our own culture. The Australians, for example, are probably much less primitive than they seem, because of their extreme introversion. I wonder if some injustice has not been made in styling them as primitive, since they have [such] a complicated mental life. The Eskimo, on the other hand, seem to us more highly developed and further advanced in culture than they really are, because their culture is extraverted, technological and non-fantastic. [Even] their mythology is more novelistic than dreamy. Thus many things in our [own] culture are better developments of things the Eskimo is already interested in, and acculturation would be expected to be easy so far as the purely cultural determinants are concerned. [The Eskimo] adapt easily to our mechanical appliances, for example.

Hindu culture too seems to be essentially introverted, for it is the most classically timeless. We seldom find dates in Hindu history, and the feeling that past and present meet — that things are not distributed in an evident sequence of years, and that there is not a before and after — is a typical sign of introversion. [The few] dates [we do have for Hindu history] are given by outside archaeologists and numismatists. In Hindu society there is an almost absurd annihilation of the external world (in contrast to Chinese culture, which is relatively [more] extraverted in its interest in dates). In India, self-contained feeling is as valuable as action; [thus] the custom of self-imposed torture for handling the world is very important. Whereas in Europe asceticism [is considered] a private problem, in India there is the feeling that this asceticism is extremely potent. This idea of the] vanity of the life of sensations is typical [of introversion, as is the associated Hindu notion that] the pleasures of the senses are sufferings. All forms of life are one; in the course of [existence] you can take different places ([i. e. become different forms of life]), for the self-existent entity is not a temporal one, [but something more like] a concept of a master idea, [or Platonic ideal. Thus] Sanskrit, [in the Hindu view, embodies] an absolute, mystic perfection of sounds and letters. It is a Platonically patternable language, a perfect pattern [against which to compare] the imperfections of reality. These mystic ad hoc realities, which for us are merely part of the stream of possibility, [illustrate introversion's charac-teristic] regression phantasy and annihilation of the difficulties of exis-tence.[20] [And just as] introverts are persuaded more by verbal formula-tions [than by sensory experience,] Hindu culture is full of verbal fetishism.

[In contrast, as I have suggested above,] American culture is essentially extraverted: in American culture action is more important than thought. Success [is measured by] fulfillment in the material world, for all values are measured with external standards. Thus a scientist gets angry because his salary does not look to him as an adequate return for his archaeo-logical work. Gandhi's passive resistance would be impossible in New Haven.

[In addition to the introvert/extravert contrast,] Jung's functional clas-sification can also be applied to culture [in the same manner, and certain contrasts between cultural configurations can thereby be brought out.] For example, there are cultures which as a whole seem to have an intellectual cast, such as the Athenian (and hence our relative ease in feeling ourselves into it, since its type of consciousness — with its intellectual values — is so much akin to ours; it is the temper of the culture, rather than the content, that we primarily appreciate). The culture of the Plains Indians, on the other hand, as contrasted [with the Greeks and also, closer at hand,] with Pueblo and Navajo culture, is characterized by a greater emphasis on the urgency of immediate feeling. The Pueblos' nostalgia [for feelings previously experienced] seems absent from the Plains because of the urgency there of immediate experience and the ease of having a vision, or enjoying ecstacy, at any time. The Plains [culture] being also extraverted, there is no privacy of feeling, and there is public boasting about visions and bravery, confessions of adultery, etc. (as among the Eskimo also). There is a tremendous rivalry regarding prestige [in these matters.]

One who was a psychological sensitive could tell in advance what types of things, games, myths, [and so on] would take [hold] in a culture, and what would not — and why. [However, it is worth repeating yet again that these] culture characterizations are not definitive, [only suggestive.]

[With this *caveat* we may continue with our typology and notice that] cultures also vary in intuitivism, although here the differences are not as great as between individuals. [Recall that on the level of the individual, the] intuitive [shows] enormous differences in the rate of movement of thought or phantasy, and in the wealth of implication. [What I mean by saying that] certain cultures are more intuitive than others is that the wealth of implication differs from one culture to another. American behavior has a remarkable wealth of implication,[21] but as to inward life it seems rather lacking in this respect as compared, for example, with the English. The English seem to assume many things without stating them and almost regard it as indelicate to make them explicit, whereas Americans would be more likely to take a practical, engineering attitude. [But] English intuitiveness is in regard to internal rather than external things; their culture is less intuitive than the American in physical matters.[22] An introverted mold, [a pattern of] whimsical fancy is characteristic of English writers, while in French culture — more intellectual [(in Jung's terms)] — epigram, not whimsy, is characteristic.

The life of sensation also varies in different cultures. In France, China, and Japan there is a tremendous emphasis on sensation values, yet there is also a selectiveness to the sensation values, and a balance of sensory enjoyment. Although an insistence on sensation for its own sake is conspicuous in French culture, the French do not go out for sensation in the way we do, because it does not have the hectic quality that it does for us. The French have educated their sensations; they are discreet and reasonable even in their license, and do not go the limit and become debauched as do Americans and English.[23] While Americans go to the extreme [when they indulge the] sensations because they feel [sensations] to be so bad they cannot be treated nicely, the French go into them restrainedly, for they do not have the good/evil dichotomy which makes us feel we may as well go the whole hog if we are going to break rules at all.

It begins to look, then, as if these various cultures had technically limited psychological possibilities. [In other words,] culture limits the opportunity for the personality to express itself in the way it is best suited. Now, how does this affect the individual? [Perhaps we must conclude that the world is full of] mute inglorious Miltons. Culture is sometimes not rich enough to give an individual an opportunity for expression.

Notes

1. The preceding two sentences are quoted from Sapir (1934b), "Personality".
2. The preceding sentence is quoted from Sapir (1934a). The sentence continues, in the 1934 publication, as follows: "...and which, as it accretes more and more symbols to itself, creates finally that cultural microcosm of which official 'culture' is little more than a metaphorically and mechanically expanded copy. The application of the point of view which is natural in the study of the genesis of personality to the problem of culture cannot but force a revaluation of the materials of culture itself." Though the idea that both personality and culture can be viewed as symbolic systems lending a distinctive configuration to experience is quite consistent with Sapir's 1937 statements, the notion that culture might be just a mechanically expanded copy of personality seems not to be.
3. The notetaker actually has, "the impossibility of understanding humor". Whose humor is concerned is not clear.
4. Here Sapir referred his audience to the psychologist Edwin B. Holt.
5. I.e., contextualization. See Chapter 5, on the "placement" of a cultural element in a cultural configuration. Sapir's discussions of context and systematic relations seem often to draw upon a geometrical model; see his letter to Benedict on Gestalt psychology and a "geometry of experience", published in Mead (1959:177).
6. The pyramid image occurs at several points in the notes on Sapir's lectures, and in his published writings as well. See, for example, the encyclopedia article on "Symbolism" (1934c): "Thus individual and society, in a never ending interplay of symbolic gestures,

build up the pyramided structure called civilization. In this structure very few bricks touch the ground."

7. See also Sapir (1937) on the "dangerous" metaphorical identification of society with a personality, or of culture with actual behavior.

8. The preceding sentence is quoted from Sapir (1937). There, it continues as follows: "... and, until his special social frame of reference is clearly established, analyzed, and applied to his behavior, we are necessarily at a loss to assign him a place in a more general scheme of human behavior."

9. The preceding sentence is quoted from Sapir (1937).

10. *American Journal of Sociology* 42 (6), May 1937, an issue of papers from a symposium of psychiatrists and social scientists discussing "social disorganization". The psychiatrist contributors were Alfred Adler, Franz Alexander, Trigant Burrow, Elton Mayo, Paul Schilder, David Slight, and Harry Stack Sullivan (see bibliography for full references). Sapir's paper, "The Contribution of Psychiatry to an Understanding of Behavior in Society", comes immediately after the psychiatrists' and comments upon them. The issue continues with articles by sociologists Herbert Blumer, William F. Ogburn and Abe Jaffe, and Mark May (see Bibliography).

11. Later writers on culture and personality used the term "norm" for a similar concept.

12. The preceding two sentences are quoted from Sapir (1937).

13. Sapir seems also to have suggested that Mead and Benedict projected their own values onto the cultural patterns they describe in psychological terms. One notetaker (M. Rouse) adds: "Benedict [assesses] Zuni from emot. evaluation | sensory type would ev. Zuni from sensory pt. of view − [emphasizing] forms − color − ritual − ..." Sapir's distinction between emotional and sensory personality types derives from Jung; see Chapter 8.

14. A notetaker adds: "(this is Mead)".

15. The preceding two sentences are quoted from Sapir (1980), a letter to Philip Selznick (October 25, 1938). The passage I draw upon begins thus: "I judge from a number of passages in your essay that you share my feeling that there is danger of the growth of a certain scientific mythology in anthropological circles with regard to the psychological interpretation of culture. I believe this comes out most clearly in Ruth Benedict's book, 'Patterns of Culture'. Unless I misunderstand the direction of her thinking and of the thinking of others who are under her influence, there is an altogether too great readiness to translate psychological analogies into psychological realities. I do not like the glib way in which many talk of such and such a culture as 'paranoid' or what you will. It would be my intention to bring out clearly, in a book that I have still to write, the extreme methodological importance of distinguishing ..."

16. One notetaker has "society" throughout this passage.

17. For one of Sapir's clearest statements about "as-if" psychology, see (n.d. [1926]), especially the following passage (from which I extract a portion, later): "We can say of all individuals who go through the forms of religious conduct that they are acting *as if* they were inspired by the feelings of those who really feel religiously, whether they really are or not ... In other words, we can look upon socialized behavior as *symbolic of psychological processes* not illustrated by the individuals themselves. ... [(after a discussion of French culture)] The point is, the psychological slant given at some time or other in the general configurations we call French culture by particular individuals became dissociated, acted as a sort of symbol or pattern so that all following have to act as though they were inspired by the original motivation, as though they were acting

in such or such a psychological sense, whether they temperamentally were or not ... So we can characterize whole cultures psychologically without predicating those particular psychological reactions of the individuals who carry on the culture" (italics original).

18. The preceding sentence is quoted from Sapir (1934a).
19. The preceding three sentences are quoted from Sapir (n.d. [1926]).
20. One notetaker (LaBarre) also mentions, "Chicago Hindu arguing about the *real* 'b' and 'p'." See Sapir (n.d. [1926]), in which this anecdote is related in detail.
21. Sapir was probably referring to Anglo-America rather than Native America here, even though one notetaker has: "Amerind [?] behavior has remarkable wealth of implication." Another notetaker (M. Rouse) has: "Much implication — action - American culture."
22. That Sapir gave some anecdotal illustration of this contrast is suggested in M. Rouse's notes: "Ques. asked about food on ship bet. Kobi & China — Stewart Richards ob. [?] all right. Of course, only imitation food. — whimsical fancy. American would attack such a ques. with engineering attitude of attacking fancied problem: then joke. Typical English attitude."
23. The notetaker adds, "who have not educated their sensations".

Chapter Ten

The Adjustment of the Individual in Society

1. [The Problem of Individual Adjustment: The General View]

[Let us turn now to] the problem of individual [adaptation] to the requirements of society: the tacit adjustment between the psychic system of the individual and the official lineaments of the [social and cultural environment.] The discussion of personality types that we have [engaged in] heretofore, [with reference to Jung's psychiatric approach, on the one hand, and with reference to its metaphorical extensions on the plane of culture, on the other,] is important not so much [for the types] in themselves as from the point of view of personality adjustment within and to a culture.

[You will recall our suggestion that] the psychology of culture has [two quite distinct dimensions:] (a) the as-if psychology, or the meaning given by culture [to one's behavior;] and (b) the actual, and much more intricate, psychology of personal action. [What we must now ask is, what is the influence of the one on the other?] What is the effect of these cultural casts on the individual, whose avenues of expression are provided by society?

[If personality were but the consequence of one's racial inheritance, or if there were no variability of temperament among the members of a society, our interesting problem would not arise. There would be little reason to distinguish between the two dimensions of the psychology of culture in the first place.][1] I believe, however, that the differences in personality are fundamental and that the variation [of personalities] is about as great in one culture as another, the variation only taking different forms in different cultures. [I find myself somewhat skeptical, therefore, about certain recent works on culture and temperament, such as Margaret Mead's writings on Samoa.] Mead's work is pioneering in the sense that she realizes that different cultures result in different personality transformations. She is entirely oblivious, however, to the play of personality differences within a primitive culture, and treats primitive personalities as being all alike on the same dead level of similarity. For example, it is likely that in actual fact there are personality misfits among Samoan adolescents brought up under the old free Samoan pattern, yet Mead has nothing to say of this and assumes all personalities developed according to one type.

Probably we have in all cultures [individuals of] the same basic personality types to deal with, such types, for example, as Jung depicts in his [book.] The problem, then, is to show the way those basic types are transformed or re-emphasized or re-aligned according to the master idea[s] of each diverse culture. This is an immense problem, [for whose solution the usual methods of anthropological work are scarcely adequate; it presents us, therefore, with] the difficulty of acquiring new techniques. The broad program would involve:

(1) A thorough study and knowledge of the cultural patterns of a group;

(2) An attempt to study personality types of selected individuals against or in terms of this background, perhaps by keeping a day-to-day diary, or [through a] case study of selected personalities in their relation to each other and in reaction to key cultural situations. But the culture must be analyzed beforehand with special reference to its master ideas. Only then can one begin the task of understanding personality transformations that occur through the impact of culture contact on native personality configurations.[2]

Defining the process of adaptation to a culture thus involves a definition both of the personality type and of the demands of the culture. [Moreover, in order to define the personality type and understand its adjustments we must remember that] there is a difference between the psychological constitution of an individual — his real characteristics — and that of his group behavior or appearance in the society as a whole.

[For example,] the group may admire male aggressiveness toward women, and demand of its male members such clearly masculine characteristics. These are socially suggested and approved in that given culture, and the different individuals reflect this pattern in a variety of forms and degrees. Of course, the prior outlines of the [person's] individuality have the utmost significance. These must be taken into consideration, [but] in order to find the true personality of the individual we have to [go through] an enormous amount of elimination of certain aspects of traits. (The more we know about the culture, the more adequately we shall be able to [speak] about the individual's real personality.) [Thus this culturally-patterned] aggressiveness appears differently in different individuals. [This is not only because individuals' nuclear personalities differ, but also because] it is in relation to others' aggressiveness in the milieu that one has to organize one's social behavior.

[In so organizing their behavior] people act symbolically and not individually. The intellectual general in the army who is an engineer or perhaps a physician is not primarily concerned with, or interested in, aggressiveness and the war affairs of his group. He is perhaps looking for new symbols for his own satisfaction, but he cannot break the social patterns that are required of him. This behavior [(the behavior that conforms with his group's aggressiveness and interest in warfare)] is an indirect expression of group loyalty. He behaves so, not in harmony with his own desires, but accommodating himself to the preferred as-if [personality dictated by the] cultural patterns of his society. Thus, [in a case like his] there is a conflict with the preferred psychological patterning of the society, and the psychological patterns of society are unreal to the personality[3] in such circumstances.

[For this reason,] no adjustment [defined simply] on the basis of an as-if psychology can be acceptable to the psychology of personal feelings. The problem of individual adjustment in society [may involve a variety of] methods of adjustment, successful and unsuccessful. [Moreover,] the energy spent in the process of adjustment to the preferred social patterns differs very much among individuals. The individual, to the extent of the difficulty he encounters, is abnormal in assimilating the psychological aspect of his culture.

[Now, suppose that a person has especially great difficulties of adjustment. The aggressiveness we were just speaking about may also arise as a consequence of this. His difficulty would display itself as] unusual aggressiveness, which is [really] cowardice. [For example, consider] an individual who, with a [wish for a] childish [form of] intimacy, wants a considerable hearing; but he cannot [have it] with every single individual member of the group. So, he hates the group and becomes excessively aggressive. He is not, therefore, normally aggressive, [only derivatively so as a result of his difficulties of adjustment. The particular nature of his aggressiveness reveals itself in his unusual acts: for instance,] he may enter the presence of a dignified and respectable elderly professor in a Napoleonic manner, making rationalizations of his own. He continues to be effectively aggressive [only] as long as his behavior is not repudiated by the group, [which it may well be. His case is different from] real aggressiveness, which belongs to the real personality, and receives some recognition among the members of the society.

[But it may be the case that the personality's adjustment to a social environment takes a different form, such as sublimation. For example,] to lie [to someone] for [reasons of] good manners is [a form of] sublimation of an original anxiety of circumstances. [One might say that because cultural patterns dictate what good manners are and when a lie is appropriate,] culture gives the key to the problem of sublimation. But individuals do not arrive at this end-point by the same means. [Moreover, some sublimations will go unnoticed because cultural patterns are available to handle them; but this is not the sum total of the sublimations effected by all the individuals in a society. We label as] perversions [those sublimations] without a cultural background into whose patterns the sublimation may be made, for those are [the sublimations] that stand out, while culturally handled perversions are absorbed. Culture gives the terrain of normal sublimation effected by the individuals [in the society, and as cultures differ so do the forms of sublimation normal to them. The introduction of] peyote and the Ghost Dance could take [hold] in the Plains but not in Pueblo [culture, therefore, since these forms of sublimation were consistent with normal cultural patterns in the one case and not the other.]

[The psychology of culture thus includes two distinct questions.] What are the general psychological roots of any culture pattern and of the as-if psychology? What is the personal psychology of [those] individuals who tend to follow the first [(the patterned as-if psychology),] and [what is the personal psychology which,] when divergent [from the cultural prescription,] will be envisaged as a morbid, obvious tendency?

We know that certain cultures act selectively with regard to certain personality types. The culture pattern, [we might say, shows a kind of] receptivity for a type. A shaman in Chukchi or Eskimo society, [for example, behaves like] an hysteric, [while] shamans are homosexual on the Northwest Coast.[4] [Other religions, such as] Christian Science, [also provide avenues and roles for the hysteric and may even capitalize on their behavior], as Arab culture capitalizes on Muhammad's neurosis. Culture acts acceptingly and electrically in response to significant personalities. The patterns of a culture make it hospitable to a [certain personality] type, but the patterns [too] are continually being tested through the adjustment of individuals to them. While a [certain type of] individual adjusts better in one culture than another, [a cultural] desire to accommodate aberrant personalities may result in new increments of social value.

[In some cases, then, we see that it is possible to] capitalize on the defects of one's personality. [This possibility is not only a question of the match between an individual and a type of society, but also of the individual's form of] compensation — and over-compensation, which is just the former to a greater degree than is necessary or customary. Such personalities [as compensate effectively] are among the most powerful members of society, for it is when in necessity that persons develop their [native endowments, such as their] genetically-endowed intelligence. The better adjustment occurs in the compensating types of personality, and less energy is consumed in the achievement. [In this process] those who associate themselves with the social order are the powerful interpreters of society — the Mussolinis, etc. The timorous man has not this identification with societal necessities, [although his compensations may be effective in other ways.] The tendency not to quite face a situation, but to translate one's lack [of ability to conform to its behavioral demands] into some other form which will be to one's own advantage, is a form of compensation.

[Everyday life is full of examples of forms of compensation. For instance,] an inability to make a flowing hand involves the compensation of [making, instead,] a very severe, fence-post handwriting. [In general, the more] rigid the law or the rules [about something, as with the handwriting] rules of this type, [the more likely they are to be] an example of an escape mechanism or compensation. [Now, to label something a] compensation is not a criticism. [Compensations are necessary and, as we have seen, they are sometimes a positive advantage. Not every personality compensates equally easily, however.] If the individual identifies himself too well with a problem and does not rely on symbolism [to find an advantageous form of behavior], then the job of compensation is harder.

Thus the society may expect the person to participate, at least to a certain level and degree, in the aesthetic requirements, to be able to play the piano for instance, and this urge may be imposed by the father upon his son who does not possess so keen an interest in the subject, and whose natural equipment may not be so favorable. This maladjusted person may turn out to be a neurotic in the major role[s] of the society. Yet another person may acquire symbols for adjustment or use, as an escape, humor which is accepted by the group. He willingly admits his defects and gets around the difficulty cleverly by reconcilement. This is overcompensation and overadjustment.

[Indeed,] humor is a good compensatory institution; [and as it is an institution, perhaps there is a sense in which] a whole culture can be described in terms of compensation. In present-day [society our] more or less strict social mores concerning sex, saloons, stag parties, and so on are [patterned like] compensations, as is the gross humor of Puritan society. Humor makes good something that has been starved out. Generally humor is valuable only to the individual, [as in the kind of case we were discussing earlier. Serving as the personality's means of adjustment or escape,] it is a purely personal matter. [On the other hand, it is also dependent on cultural patterns, so a certain] cultural adjustment is necessary before certain kinds of humor can be appreciated. The mother-in-law joke [will hardly be appreciated in a culture where the mother-in-law is] taboo.

[These considerations about compensation illustrate the complexity of the problem of individual adjustment to the demands of culture. And it is fundamental to bear in mind that] the culture is not just an inert psychological value. [From one point of view, of course,] culture is merely a pattern; it is in process only when the individual participates. These patterns, however, themselves are psychological problems and impinge upon the individual at a very early age. And the various types of adjustment [which the various types of personalities effect] give us a very large number of social-psychological processes.

[The variety of] methods of adjustment, successful and unsuccessful, [in turn affect the patterns of culture. As we have said,] culture patterns [— though they are historically derived —] are continually being tested in the adjustment of individuals [to them. Which plays the greater role — the weight of anonymous tradition, or the act of the individual?] The anonymity of anthropological method [stands starkly opposed] to the Carlylism of historians [who see history in terms of the acts of great personalities. I should prefer to suggest, however, that] the stability of culture depends on the slow personal reinterpretations of the meanings of patterns. Adjustment consists of the linking of the personal world of meanings onto the patterned, social world of meanings. Thus one's personal culture is a pattern [seen] for what it means to the individual, [who places] personal emphasis on some values as opposed to others; [and this in turn affects] the viability of the values [over the long term. Cultural] vitality [is made] not of impersonal sequences of events, but a pooling of these many case-histories and statistical ironings-out.

[Perhaps we can say something more about] the personal world of meanings, [if we consider] the field of child development. As soon as we set ourselves at the vantage-point of the culture-acquiring child, [with] the personality definitions and potentials that must never for a moment be lost sight of, and which are destined from the very beginning to interpret, evaluate, and modify every culture pattern, sub-pattern, or assemblage of patterns that it will ever be influenced by, everything changes. Culture is then not something given but something to be gradually and gropingly discovered. We then see at once that elements of culture that come well within the horizon of awareness of one individual are entirely absent in another individual's landscape.[5]

[If we are to understand the transmission of culture, or indeed the whole problem of culture from this developmental point of view,] the time must come when the cosmos of the child of three will be known and defined, not merely referred to. The organized intuitive organization of a three-year-old is far more valid and real than the most ambitious psychological theory ever constructed. [Yet, our three-year-olds are not all the same.] Our children are fully developed personalities very early. [We do not quite know how this comes about, but it depends considerably on] the interactions between the child and his early environment up to the age of three.[6] [Even within the same family, each child's] world is a different kind of a thing because the fundamental emotional relationships were differently established [depending on his status] as first or second child.

In the child's cosmos, patterns of behavior are understood emotionally, [in terms of a particular constellation of relationships].[7] The genetic psychology[8] of the child will show specific emphases of meanings of patterns which are used to handle and control the people and events of the social world. [Thus words and other symbols do not have exactly the same meaning for the child as they will for the adult, for in the child's world] various words have special values and emotional colorations, [taken on through their] absorption [in the child's] emotional and rational [concerns]. Later additions of meanings must be seen in the light of the nuclear family complex and its effect on personality development. It is obvious that the child will unconsciously accept the various elements of culture with entirely different meanings, according to the biographical conditions that attend their introduction to him. It may, and undoubtedly does, make a profound difference whether a religious ritual comes with the sternness of a father's authority or with the somewhat playful indulgence of the mother's brother.[9] [So it is only through patient studies of child development, concerned with a limited number of specific individuals, that we may really begin to understand the connections between] childhood constellations and religion, between infantile *apperzeptions-masse* [and the meaning of] adult activities,[10] [between the child's] hunting in closets and [the adult's] scientific interest in crystallography.

It has been suggested by Dr. Sullivan that studying a limited number of personalities, for about ten years, by different representatives of the fields of social science will, no doubt, be of great help to understand more clearly the problem of personality. [The same is true for the problem of culture.] This study will take the individual as early as possible in life and follow him through for quite a considerable period of time with utmost care and with cooperation and mutual aid of each system and method of approach involved.

Study the child minutely and carefully, from birth until, say, the age of ten, with a view to seeing the order in which cultural patterns and parts of patterns appear in his psychic world; study the relevance of these patterns for the development of his personality; and, at the end of the suggested period, see how much of the total official culture of the group can be said to have a significant existence for him. Moreover, what degree of systematization, conscious or unconscious, in the complicating patterns and symbolisms of culture will have been reached by this child? This is a difficult problem, to be sure, but it is not an impossible one. Sooner or later it will have to be attacked by the genetic psychologists. I venture to predict that the concept of culture which will then emerge, fragmentary and confused as it will undoubtedly be, will turn out to have a tougher, more vital importance for social thinking than the tidy tables of contents attached to this or that group which we have been in the habit of calling "cultures".[11]

If we take the purely genetic[12] point of view, ... problems of symbolism, of superordination and subordination of patterns, of relative strength of emotional character, of transformability and transmissibility, of the isolability of certain patterns into relatively closed systems, and numerous others of like dynamic nature, emerge at once. We cannot answer any of them in the abstract. All of them demand patient investigation and the answers are almost certain to be multiform.[13] [For, a part of what we are investigating is the emergence of a personal cosmos and, in an important sense,] a personal cosmos — a personal world of meanings — is a separate culture. The totality of culture is more many-chambered and complex than we suspect. We take meanings that apply to the majority of individuals in a group and thus create the illusion of an objective entity which we call "culture" or a collective body of meanings. But it is an imaginative abstraction. Thus [— to recall an argument we made in an earlier lecture —] it is so hard to speak of the causes of historical events. Culture history has fate [perhaps, even] necessity, but no causation. The "reasons" [we give to cultural forms are] only harmonizations of our [own] ideas. The true reasons [we draw the abstractions we do] are difficult [to recognize, and] many times would be embarrassing and dangerous [for us were we to do so.][14]

[Investigating] the problem of individual adjustment in society [has thus led us inevitably to] the concept of pluralism of culture in a given society. [For the patterns of culture are subject to] endless revaluation as we pass from individual to individual and from one period to another. [We have also seen something of the relationship between] individual and cultural configurations: how they [may] correspond, reinforce each other, overlap, intercross, or conflict. [In this process, culture is reinterpreted and its patterns respond to the individuals adjusting to them; personality does likewise.] While several factors may be responsible for individual differences in personality the one of considerable importance socially is to find what the general social patterns mean to individuals who participate in them.[15]

[In sum,] the thesis is that the degree of agreement between the meaning which the individual comes to see in social patterns and the general meaning [which] is inherent (for others) in those patterns is significant for an understanding of the individual's process of adjustment, as revealing harmony or conflict.[16]

2. [Individual Adjustment to Changing Conditions]

It is said that for one individual one type of society is best; [in fact, we have implied as much in earlier pages.] But this [statement, if it is to be taken as anything more than the acknowledgement that some personalities find adjustment to their social environment particularly difficult,] involves a need for correct analysis of two societies plus one individual — analyses which are not easy to make.

[Suppose however that we consider the case of some one individual who happens to emigrate to a new social environment. Suppose that he is a scatterbrain and, finding that his fellows in his native setting react unfavorably to his behavior, he moves to Paris, where his life is easier.

Is he now better-adjusted?] A scatterbrain in Paris does not adjust better there; his adjustment is the same as before. But the type of judgement [the members of the surrounding society make] of his adjustment is more lenient. Such a thing as a foreign accent will [actually] help [his] adjustment, [or rather it will] lessen his own problem of adjustment, by reducing the demands of others. [Their] judgement [is more lenient because, hearing the accent, they recognize him as a foreigner and expect less of him. In this case it is not the mode of adjustment that is at issue, only the society's tolerance of foreigners.] Indeed, if one cannot adjust to the society in which one has been nurtured, how can one adjust better to one in which one has come at a late date, except in the way above of charitable misunderstanding on the part of the host society?

[At first glance all instances of immigration might appear to be the same as this one. But that is not so.] In contemporary America especially, a society where institutions are changing, important theoretical advances may be made concerning the relation between culture and personality. Where conditions are not very stable, as in the United States, the relation between personality and culture becomes very important. Contrary to Europe, the individual has a choice of several as-if psychologies. There is a remarkable flux of status and function and a remarkable "selfness" of the individual. [Now, while great] importance [is placed on] the individual, and we are meeting individual peculiarities much more hospitably than ever before, [what looks like hospitable accommodation by society to the individual personality in one sense is part of a particular cultural pattern, in another.] It is part of the extraverted, intuitive character of American life. [Ours is a] rapid pace, pretty much in the open; and this can be thought of as exhilarating or as shallow.

What Europeans will accommodate themselves best [to American life? Perhaps they are] those who have the least to lose [by accommodation] — sometimes those least adapted to the older system. There will be an attempt to recapture the old [cultural] symbols in the new context; where this is not possible, the old will quite degenerate. There is, then, a tendency for those who become successful to adapt themselves by really adopting the new culture. In America, complete transvaluations ([i. e., cultural shifts, or] acculturation) are commonplace. This acculturative process must be strictly distinguished from the [case of our scatterbrain in Paris, or, analogously, the] process by which the American culture simply makes itself hospitable to, say, an Englishman who preserves or even accentuates his differences from his American fellows.

There is no significant acculturation that is not painful, however. [As we have just said,] if the attempt to recapture old symbolisms in new terms cannot be achieved, disintegration results. Indeed, all the processes of adjustment of the individual to society involve some sacrifice. [There is always some] clash between the demands of a personality and those of a culture. The process of [actively] adjusting or passively conforming to the culture [can be the source of what appears to be merely a] personality problem.

Thus the theory that unless one is a neurotic one can adjust to any culture cannot be absolutely correct. I believe people differ fundamentally in personality − though it is fashionable to believe otherwise − and that personality can be read in terms of explicable factors. Cultures [also vary, so that some cultures,] because of certain values [central to them,] are not as suitable to some personalities as to others. No theory of neurosis is needed to account for the difficulty of the individual in adjusting to the culture. We are too quick to brand many of these personalities as abnormal. Actually, every one of them might be perfectly adapted to some one as-if cultural psychology, [had it but found itself in the right cultural environment].

[If it is the process of adaptation, and not necessarily just the personality itself, that may be the source of maladjustments, there may actually be] two ways maladjusted people can be helped. One [of these] is to change the personality; the other, to change the patterns or concepts [by means of which the personality interacts with its environment. But] perhaps just as some [people are constitutionally] too delicate to survive physically [in the geographical environment in which they find themselves], in the cultural landscape the same may be true of personalities. A certain amount of [psychological] death rate in adjusting the personality to the cultural climate [must be expected, just] as in adjusting physique to [physical] climate. While the strategic placement of the individual in [just the right type of] society may be a possibility theoretically, it is hardly so in practice.

3. Can There Be a True Science of Man?

[We have now spent some time discussing] the tacit adjustment between the psychic system of the individual and the official lineaments of the [social and cultural] environment. [It is clear that the life of the individual in society can never be just a simple and direct expression of his own nuclear personality, for it must always take social pressures into account.] The organization of [social] force [impinging on the individual [comprises] many [forms of coercion,] from the tyranny of one's little boy to governmental force. [From these pressures] we are too cowardly ever to be free.

The factors of inner adjustment are difficult to know. The process of adjustment is not only the matter of finding a place in the cultural setting, [a problem each individual might face equally] regardless of what the individual personality needs are. [It is also a problem of] the adjustment of the personality [itself, and the form of one's participation in society.][17] Those who are well-adjusted because [their participation subjects them to] less thwarting — [perhaps because their] professional [situation,] etc., [satisfies their personality needs] — are unaware of the concept of carrying around a psyche that is always fighting for psychic existence.[18]

[So, how are we to approach these problems, from an analytical point of view? What scientific discipline, if any, might] take on the character of [a sufficiently] inclusive perception of human events and personal relations? [Many of the disciplines constituted as special sciences of man's physical and cultural nature will disappoint us if we look to them for help. Tending to create a framework of tacit assumptions about the nature of man which enable their practitioners to work with maximum economy and generality, they present only fragmentary pictures of man, pictures which are not in intelligible or relevant accord with each other and which tend to become more and more estranged from man himself.] The classical example of this unavoidable tendency is the science of economics, which is too intent on working out a general theory of value, production, flow of commodities, demand, [and] price, to take time to inquire seriously into the nature and variability of those fundamental biological and psychological determinants of behavior which make these economic terms meaningful in the first place. The sum total of the tacit assumptions of a biological and psychological nature which economics makes get petrified into a standardized conception of "economic man", who is endowed with just those motivations which make the known facts of economic behavior in our society seem natural and inevitable. In this way the economist gradually develops a peculiarly powerful insensitiveness to actual motivations, substituting life-like fictions for the troublesome contours of life itself.[19]

The economist is not in the least exceptional in his unconscious procedure[20] [which creates an] economic theory in which psychological factors are not recognized. In linguistics, abstracted speech sounds, words and the arrangement of words have come to have so authentic a vitality that one can speak of "regular sound changes" and "loss of genders" without knowing or caring who opened their mouths, at what time, to communicate what to whom. ... The laws of syntax acquire a higher reality than the immediate reality of the stammerer who is trying to "get himself across";[21] [but his] speech errors cannot be described or explained, [let alone] escaped, only linguistically. There are psychological reasons [for them too — reasons linguistics has excluded from its concerns.] One can go far in a discipline without placing it in the cosmos of man.

[Perhaps] cultural anthropology and psychiatry [are better placed to make formulations about man and his place in society which can prove accurate when tested by the experience of the individual.] Each of these disciplines has its special "universe of discourse" but at least this universe is so broadly conceived that, under favorable circumstances, either of them can take on the character of a true science of man. Through the sheer weight of cultural detail and, more than that, through the far-reaching personality-conditioning implications of variations in the forms of socialized behavior, the cultural anthropologist may, if he chooses, advance from his relatively technical problems of cultural definition, distribution, organization, and history to more intimate problems of cultural meaning, both for individuals and for significantly definable groups of individuals. And the psychiatrist may, if he chooses, advance from theories of personality disorganization to theories of personality organization, which, in the long run, have little meaning unless they are buttressed by a comprehension of the cultural setting in which the individual ceaselessly struggles to express himself. The anthropologist, in other words, needs only to trespass a little on the untilled acres of psychology, the psychiatrist to poach a few of the uneaten apples of anthropology's Golden Bough.[22]

[Perhaps it will be possible to see where the middle ground between our two disciplines might lie if we consider the problem of the relationship between] personality demands and symbols. [It takes no long acquaintance with psychiatry to discover that a human being's] personal strength is augmented by touching society's [symbols] and the individual['s own] symbols at some points. [But what the psychiatrist may overlook is that there are] two orders of symbols — individual and social. [Let us remind him that he needs to concern himself with both, and to recognize that the social plane of symbols touches intimately on the individual's motives and experience, for those symbols are fundamentally involved in our everyday interactions with other members of our society. As individuals whose lives intertwine with others,] we use the same symbols as others do so that we can advance our own interests. [It is not because we have transcended those interests and moved into an exalted realm in which we] care about society's welfare − [a matter about which, in any case, we can have no impersonal judgement; we] only have [personal] preferences. [Indeed, the nature of your] individual adjustment colors your philosophy of society. It is the process of adjusting your personality, not your cultural role, [that is so influential in organizing the world of meanings which includes your conception of "society" itself, and in terms of which personal action is undertaken and interpreted].

[By the same token, the cultural anthropologist whose primary interest in symbols lies on their social plane needs to recognize that] cultural considerations alone can never explain what happens from day to day − they are inadequate for predicting or interpreting any particular act of an individual. [The reason for this, in a nutshell, is that in those particular acts] the individual is not adjusting to "society", but to interpersonal relationships.

[Faced, therefore, with] the difficulty of segregating the [psychological and the social] systems, [and convinced that] the gap between the sociological approach and the psychological approach must be filled and both systems must be used, [I find that] I am particularly fond of Dr. Harry Stack Sullivan's pet phrase of "interpersonal relations." The phrase is not as innocent as it seems, for, while such entities as societies, individuals, cultural patterns, and institutions logically imply interpersonal relations, they do little to isolate and define them. Too great agility has been gained over the years in jumping from the individual to the collectivity and from the collectivity via romantic anthropological paths back again to the culture-saturated individual. Reflection suggests that the lone individual was never alone, that he never marched in line with a collectivity, except on literal state occasions, and that he never signed up for a culture. There was always someone around to bother him; there were always a great many people whom his friends talked about and whom he never met; and there was always much that some people did that he never heard about. He was never formed out of the interaction of individual and society but started out being as comfortable as he could in a world in which other people existed, and continued this way as long as physical conditions allowed.[23]

[The study of] interpersonal relations is the problem of the future. It demands that we study [seriously and carefully just] what happens when A meets B − [given that] each is not only physiologically defined, but each [also] has memories, feelings, [understandings,] and so on about the symbols [they can and must use in their interaction]. It is also necessary to study variations in individual behavior in different circumstances, [for] the individual's whole behavior is modified in a new situation, and even his facial expressions change. [And it is also necessary that we study the consequences of the fact that] the differences between individuals make different things happen when A and B are different people, or when someone else, C, is with them. Thus A may be very friendly to B when alone and yet not friendly when C is present. And what happens when C substitutes for A? When all three meet? When one of the three is removed and another added? [In each case you have] a new situation. [In any situation] when two people are talking, they create a cultural structure. [Our task, as anthropologists, will be to determine] what are the potential contents of the culture that results from these interpersonal relations in these situations.[24]

I think we should abandon [our present] abstract terminology [for a while] and study each situation as it occurs. In this way we will be able to study the values of behavior [in both] individual and cultural [dimensions — the first of] which anthropologists now carefully avoid. [We would be recognizing that we do not have, as our immediate object of study, a culture adapting to a physical environment, but human beings adjusting to actual situations, by means of structures of symbols. It is not usually the physical environment itself that we adjust to in any case, but what we see as environment.] Secondary symbols of the environment are most important, [then, and these are] things we have invented.

To do this thoroughly — [to study each situation and all its implications —] is, of course, impossible. But the students of culture must not leave these [considerations] out of account. The student must proceed as follows: (1) study the individual behavior [arising in a particular situation, in] the relation between A and B, etc.; (2) abstract the cultural patterns from it; (3) make the generalizations [that turn out to be pertinent at the level of the totality of culture]. At present most anthropologists work from (3) to (1). [But I think it is not unreasonable to suggest that] every student of culture ought to have [some] feeling for the relationships of people — [and only] then abstract the forms [we call culture.]

[What I wish to propose is that we take seriously the proposition that] cultural, linguistic, and historical patterns are derivative of interpersonal relations, though they are meaningful. [Until we are sure of their] testability in behavioral terms, [we will never be sure of the] import of the cultural "phenomena" abstracted by anthropology.

Notes

1. See Sapir (n.d. [1926]) on the "mentality of races", and Chapter 13's statement (from the concluding lecture of the Rockefeller Seminar): "To study the problem of the relations of 'culture' and 'personality' means that one does not consider personality as the mere unfolding of a biological organism."

2. See also the various research proposals Sapir wrote, or to which he contributed, for the Social Science Research Council and the National Research Council; for example Sapir (1930).

3. I.e., not native to it?

4. It is not clear whether Sapir claimed the Chukchi shaman actually is an hysteric, who happens to enjoy an acceptable role, or whether the label "hysteric" applies only to our own evaluation of the cultural pattern of Chukchi shamanistic behavior. Compare Sapir (n.d. [1926]): "We find among the Eskimo the Shaman or medicine man acts as if he were a hysteric. He goes through all the motions of hysteria, and perhaps he is, I don't know, I am not a psychiatrist. Their pattern of medicine man activity demands hysterical conduct. He autosuggests a hysteria complex. I am not in a position to disentangle what happens. The diagnosis of that hysteria is not the same as that of hysteria among ourselves, because the cultural background is notably different in the two cases... [example of homosexuality among medicine men] ... It isn't necessary to suppose that you are really dealing with types of personality that lead to that kind of behavior naturally."

5. The preceding passage, starting from "the field of child development", is quoted from Sapir (1934a).

6. This passage comes from the Rockefeller Seminar. Notes on the discussion period of this seminar session further show that "Mr. Dai raised the question of the development of Personality types. Dr. Sapir answered in brief the three stages: 1. Heredity, the somatic implications may mould the character. (Not so important from our point of view.) 2. The maturing period, we do not know quite about, but very important. 3. Interactions between the child and his early environment up to the age of three."

7. The notetaker actually has, "In the child's cosmos, Chinese patterns of behavior are understood emotionally." Sapir presumably contrasted the emotional outlook with the ethnological here, as in Sapir (1934a) and in the Lecture to the Friday Night Club, which begins, "I cannot be ethnological and be sincere in observing my little boy play marbles. I cannot watch a Chinese mandarin and be psychological." The child does not understand a particular mode of behavior as representative of a culture, Chinese for instance, but in terms of its emotional significance for him or her.

8. I.e., developmental psychology.

9. The preceding two sentences are quoted from Sapir (1934a). On this point see also Malinowski (1927), *Sex and Repression in Savage Society*.

10. Here Sapir apparently referred the class to the work of Edwin Holt.

11. The preceding paragraph is quoted from Sapir (1934a).

12. I.e., developmental.

13. The preceding passage, from "If we take the purely genetic point of view", is quoted from Sapir (1934a).

14. Beaglehole's notes have: "Culture history has fate, necessity, but no causation. True reasons are difficult, many times humiliating." LaBarre has: "Thus so hard to speak

of 'causes' of historical events. [new paragraph] 'Biography' of Julius Caesar full of cliches of Roman culture, tell us nothing of the personality. History has 'fate' inherent in it, pragmatically no 'cause' for it; for us only 'necessity.' [new paragraph] Interest in ethnology, a running away from the ethnologist's own personal problems: escape from responsibility (Margaret Mead) 'reasons' only harmonize our ideas, real reasons are sometimes embarrassing and dangerous." Sapir seems to have been asserting that statements as different as Caesar's (auto)biography and Mead's ethnography are equally pervaded by ideology and their authors' personal agendas. It is unlikely, however, that Sapir would have included so rancorous a statement about Mead in any published text.

15. The preceding sentence is quoted from Sapir (n.d. [1930]).
16. The preceding sentence is quoted from Sapir (n.d. [1930]).
17. I believe Sapir meant to imply that to understand an individual's adjustment it is not sufficient to consider merely his/her sociological role, but more important to consider the personality and how that is adjusted to society in general (including one's role). I do not think Sapir means that one's sociological role is utterly irrelevant (see the later passage on "professionals", and Sapir [1939a]).
18. Compare passages toward the end of Sapir (1939a), for a similar argument.
19. This paragraph is quoted from Sapir (1939a).
20. The preceding portion of this sentence is quoted from Sapir (1939a).
21. The preceding two sentences are quoted from Sapir (1939a).
22. The preceding paragraph is quoted from Sapir (1939a).
23. The preceding passage, from "I am particularly fond ...", is quoted from Sapir (1937). A notetaker (M. Rouse) has some similar material.
24. Compare the concluding passage of Sapir (1937): "If we could only get a reasonably clear conception of how the lives of A and B intertwine into a mutually interpretable complex of experiences, we should see far more clearly than is at present the case the extreme importance and the irrevocable necessity of the concept of personality. We should also be moving forward to a realistic instead of a metaphorical definition of what is meant by culture and society. One suspects that the symbolic role of words has an importance for the solution of our problems that is far greater than we might be willing to admit. After all, if A calls B a 'liar,' he creates a reverberating cosmos of potential action and judgment. And if the fatal word can be passed on to C, the triangulation of society and culture is complete."

Chapter Eleven

The Concept of "Primitive Mentality"

[One of my aims in these lectures has been to] try to establish a more intimate relation between the problems of cultural anthropology and those of psychiatry than is generally recognized.[1] [In the study of interpersonal relations,] it looks as though psychiatry and the sciences devoted to man as constitutive of society were actually beginning to talk about the same events — to wit, the facts of human experience.[2] [But before we allow ourselves so comfortable a conclusion, it will be well to consider a problem with regard to which psychiatry and cultural anthropology have shown themselves to be much less compatible bedfellows. This is the problem of the so-called] "primitive mentality". In presupposing a special primitive mentality, [an archaic psychological regime supposedly explaining modes of behavior in the neurotic and among the primitives,] psychoanalysts welcome the contributions of cultural anthropology but it is exceedingly doubtful if many cultural anthropologists welcome the particular spirit in which the psychoanalysts appreciate their data.[3]

[Now, how did Dr. Freud, the founder of psychoanalysis, arrive at his version of "primitive mentality", the common ground of his] inevitable triad of children, neurotics, and savages?[4] For a long time psychiatry operated with a conception of the individual that was merely biological in nature. This is easy to understand if we remember that psychiatry was not, to begin with, a study of human nature in actual situations, nor even a theoretical exploration into the structure of personality, but simply and solely an attempt to interpret "diseased" modes of behavior in terms familiar to a tradition that was operating with the concepts of normal and abnormal physiological functioning.[5] It is necessary to keep in mind, then, that psychoanalysts are pathologists. They are medical men, not usually psychologists, [and they have often] not been willing to generalize their theories outside of pathology. [This colors their entire approach.]

[When we recall that] Freud was a clinical doctor at first, [we will more easily see that] his [early] reports are not really psychological [in any sense in which we might now understand that term] but [represent] a jump from clinical notes to vaguer cultural institutions. Hypnotism was in vogue at that time [among the clinicians with whom Freud trained], but [after some initial experimentation] Freud didn't go [in] for that. [Instead,] his idea was that of an early awakening − of [the organism's] going back to early reactions in an attempt to start anew and adjust [to a situation of stress.] As a result of his clinical training he dealt with physical systems; hysteria was his field, [initially,] not so much neurotic obsession. [The concepts of regression and repression that are so fundamental to psychoanalysis emerged in this context of the clinical setting and this emphasis on] the physiological approach to behavior, [rather than] the psychological approach, [although the further exploration of regression and repression led far beyond the organic level.][6]

[Like Freud,] Adler and Jung were also medical students in Germany and Austria, [and just as the medical background can be traced in the work of all three, so can the cultural.] The German scholar is very factual, on the one hand, [yet he is often enough to be found] mystically chasing the blue flower, on the other. [It is consistent with this propensity that] Freud never dismissed anything as trivial, but worked out a great deal of meaning in trivialities. [And it is also consistent with his own social environment that] many of his [ideas and arguments relate to] a background of European culture − the Oedipus complex, for example. This is purely European, [a reflection of the European] patriarchal [family structure. But if we can succeed in putting aside the particular cultural setting we can see how Freud] attaches a great deal of importance to the tangles of early life − the relationships of the child within the family. Among the more readily defined and generally recognized insights that we owe, directly or indirectly, to Freud are the genetic analysis and the treatment of the neuroses;[7] the basic importance of the psychic sexual constitution, not merely in its proper functional sphere, but also in connections that seem unrelated; the far-reaching importance of infantile psychic experiences in adult life and the ever-present tendency to regression to them; and the general light thrown on the problem of mental determinism.

It is the great and lasting merit of Freud that he freed psychiatry from its too strictly medical presuppositions and introduced an interpretative psychology which, in spite of all its conceptual weaknesses, its disturbingly figurative modes of expression, and its blindness to numerous and important aspects of the field of behavior as a whole, remains a substantial contribution to psychology in general and, by implication, to social psychology in particular. His use of social data was neither more nor less inadequate than the use made of them by psychology as a whole. It is hardly fair to accuse Freud of a naivete which is still the rule among the vast majority of professional psychologists. It is not surprising that his view of social phenomena betrays at many points a readiness to confuse various specific patterns of behavior, which the culturalists can show to be derivative of specific historical backgrounds, with those more fundamental and necessary patterns of behavior which proceed from the nature of man and of his slowly maturing organism. Nor is it surprising that he shared, not only with the majority of psychologists but even with the very founders of anthropological science, an interest in primitive man that did not address itself to a realistic understanding of human relations in the less sophisticated societies but rather to the schematic task of finding in the patterns of behavior reported by the anthropologist such confirmation as he could of his theories of individually "archaic" attitudes and mechanisms.[8]

Hence it is important for the psychoanalyst, [according to Freud and his followers,] to study primitive mentality to see just what familial attitudes remain constant with the European, and so on. Neurotic and psychotic, through the symbolic mechanisms which control their thinking, are believed to regress to a more primitive state of mental adjustment than is normal in modern society and which is supposed to be preserved for our observation in the institutions of primitive peoples. In some undefined way which it seems quite impossible to express in intelligible biological or psychological terms the cultural experiences which have been accumulated by primitive man are believed to be unconsciously handed on to his more civilized progeny.[9] [Thus the idea of regression, central to psychoanalytic thinking, connects the neurotic with the child; and when the Freudian] uses [the same logic as] the old evolutionary anthropologists and places the primitive with the child, [the triad is complete.]

The cultural anthropologist can make nothing of the hypothesis of the racial unconscious nor is he disposed to allow an immediate psychological analysis of the behavior of primitive people in any other sense than that in which such an analysis is allowable for our own culture.[10] And he is disposed to think that if the resemblances between the neurotic and the primitive which have so often been pointed out are more than fortuitous, it is not because of a cultural atavism which the neurotic exemplifies but simply because all human beings, whether primitive or sophisticated in the cultural sense, are, at rock bottom, psychologically primitive, and there is no reason why a significant unconscious symbolism which gives substitutive satisfaction to the individual may not become socialized on any level of human activity. The cultural anthropologist's quarrel with psychoanalysis can perhaps be put most significantly by pointing out that the psychoanalyst has confused the archaic in the conceptual or theoretical psychologic sense with the archaic in the literal chronological sense.[11]

[The same criticism we make of psychoanalysis can be made of other] theories that presuppose a special primitive mentality, [such as that] of Lévy-Bruhl. The fact that a method is lacking in sophistication doesn't make it primitive, [nor does it reveal an archaic mentality in its practitioner. We have only to consider] Aristotle trying to do multiplication, [to recognize the absurdity of assigning him a primitive mentality on such a basis.] The apparent differences of behavior [between primitives and ourselves] are due to differences in the content of the respective cultural patterns, not to differences in the method of mental functioning in the two supposedly distinct levels.

In passing through Chicago once, Lévy-Bruhl said that he had never met a primitive man and hoped he would be able to stop off for a day or two to see some Indian tribe. Lévy-Bruhl has never visited a primitive group; he does not know primitive man. [So it is not from direct experience that he] was so very impressed by the "pre-logical mind", that "primitive mentality" about which he has speculated so much and has seen so little. Anyone who has been in contact with natives knows, [unless he is so devoted to his prejudices as to pay no heed to his observations,] that the pre-logical mind does not exist in them. [At least, it does not exist in them more than in ourselves.] Modern man is just as illogical as primitive man in many respects — politics, for example. The only difference [between primitive man and ourselves lies not in the processes of our thinking but in the fact that] we appeal to more sophisticated supernatural beings [and that we have accumulated a larger store of technical knowledge.] It seems obvious that we must control the brute facts in our environment more than does primitive man; [and once we have acknowledged this, the supposed] naive feeling of [primitive] man as opposed to the sophisticated thinking of civilized man is perhaps not [any longer a tenable] distinction. To say that a primitive man's experience of the world is considerably less potent than ours is all that needs to be said about "primitive mentality". [He simply] knows less about the world we live in.

Now, the less one knows of the potential factors of the environment [that influence the outcome] of a situation, the more one must speculate — fill in [the gaps in one's knowledge] with symbols. [In this regard] scientific and magical statements are hardly distinguishable. Whether they be science or magic, [such statements reflect] the desire to control the world, [on the basis of experience where possible but on the basis of a symbolic cosmology otherwise.] Is not the atomic theory, [and other theories about our environment in which we postulate the existence of invisible entities and forces,] really magic, [in its reliance on the speculative? — But what about the scientific method, you may ask, with its] revision of formulations on the light of more experience? Indeed, if a negative instance does not cause you to revise [your formulation] you are stupid. But such revisions, such reformulations of the magical explanation of unknown phenomena, are constantly occurring in primitive groups. [So they are just as scientific in this sense as we are, while] we are just as magical as primitive man. The primitive has had less experience with the potential factors which influence the situation, but when he fills in what is not known with abbreviated, [speculative] processes the native [proceeds] just as we do.[12] Both [they and we] use reason, and both [they and we] use magic. For if this wish-fulfilling interpolation is a magical thought-process, then in being scientific you have to be magical [as well]. That is, you have to act on what knowledge you have, [and fill in the rest as best you can.]

It has been pointed out to Lévy-Bruhl that the primitive is very logical in any technological process. Indeed, primitive man has the nicest feeling of the adaptation of means to ends, as Boas [showed us in his studies of the] technology of the Kwakiutl Indians. The primitive is as logical as we are where he can be. [Thus we need not speak of him as if he were a distinct kind of human being with respect to his psychical functioning, for it is no different from our own.] We are all logical where we can be, and we all fill in the rest with magic. All we know is that certain things will happen given certain circumstances. We are logical only in regard to those particular [areas of life] in which we have experience and which we have analyzed. Over these things we have control; in all other cases, we work on faith.

[Surely many of the supposed differences between] magic, science, and religion are really a matter of terminology and not of essence.[13] It is vain to look for fundamental psychic differences in human beings; the difference [lies] only in knowledge, [not in the logic of thought processes.] The primitive [is as disposed to be logical as we are, but he] is not able to be logical in as many places. All human beings, primitive and sophisticated, have a profound conviction of the causal and logical nexus of their experienced universe, a belief that comes from the continuum of nature and [their] natural wants. Where we don't actually succeed in manipulating [the world] as we wish, we express the wish in a formula, [and try to manipulate the world with its aid.]

[Everywhere you look among human beings you will see the] interpolation of quotidian faith in the daily procedure of our lives. [It is an interpolation based] little on the personal application of knowledge, [much more on] the patterns of culture. [In our own case, like any other,] our scientific thinking — [over which we have no monopoly —] does not explain our own culture [patterns.]

[For all these reasons, then, Lévy-Bruhl's speculations about primitive mentality] seem important to the psychoanalyst but not to the anthropologist. [Many anthropologists would prefer to dispense with the idea of a special primitive mentality altogether. But before we can do so, we must consider one other version of it that has even attracted some following within anthropology itself. It is a version based on the idea that language plays a quite different role in the mental life of primitives than among ourselves. According to Malinowski, the primitive's exercise of magic comes about because the pragmatic and affective functions of language overwhelmingly predominate in determining the meaning of his speech. Primitive man is not taught the forms of grammar in school, so his speech, we are told, is more closely governed by his hopes and fears and his social purposes, than is our own.][14]

[It is true that] language has more far-reaching implications than are [generally] assigned to it [by philologists.] Language is only in part a coherent system of symbolic reference. To a far greater extent than is generally realized language serves also affective and volitional purposes. [But even if] the *function* of language is not in practice a purely symbolic or referential one, is it not a highly significant fact, nonetheless, that its *form* is so essentially of symbolic pattern?[15] The outstanding fact about any language is its formal completeness. This is as true of a primitive language, like Eskimo or Hottentot, as of the carefully recorded and standardized languages of our great cultures.[16]

Malinowski is an anti-formalist, [however, and in this he is far from alone.] The normal man of intelligence has something of a contempt for linguistic studies, convinced as he is that nothing can well be more useless.[17] Everybody hates grammar [who has had to endure in school the traditional mode of procedure which laboriously dissects sentences and arranges Greek aorists into patterns. In reaction to this apparently frigid and dehumanized process][18] everybody hates form — you're interested in the color of the word, its function, not whether it is a noun or a verb. We not only dislike it implicitly, but explicitly because we had to learn it in school. [But Malinowski] does not distinguish between the grammar that is inherent in our speech, and grammar as it is taught.

[The fact that grammar is taught in schools only for the languages of the sophisticated peoples of the classical world and Europe does not mean that other languages have only form, or that European languages have no function.] The psychological problem which most interests the linguist is the inner structure of language, in terms of unconscious psychic processes. ... To say in so many words that the noblest task of linguistics is to understand languages as form rather than as function or as historical process is not to say that it can be understood as form alone. The formal configuration of speech at any particular time and place is the result of a long and complex historical development, which, in turn, is unintelligible without constant reference to functional factors. All languages are set to do all the symbolic and expressive work that language is good for, either actually or potentially. [Whether it is spoken by an Eskimo or an Englishman,] the formal technique of this work is the secret of each language.[19]

[It is not in the study of language, then, that you will find support for] theories presupposing a special primitive mentality. [As we have said,] the apparent differences of behavior [between "primitives" and ourselves] are due to differences in the content of the respective cultural patterns, not to differences in the method of mental functioning in the two supposedly distinct levels.

[Thus our exploration of mental functioning has led us back once again to the importance of cultural patterning and of cultural form.] No matter where we turn in the field of social behavior, men and women do what they do, and cannot help but do, not merely because they are built thus and so, or possess such and such differences of personality, or must needs adapt to their immediate environment in such and such a way in order to survive at all, but very largely because they have found it easiest and aesthetically most satisfactory to pattern their conduct in accordance with more or less clearly organized forms of behavior which no one is responsible for, which are not clearly grasped in their true nature, and which one might almost say are as self-evidently imputed to the nature of things as the three dimensions are imputed to space.[20] [To explain our culture or any other it will help us but little to center our attention on a person's biological makeup, or temperament, or conscious purposes in behaving in some particular way.] [In a sense] culture is self-explaining; [its form cannot be attributed to external causes. Instead, we might do just as well to consider cultural form in terms of the] springs for art in every human being. [For to an extent as yet insufficiently appreciated, aesthetic] imagination is the unconscious form-giver of culture. [Even such a thing as the] musical ability of the Negro, [so often explained as due to the physiology of the race, is far better interpreted as fundamental to his] cultural heritage.

[What role can we envision for the individual, then, in the formation of these patterns of culture?] It is an unfortunate thing that in arguments about the relative place of cultural conditioning versus biological determinants and fundamental psychological conditioning too little account is taken of the extremely complicated middle ground.[21] [From the standpoint of the personality, I believe that] the struggle for significant form in culture unconsciously animates all normal individuals and gives meaning to their lives. [And just as the individual personality's] tendency to expression may, when sublimated, give rise to patterns [of behavior, so, among constellations of significantly interacting individuals, there is evidently] some kind of a cumulative process, some principle of selection, according to which certain tendencies to change human activities are allowed unconsciously by society, insofar as it patterns its conduct, and certain others are not allowed. ... I don't think any of us are powerful enough to quite understand what that means, but the actuality of these drifts, these cumulative processes, cannot be doubted by anyone who has studied history, language, or whatever type of patterned activity he may take up.[22] [These are the] cultural patterns [whose emergence, whose locus in specific interactions of individuals, and whose import for the personality we are only just beginning to see.]

Notes

1. The preceding sentence is quoted from Sapir (1932a).
2. The preceding sentence is quoted from Sapir (1937).
3. The preceding sentence is quoted from Sapir (1932a).
4. This expression is quoted from Sapir (1928a).
5. The preceding passage, from "For a long time", is quoted from Sapir (1937).
6. See also Sapir (1932a): "The locus of psychiatry turns out not to be the human organism at all in any fruitful sense of the word but the more intangible, and yet more intelligible, world of human relationships and ideas that such relationships bring forth."
7. The preceding passage, from "Among the more readily defined ... " is quoted from Sapir (1917b), as is the remainder of the sentence. I omit the following passage, included in the original text at this point: "to a much smaller extent also of the psychoses (forms

of insanity); the frequency and radical importance of symbol-formation in the unconscious mind, understanding of which is sure to prove indispensable for an approach to the deeper problems of religion and art; the analysis and interpretation of dreams".

8. The preceding paragraph is quoted from Sapir (1937).

9. The preceding two sentences are quoted from Sapir (1932a).

10. The preceding passage, from "the cultural anthropologist can make nothing", is quoted from Sapir (1932a). The original text adds: "He believes that it is as illegitimate to analyze totemism or primitive laws of inheritance or set rituals in terms of the peculiar symbolisms discovered or invented by the psychoanalyst as it would be to analyze the most complex forms of modern social behavior in these terms."

11. The preceding paragraph is quoted from Sapir (1932a).

12. In a course on religion (Yale, notes by David Mandelbaum) Sapir made some of the same points as in the present discussion. From Feb. 6: "Belief as such never constitutes religion. Very few of our beliefs are tangibly contextual to our senses. Our beliefs become interwoven and become a smooth weave of existence. At no point does it pay us to deny our beliefs. Thus in the social world as well as in the physical world, when you get enough people to say so then you just don't deny. Thus electricity and god are exactly analogous beliefs. Most of the things I believe I know about history and science (is not different from my belief in God) — is built up on my dependability in secondary sources." From March 23: "Our formal processes of education very closely approaches religious ritual. Despite the pragmatism of our age, we do not as a rule test the validity of our education by watching its effects. There seems to be a universal impulse in men to create abbreviated patterns of conduct in a formalized manner and to abide by these stringently."

13. For a somewhat different discussion of science and religion, see Sapir (1928b), "The Meaning of Religion".

14. The class notes move from a critique of Lévy-Bruhl to a critique of Malinowski's view of language. Presumably Sapir first indicated what Malinowski's position was. The bracketed material, inserted to connect the two discussions, presents a version of Malinowski's position based on Sapir's subsequent critique of it. The work Sapir probably had most in mind here was "The Problem of Meaning in Primitive Languages", Malinowski's (1923) paper published as a supplementary essay in Ogden and Richards' *The Meaning of Meaning*. Sapir had reviewed Ogden and Richards' book in "An Approach to Symbolism", Sapir (1923). I draw on that review to fill out the reconstructed lecture text.

15. The preceding three sentences are quoted from Sapir (1923a). Italics are original.

16. The preceding two sentences are quoted from "The Grammarian and His Language," Sapir (1924a). Although the theme of this paper is relevant to Sapir's Yale lectures, it seems less clear whether, by 1937, Sapir would still have spoken of a "primitive language" or of "great cultures". What he evidently means by those expressions in the quoted passage is a language spoken by "primitives", and the cultures of complex societies with literary traditions.

17. The preceding sentence is quoted from Sapir (1924a).

18. The wording of the bracketed passage derives from Sapir (1924a).

19. The preceding paragraph is taken from Sapir (1924a).

20. The preceding passage, from "No matter where ...", is quoted from Sapir (1927c).

21. The preceding sentence is quoted from Sapir (n.d. [1930]).

22. The preceding passage, from "some kind of a cumulative process," comes from Sapir (n.d. [1926]).

Part III

Symbolic Structures and Experience

(1933 – 34)

Chapter Twelve

Symbolism

[Part I: 1933]

1. [The Symbol]

What is referred to by the word "symbol"? It is not so easy to tell. [Suppose we start with an example: someone bangs on a table and another person calls this action a symbol of violence. Now, if we interpret the action in that way,] a bang on the table has for us no direct connection either with the muscular movement [of the person who bangs] or with the sound waves [he produced. These do not really matter to us; what we are thinking of is the meaning.] It is a direct meaning in an indirect behavior, understandable by a certain convention. The banging of the table may be rather inadequate as expression, but it is a conventional symbol for violent expression.

[Still, it is not impossible to pay attention to the physical activity itself, should we wish to. There are two aspects or sides to the behavior, and] it can be turned to its "natural" side or turned to its conventional side, since it may be looked upon [either] as non-symbolic (natural) or as symbolic (conventional). How we consider it is a question of tendency.

[So perhaps what we need to be concentrating upon is not, at least in the first instance, the symbol itself but in what way human behavior can be understood as symbolic, and when the human mind can be said to be reacting symbolically. Let me offer an initial] definition. The human mind is reacting symbolically when some component of experience — [be it] an object of the external world, an idea, an event, [even] a personality, or a behavior pattern — elicits beliefs, ideas, emotions, sentiments or ways of behavior which refer to the meaning of this experience [rather than to its objective characteristics.] There is a symbolic reference, [in other words — a leap from] the symbol to the meaning of the symbol. There are all kinds [of behaviors that can be symbolic. What is] constant in symbolism [is not the behavior itself but the fact that it] always substitutes for some closer intermediating kind of behavior. If a given behavior is substitutive to a more direct expression, there is already a symbol. [Moreover, symbols take part in a whole structure of ideas. So] it may also be said, that if you rationalize [in any way about an action or event,] you have already declared your faith in symbols.

[Because the object or behavior itself is not the issue in symbolism but the assignment of meaning to it, all kinds of apparently dissimilar things can be] examples [of symbolism]. Mathematical and algebraic signs and figures [are symbols]; colored lights and flags [are symbols, while] the green, red, or white [colors of those flags and lights may have symbolic meaning too in their own right.] There are purity symbols – flowers or dresses [of a certain kind] – and the numbers [we just alluded to as mathematical signs may also have other kinds of significance,] such as [the bad luck attaching to the number] thirteen. [The physical characteristics of these symbols, such as the scratches on paper representing "13", will not take us very far in explaining the significance attached to them, as we may easily see if we consider that] the handshake, the olive branch, and the palm branch [can all be said to symbolize peace even though their natural aspects are quite dissimilar.]

[Although some symbols may arouse little feeling in their users others are deeply attached to personal or social significance. For instance, symbols like] national flags and the Christian crucifix [bear a great emotional potency for the social groups with which they are associated. Among symbolisms of this kind we should probably also include the] trappings of royalty, such as the crown, scepter, and so on, [trappings that can even mean or represent the state itself]. Totemic animals and college animals [are symbols of an analogous kind in their representation of social groups and the feelings one has as a member of the group. And while some people are fond of interpreting objects and events as] psychoanalytic sex symbols, [we must not lose sight of the possibility of interpreting] home and mother [not as irreducible meanings but as symbols in their own right,] symbols of respectability.

[Disparate as these examples may be, it is not impossible to attempt a] classification. [First of all, to the extent that the "natural" aspect of the symbol or symbolic behavior, that is its physical characteristics, has some connection with its meaning,] it is convenient to distinguish between (1) primary symbols, and (2) dissociated symbols. For example, we have a primary [symbol] when the symbol of a cow is a drawing of a cow; a dissociated [symbol,] when any sign may stand for a certain sound. There is no complete break [between these types,] but a continuous line from the one to the other. [Actually, it might be more accurate to say that] there is a hierarchy of symbols ranging from the [most] direct expression to [the most] highly institutionalized, dissociated, reintegrated forms. [Among these last,] the symbolic meaning may depend upon [the symbol's] belonging to a certain plateau [in the symbolic structure.]

[Actually, primary and dissociated symbols can be thought of as taking part in a] classification [of another sort. We might call both of them] *signatory* symbols: [whether dissociated or not,] signatory symbols tend to be simple signs without significant [affective] overtones. [Symbols of this kind contrast with] *assimilative* symbols, [by which I mean those where strong] overtones of feeling are assimilated to the sign. These symbols become foci of emotional grouping and favor the formation of sentiments.

There is, however, a long way [from a single symbol] to a symbolic system, [which incorporates another degree of dissociation through con-figurative patterning.] The symbolic system is far removed from and dissociated from the original function, but associated within itself. Take for instance the red and green traffic light, the simplest symbolic system. It is highly dissociated, but highly complete in itself; it is not a mirror of reality, but a convenient scheme for orientation [to it]. It is important [to recognize] that the symbolic system as such is highly dissociated from the elements in which it is expressed, but it has its own logic. The most completely dissociated system is mathematics, but language too is a very complicated system of this kind. It must not be too rigid, however, if it is to allow the development of a rich treasure of symbols.

[Formal patterns, that is to say symbolic systems, thus contain a certain complexity. They are not merely assemblages of individual symbols.] A second important quality of a strict symbolic system is the homogeneity of its materials. [With the traffic signals, for instance, the elements of the system consist of] light, in both cases − [either] red or green. Language and mathematics [are perhaps the prime examples that] show this absolute homogeneity. [In contrast, consider some examples of systems that are] not homogeneous, [such as] Casella's music, [with its inclusion of] a real nightingale, and the use of real shell and real hair in connection with a usual oil painting.

[In sum, depending on the nature of their connection with a symbolic] structure, symbols differ in certain respects:

(1) There may be a one-to-one correspondence [between the symbol and its meaning,] as compared with over-determination, conditioning [by

other dimensions of a symbolic structure,] or assimilation [of affective overtones].

(2) There may be poverty of content as compared with richness of content.

(3) Symbols may be more social than individual and vice versa.

(4) They may be more conscious than unconscious and vice versa.

(5) [Symbols that participate in a symbolic configuration] may be relatively homogeneous or the reverse, consistent or inconsistent [with one another in their physical components].

2. Signs and Symbols

My intention was to use the first lecture on symbols as a way to show what an interesting, but also very difficult and complicated, field this is, and, in a way, to clear the ground for the following hour. [Now we can consider some particular topics within this field, such as the distinction between] sign and symbol, and the many [problems] involved in these concepts.[1] [We have already indicated that] when the human mind is reacting symbolically, this means that] words, action, gestures coming either from us or from the people around us, [even] objects, in a word all the elements of the environment, stand not only for themselves, but [also] for something else of which they are the sign. [They have not only a natural character but also a] semiotic character. At a certain point of dissociation of the sign from the physical experience, the symbol will appear. [To put this another way,] the sign becomes symbol when it no longer has a perceptible causal relation with what it refers to.

If the distinction is between an actual relation (the sign) and an imputed one (the symbol), can there be any genetic relationship between sign and symbol? There is certainly a difference between the contextual sign and the full-grown symbol, but it is a logical difference, a difference of definition. [It does not mean that symbols cannot have their genesis in signs.] In fact, symbols have grown out of sign situations by dissociation. For example, [when you shake] the fist to threaten a person out of reach, the action is not completed; a part of it has been dissociated. There is an interruption. [And eventually, shaking the fist at an imaginary enemy becomes a symbol for anger itself when no enemy, real or imaginary, is actually intended.][2] One must establish a great distinction between the logical and the genetic viewpoints.

The threat of the fist, considered in its primary meaning, is merely a sign of trouble. It becomes a symbol when the adversary is out of reach, when the situation takes a hypocritical character. But there are many intermediate degrees, and they represent the genesis of the symbol from the sign. If it often happens that the threatening does not lead to action, it comes to be considered as a substitute for action. That is [simply a product of] the process of socialization. The part of the situation which is dissociated from [the action] and substitutes for it is not necessarily the most important. For example, in a situation of anger the secretion of the endocrine glands, or other bodily phenomena, are more important [parts of the experience] than the clenching of the fist. So sign and symbol must not be taken as an actual antinomy, but as two poles between which the concrete thing or event moves.

The sign devoid of its context is always ambiguous. The ambiguity of the sign sometimes leads to a stiffening of the meaning [it bears, and] thus symbols may appear.

[Clearly,] the field of signs and symbols presents many interesting questions. [Now] I shall read some of the statements made by members of the seminar and point out some of the problems involved in the examples given.[3] These are cases of symbol genesis, [in which members of the seminar have] presented instances of a sign which by dissociation has become a symbol.

First, the example given by Mr. Marjolin: "Before the War,[4] people in France used to have on Sundays a special kind of cake in the form of a crescent, just a little bit different from the ordinary bread. It was a sign of good times. During the War food was scarce, and people could no longer afford to have this special kind of cake on Sundays. But after the War this crescent form of cake was revived, and this was done with great enthusiasm, almost approximating a religious ceremony. People associated this crescent with the old golden days of peace and happiness. Thus the cake became a symbol. Although the material out of which the revived crescent was now made, and the way it was made, may have been different from pre-war practices, the form remained [and it was this form that became the symbol.]"

This is a fair example showing how a symbol may grow out of a sign. As a matter of fact, we cannot tell when the sign ends and when the symbol begins; the transition is gradual. But there is always a historical connection somewhere, in which the sign is dissociated from its original meaning, although this historical connection is seldom clear.

Now, the example given by Mr. Ferrero: "Before the War the three-colored Italian flag was beautiful — it was associated in my mind with beautiful thoughts. But after the War the Italian flag belonged to a party of violence, and it is [now] associated in my mind with bloodshed, persecution, corruption and policemen. I saw the police beat people. The new flag becomes to me, therefore, a symbol of violence."

This example [given by] Mr. Ferrero is more personal than the one given by Mr. Marjolin, although there may be many other people in Italy who share this feeling. [However, the fact that an example involves personal feelings does not mean it cannot be a symbol, for] there are private symbols [as well as those that are accepted by a whole group. Even among signs that have become socialized and have become social symbols in the clearest sense,] most of the time the socialization takes place for the material of the symbol, not for its reference. To be sure, everything in this realm of symbolism is partly social, partly individual. Social symbols can [even] give birth to private symbols.[5] In psychotics we see more spectacularly the process of personal affective evaluation of a common symbol. But the world of the individual is never dissociated from the life of society; and the life of "society" is after all a figure of speech — it is a total of private worlds. All symbols therefore have both social and individual values, although there is always an antagonism between the social and the individual interpretations.

We don't know how far we can go in the use of private symbols. For example, there have been poets who have not been understood, because of the private symbolism which they used. [On the other hand,] even the private world of meaning of a psychotic patient has its roots in culture — the culture as manifested in his family relations, for example. Therefore we should not draw too hard and fast a line between the affectively-laden symbolism and social symbolism. Nor do we want to make too [sharp] a distinction between conscious and unconscious symbols, or even between signs and symbols.

[Let us turn now to] the example given by Dr. Maki: "I am greatly impressed by the way Americans use certain humming sounds in connection with their speech, such as *m* ..., *n* ..., etc. In Finland, this mixing of unvoiced sounds with clearly enunciated words would be considered impolite."

This is an example of the reinterpretation of symbols. In America the use of such "unvoiced sounds" is considered an individual mannerism, not so much as a sign of impoliteness. Women in particular have such mannerisms. Sometimes they make a certain sound by inhaling, in order to show their attention to a man's talk. This may be a kind of primary symbolism.

[Let us now consider] the case of symbol genesis presented by Dr. Beck:[6] "Once I had a rather tiresome talk with a prisoner, and [in greeting him] I quite involuntarily played with the prison's keys that I carried around. On noticing this, the prisoner remarked that he realized that he was in prison but that one day he would be free, etc. This involuntary act on my part, therefore, was taken as a sign of institutional power."

Dr. Beck presents the instance of a sign which by dissociation has become a symbol. The greeting which he addressed to the prisoner in coming to his cell stands for its whole ordinary context, that is, the world in which the prisoner was living before going to jail. This greeting has a meaning so dissociated, so remote from its intrinsic value that it becomes a symbol. [But there is probably more to say about this example too.] The use of hands in various connections, and gesture in particular, [deserve a considerable discussion.] They represent a kind of symbolism that has not been carefully studied.[7]

[So although these cases were supposed to illustrate relationships between sign and symbol, now that we have looked at them] the mere opposition between sign and symbol appears too poor to express the reality. We must distinguish several points of view: the relative degree of dissociation; the relative degree of socialization; and so on, [perhaps other dimensions as well.] We need a more elaborate nomenclature, [it seems, and even the examples that seemed at first glance to be the simplest may turn out to be quite complicated.]

Take, for instance, the implication of the word "door". It does not merely stand for the single object (of wood, that can be moved on hinges, etc.), but at the same time it also suggests something else — a hall, a corridor, or a room — from which or to which the door is leading. [The word is a symbol for the door, but the door itself] may be a sign for "activities to be completed". [So how are we to describe its semiotic character?] [As we have just said,] the symbol will appear at a certain point of dissociation of the sign from the physical experience; but there is no limit to the transformation of the symbol. Thus the door can become the symbol of the corridor and have "exist" as its only meaning [(i. e., "a corridor exists")]. The implications [of the door take precedence and there is a dissociation from the physical thing. We react to the implications rather than to the physical object. In the same way] a gesture, [no matter what sort of muscle movement it may involve — and even if it is very gracefully executed −] may be displeasing because of its remote implications.

[Now, as soon as we find that we have to mention these remote implications,] that raises the problem of the immediacy of meaning. [If meaning does not lie in the gesture, object, or behavior itself, what is the set of implications in which it does lie?] What is the context of our experience, [from which we are to derive its meaning]? For, any experience must be placed in a totality from which it takes all its significance. And what contexts people see may be very different. [If I speak about an object (such as a door) in the environment,] what ideas and feelings am I raising in the minds of others when I speak? An element of the same environment may not be the same for two persons experiencing it [if they place it in different contexts. I think that if we really tried to study this problem thoroughly] we should find, at last, that the environment is not the same for all the individuals [who experience it.] Any experience has a different meaning for each person, because each of them gives a private sense to a physical thing or event, the meaning of which would seem at first to be universal. That does not mean that there is no possible understanding between them, for the meaning of a part of this environment becomes socialized by convention − the most powerful instrument of which is language.

This discovery of the private meanings of things and events leads [us to see the inevitable futility of any] endeavor to understand anything [in human life] by a mere survey of the physical behavior [concerned in it]. It also leads to caution in our dealings with children, [for as an adult] one does not apprehend the true context in which their acts must be placed. [Not yet fully socialized, they do not share the socialized meanings we can attribute to behaviors.] Furthermore, the socialized meanings themselves are different from one culture to another − the meaning of intimacy, for example.

[Surely] the study of symbolism will throw light upon the growth of culture, therefore. We must be aware of the semiotic nature of all elements of experience. As signs they speak a language of implications, and the real language is supported by this anonymous language of signs, with all the implications of meaning.

[Now as you think about this you may find it instructive to] try to suggest situations where the sign-implications for two persons may be quite different.[8] [This may help you avoid the great] danger [in the study of symbolism, which] is to overemphasize its social character. The social relations [of the meanings of symbols] are but fragmentary; what can be expressed and understood [in common] is relatively little. The illusion [that meaning, and culture, are shared] comes from this marvelous tool which is language.

In the last analysis, the study of culture has to be the study of individual lives. What is generally thought of as culture may be said to be an illusion of objectivity, [fostered by language]. The complete, impersonalized "culture" of the anthropologist can really be little more than an assembly or mass of loosely overlapping idea and action systems which, through verbal habit, can be made to assume the appearance of a closed system of behavior.[9] [Attention to symbolism should reveal to us, then, that] even in a social situation we are reacting to personalities. [We are reacting in terms of meanings and] cultural definitions which do not apply to all the members of [our] group, which even, in specific instances, apply to [ourselves] alone.[10] On the other hand, symbolism manifested by individuals, even in such trivial things as posture, often has a cultural background that is frequently overlooked. [There is no contradiction between these two observations.] It is not the concept of culture which is subtly misleading but the metaphysical locus to which culture is generally assigned.[11]

3. Speech as a Symbolic System

Reading poetry we frequently experience [the way in which] the words as well as the whole evocative structure of the spoken poem have symbolic values. [Leaving the question of the poem's overall structure aside,] the symbolism of words is highly dissociated, highly abstracted. [Now, the symbolism in them that is most often and easily experienced is the] referential — referring, that is, to meanings which are not given in the sounds themselves and that are not "primary", [to use the nomenclature I proposed in an earlier lecture. The referential is often taken to be the essential form of symbolism in language, what we might even call linguistic symbolism *par excellence*.] But in the person speaking, there appear symbolisms very different from the referential symbolism of language, primary symbolisms which are over and above linguistic symbolisms, and which are frequently used consciously or subconsciously by poets and actors, [in their management of] sounds, rhythm, and intonation, [for example. The meanings conveyed with these symbolisms may turn out to be quite at odds with what the words express referentially. As they say,] it is the actor's art to use any word to express anything.

This observation leads to the question, have sounds as such a potential quality aside from what they mean? In 1929 I started an experimental investigation in this point, a preliminary report on which is published under the title "A Study in Phonetic Symbolism".[12] These studies are still going on, [thanks to] Dr. [Stanley] Newman, [who has taken over the work.]

[In the course of] that study it became obvious that there is [something we might call] a natural phonetic alignment — that is, that certain meanings which don't come from the situation [itself] are applied to certain sounds. [We found that] there exists a "phantasy vocabulary," that certain vowels [seem to] sound bigger ([or smaller,] etc.) than others. For instance, the contrast between the vowel *a* and the vowel *i* (the phonetic or continental values are intended) was illustrated in every one of sixty pairs of stimulus words, the subject being requested to indicate in each case which of the two in themselves meaningless words meant the larger and which the smaller variety of an arbitrarily selected meaning. For example, the meaningless words *mal* and *mil* were pronounced in that order and given the arbitrary meaning 'table.' The subject decided whether *mal* seemed to symbolize a large or a small table as contrasted with the word *mil*.[13] About 80% of the subjects' answers attached the imagined [connotation] of something large or big to the vowel *a* ([pronounced] as in "saw"), and the imagined [connotation] of something small to the vowel *i* (as in "it"). The more remote the sounds were from each other, within the scale from *a* to *i* — the larger the contrast-step, that is — the more certain and distinct was the meaning attached. It is important to note that the words were so selected as to avoid associations with meaningful words.[14]

[These experiments were never intended to contradict the well-established philological fact that] languages are not built on such principles [as sound symbolisms.] There is no stable and distinct relation between sounds and the real linguistic meanings of words. [Instead, what the studies show is that] this vowel symbolism occurs as an unconscious symbolism which may be conditioned either acoustically or kinaesthetically. There are of course linguistic interferences, and individual differences (probably conditioned by different degrees of sensitivity), which should be and will be studied. Furthermore, the studies should be extended to very young children and to foreign languages.[15]

[Earlier in our discussion an example offered by Dr. Maki similarly brought to mind a type of expressive symbolism as contrasted with the merely referential symbolism we normally recognize.[16] It was what Dr.

Maki called "unvoiced sounds", such as the] mannerisms of women who make a certain sound by inhaling, in order to show their attention to a man's talk. This may be a kind of primary symbolism [too, like the sound symbolism of vowels. Something rather like this behavior also occurs] in an Indian tribe in northern California, among whom, for example, men and women observe different phonetic rules.[17] Thus when a man says 'moon', he says *wak!āra*, while a woman says *wak!āR^a*,[18] the last sound being produced probably by inhaling. I really have no [definite] theory [explaining] this "unvoiced speech" of women. Such sounds may belong to a category other than ordinary language. Possibly they may represent a kind of primary symbolism, [perhaps] due, [if we are to believe the psychoanalysts,] to women's masochistic tendency.[19]

[Of course the Yana man or woman who produces one or other of these forms is referring to the moon at the same time as symbolizing maleness or femaleness.] It goes without saying that in actual speech referential and expressive symbolisms are pooled in a single expressive stream.[20] [We might even distinguish among levels of referential symbolism as partaking of this kind of expressiveness.] For instance, [suppose you have an acquaintance who has been your intimate friend; but you sense that he has changed toward you, and you deduce this from his] use of a vocabulary marking a greater social distance than previously. [Notice here that] the referential meanings of language above the average level do not need a special situation to be understood. There can be a direct implication, [so that you deduced the change of attitude directly from your friend's speech.]

[It seems then as if there are in speech] many levels on which expressive patterns are built. ... [And] quite aside from specific inferences which we may make from speech phenomena on any one of its levels, there is a great deal of interesting work to be done with the psychology of speech woven out of its different levels.[21]

4. Symbolism and Social Psychology

[The study of language is probably one of the most important avenues to take if we wish to explore the relationship of] symbolism and social psychology. [But let us speak about that relationship more broadly. First of all, what is social psychology?] Social psychology deals with:

(1) the distinctive elements in the human mind which determine man's social relations;

(2) interpersonal relations; and

(3) the reaction upon the mind of social relations and the recognized and established usages of social life (institutions, that is).

The study of symbolism is one means of understanding (2) and (3), or, in other words, the relations between the individual and society. This may be done by studying the locus of the symbolic complex. The latter may belong to the field of institutions, to unconscious social patterns, or to individual patterns, conscious or unconscious; its relative position depends upon analysis. But in any case, neither the individual nor the social is an isolated entity and the locus is never found entirely and ultimately in the individual mind, nor again in an institution. The distinction between these two is [a distinction between a] relatively minor or [relatively] major extent of the locus. The individual hooks onto society through [his or her] participation, to a greater or lesser degree, in the social symbol.

[A study of symbolism must therefore not take too seriously a classification of symbols into the social and the personal, (say) the psychoanalytic. Although the latter type may appear to concern only the individual personality,] symbolism of a psychoanalytic character is a dynamic cultural fact nevertheless, a fact which is for the time being relatively private and obsessive though it may easily become socially accepted.

On the other hand, the [extent or even] universality of response to a symbol is a measure of the homogeneity of a culture; though here again [it must be pointed out that] relatively few people in a given society fully participate in all the major symbolic patterns of the society (for example its patterns of religious, political, aesthetic, and legal [activity], and so on). This means that there is a drawing together into smaller groups of all those who share to a required degree in one or more of these major symbolisms.

No problem of social psychology that is at all realistic can be phrased by starting with the conventional contrast of the individual and his society. Nearly every problem of social psychology needs to consider the exact nature and implication of an idea complex, which we may look upon as the psychological correlate of the anthropologist's cultural pattern, to work out its relation to other idea complexes and what modifications it necessarily undergoes as it accommodates itself to these, and, above all, to ascertain the precise locus of such a complex. This locus is rarely identifiable with society as a whole, except in a purely philosophical or conceptual sense, nor is it often lodged in the psyche of a single individual. In extreme cases such an idea complex or cultural pattern may be the dissociated segment of a single individual's mind or it may amount to no more than a potential revivification of ideas in the mind of a single individual through the aid of some such symbolic depositary as a book or museum. Ordinarily the locus will be a substantial portion of the members of a community, each of them feeling that he is touching common interests so far as this particular culture pattern is concerned.[22]

Thus the study of symbolism provides one of the most valuable and [fruitful] methods of approach to the basic problems of social psychology.

[Part II: 1934][23]

The term "symbolism" covers a great variety of apparently dissimilar modes of behavior. In its original sense it was restricted to objects or marks intended to recall, represent, or direct special attention to some larger and more complex phenomenon − [some] person, object, idea, event or projected activity associated only vaguely or not at all with the symbol in any natural sense. By gradual extensions of meaning the terms "symbol" and "symbolism" have come to include not merely such trivial objects and marks as the letter t [to indicate a particular sound in speech], black balls, to indicate a negative attitude in voting, and stars and daggers, to remind the reader that supplementary information is to be found at the bottom of the page, but also more elaborate objects and devices, such as flags and signal lights, which are not ordinarily regarded as important in themselves but which point to ideas and actions of great consequence to society. Such complex systems of reference as speech, writing and mathematical notation should also be included under the term "symbolism", for the sounds and marks used therein obviously have no meaning in themselves and can have significance only for those who know how to interpret them in terms of that to which they refer.[24] A certain kind of poetry is called symbolic or symbolistic because its apparent content is only a suggestion for wider meanings. In personal relations too there is much behavior that may be called symbolic, as when a ceremonious bow is directed not so much to an actual person as to a status which that person happens to fill. The psychoanalysts have come to apply the term "symbolic" to almost any emotionally charged pattern of behavior which has the function of unconscious fulfillment of a repressed tendency,[25] as when a person assumes a raised voice of protest to a perfectly indifferent stranger who unconsciously recalls his father and awakens the repressed attitude of hostility toward the father.

Amid the wide variety of senses in which the word is used there seem to emerge two constant characteristics. One of these, [which we have already mentioned,] is that the symbol is always a substitute for some more closely intermediating type of behavior, whence it follows that all symbolism implies meanings which cannot be derived directly from the contexts of experience.[26] The second characteristic of the symbol is that it expresses a condensation of energy, its actual significance being out of all proportion to the apparent triviality of meaning suggested by its mere form. This can be seen at once when the mildly decorative function of a few scratches on paper is compared with the alarming significance of apparently equally random scratches which are interpreted by a particular society as meaning "murder" or "God". This disconcerting transcendence of form comes out equally well in the contrast between the involuntary blink of the eye and the crudely similar wink which means "He does not know what an ass he is, but you and I do." The wink is a symbol, the blink [merely] a reflex.

It seems useful to distinguish two main types of symbolism. The first of these, which may be called referential symbolism, embraces such forms as oral speech, writing, the telegraph code, national flags, flag signaling and other organizations of symbols which are agreed upon as economical devices for purposes of reference. The second type of symbolism is equally economical and may be termed condensation symbolism, for it is a highly condensed form of substitutive behavior for direct expression, allowing for the ready release of emotional tension in conscious or unconscious form. Telegraph ticking is virtually a pure example of referential symbolism; the apparently meaningless washing ritual of an obsessive neurotic, as interpreted by the psychoanalysts, would be a pure example of condensation symbolism. In actual behavior both types are generally blended. Thus specific forms of writing, conventionalized spelling, peculiar pronunciations and verbal slogans, while ostensibly referential, easily take on the character of emotionalized rituals and become highly important to both individual and society as substitutive forms of emotional expression. Were writing merely referential symbolism, spelling reforms would not be so difficult to bring about.

Symbols of the referential type undoubtedly developed later as a class than condensation symbols. It is likely that most referential symbolisms go back to unconsciously evolved symbolisms saturated with emotional quality, which gradually took on a purely referential character as the linked emotion dropped out of the behavior in question.[27] Thus shaking the fist at an imaginary enemy becomes a dissociated and finally a referential symbol for anger when no enemy, real or imaginary, is actually intended. When this emotional denudation takes place, the symbol becomes a comment, as it were, on anger itself and a preparation for something like language. What is ordinarily called language may have had its ultimate root in just such dissociated and emotionally denuded cries, which originally released emotional tension. Once referential symbolism had been established by a by-product of behavior, more conscious symbols of reference could be evolved by the copying in abbreviated or simplified form of the thing referred to, as in the case of pictographic writing. On still more sophisticated levels referential symbolism may be attained by mere social agreement, as when a numbered check is arbitrarily assigned to a man's hat. The less primary and associational the symbolism, the more dissociated from its original context, and the less emotionalized it becomes, the more it takes on the character of true reference.

A further condition for the rich development of referential symbolism must not be overlooked — the increased complexity and homogeneity of the symbolic material. This is strikingly the case in language, in which all meanings are consistently expressed by formal patterns arising out of the apparently arbitrary sequences of unitary sounds. When the material of a symbolic system becomes sufficiently varied [(i. e., complex)] and yet homogeneous in kind, [therefore,] the symbolism becomes more and more richly patterned, creative and meaningful in its own terms, and referents tend to be supplied by a retrospective act of rationalization. Hence it results that such complex systems of meaning as a sentence form or a musical form mean so much more than they can ever be said to refer to. In highly evolved systems of reference the relation between symbol and referent becomes increasingly variable or inclusive. There is never, [in such systems, merely] a one-to-one relation of symbol and referent; [the relation is much more complicated] because of the configurative richness — [the involvement of an entire] "as-if" parallel system [or orientational scheme in which the symbol participates].[28]

In condensation symbolism also richness of meaning grows with increased dissociation. The chief developmental difference, however, between this type of symbolism and referential symbolism is that while the latter grows with formal elaboration in the conscious, the former strikes deeper and deeper roots in the unconscious and diffuses its emotional quality to types of behavior or situations apparently far removed from the original meaning of the symbol. Both types of symbols therefore begin with situations in which a sign is dissociated from its context. The conscious elaboration of form makes of such dissociation a system of reference, while the unconscious spread of emotional quality makes of it a condensation symbol. Where, as in the case of a national flag or a beautiful poem, a symbolic expression which is apparently one of mere reference is associated with repressed emotional material of great importance to the ego, the two theoretically distinct types of symbolic behavior merge into one. One then deals with symbols of peculiar potency and even danger, for unconscious meanings, full of emotional power, become rationalized as mere references.

It is customary to say that society is peculiarly subject to the influence of symbols in such emotionally charged fields as religion and politics.[29] Flags and slogans are the type examples in the field of politics, crosses and ceremonial regalia in the field of religion. But all culture is in fact heavily charged with symbolism, as is all personal behavior. Even comparatively simple forms of behavior are far less directly functional than they seem to be, but include in their motivation unconscious and even unacknowledged impulses, for which the behavior must be looked upon as a symbol. Many, perhaps most reasons are little more than ex post facto rationalizations of behavior controlled by unconscious necessity. Even an elaborate, well documented scientific theory may from this standpoint be little more than a symbol of the unknown necessities of the ego. Scientists fight for their theories not because they believe them to be true but because they wish them to be so.[30] Even objectivity must be motivated.

[From the perspective of unconscious motivation] the fundamental necessity of the human organism is to express the libido — and all cultural patterns are [oriented] in one way or another in that direction and operate via the mechanisms of symbolism. By an unconscious mechanism of symbolic transfer, an endless consecutive chain of symbols [is built up] in a richly configurative [symbolic structure.] Thus individual and society, in a never ending interplay of symbolic gestures, build up the pyramided structure called civilization. In this structure very few bricks touch the ground.[31]

[Perhaps this suggestion will be more convincing to you if we consider an example] of some of the less obvious symbolisms in socialized behavior — [such as those that are conveniently summarized as etiquette.] Etiquette has at least two layers of symbolism. On a relatively obvious plane of symbolism etiquette provides the members of society with a set of rules which, in condensed and thoroughly conventionalized form, express society's concern for its members and their relation to one another. There is another level of etiquette symbolism, however, which takes little or no account of such specific meanings but interprets etiquette as a whole as a powerful symbolism of status. From this standpoint to know the rules of etiquette is important, not because the feelings of friends and strangers are becomingly observed but because the manipulator of the rule proves that he is a member of an exclusive group. By reason of the richly developed meanings which inhere in etiquette, both positive and negative, a sensitive person can actually express a more bitter hostility through the frigid observance of etiquette than by flouting it on an obvious wave of hostility. Etiquette, then, is an unusually elaborate symbolic play in which individuals in their actual relationships are the players and society is the bogus referee.

[Now, it is also possible to treat the subject of etiquette as an example of a realm of symbolic behavior and to consider how we might approach its study.] Four kinds of approach [may be compared:]

(1) [One way to study etiquette would be to try to discover the recognized] rules of etiquette [in a given society. This is] the ethnological objective.

(2) [In another type of study,] the rules are assumed; what you try to discover, instead, is how the individual would react to them. This is the psychological type [of inquiry, and it] needs a huge mass of material [if it is to be properly conducted.]

(3) [Another approach would involve] testing the etiquette of the group in definite contexts, [and seeing what kind of] rationale emerges. On the whole, this is the most difficult way [to approach the subject.]

(4) [A fourth possibility would be] a reasoned inquiry into the nature of etiquette itself, and its psychological basis. [Let us pursue this avenue a little way now.]

[It is sometimes said that etiquette is a kind of] luxury of behavior, inherently and obviously trivial. Otherwise it passes over into morals, techniques, or law. But can you conceive of society without etiquette? Historically etiquette was no luxury, [but a matter of deadly seriousness for the individuals whose social fortunes depended on its observance. Perhaps in some quarters] etiquette [is seen] as a game − a diversion [from the sober necessities of life. But it is a special kind of game, then, if] I may play at etiquette, but not flippantly. [What is fundamental to etiquette is not that it is actually a trivial aspect of life but that it is *seen* as] inherently trivial − that its triviality is recognized. [Indeed, its rule is actually so stern that despite the supposed triviality it amounts to a form of] compulsive tyranny as real as the tyranny of morality, with which it shares a basis in ego-anxiety, [and with which it shares a function of] simplifying human relationships. [Actually, from this quasi-political point of view that assesses etiquette's tyrannical governance of human affairs we might look at] etiquette as a passport [governing the individual's access to social groups outside his circle of intimates. The forms of] etiquette [pertaining to contacts] between classes [are particularly inter-esting, therefore, with their symbols of the] rights of status. [In such contacts we are likely to get a good view of the] advantages and disad-vantages of familiarity and unfamiliarity with etiquette.

[Another property of etiquette that bears a paradoxical relationship to its compulsiveness is the] freedom of choice [that one supposedly exercises in following its forms,] as if [one behaved not out of necessity at all but out of] spontaneity and gratuitousness. [But like the notion of the] free gift, [in the rules of etiquette we have only] the fiction of freedom — only theoretically a freedom of choice.

The paradox of etiquette, then, is that it combines an obvious triviality with a strong moral necessity and tyranny and a felt element of choice. The strength of the moral necessity depends upon symbols of interper-sonal status. [But its presence, and its hidden compulsion, are evidenced in the fact that] breaches of etiquette can rarely be atoned for in any thoroughgoing manner. [True, our] society provides [us with a supposed form of atonement in] the apology, but this is never really satisfactory. In societies where breaches of etiquette are atoned for [by harsher means, such as the imposition of] fines, and so on, etiquette merges with morality. So it seems that where the triviality is ostensibly important we have etiquette; where the tyranny is overtly emphasized we have morality.

In this connection [it would be a useful project] to check up etiquette situations in Polynesia, especially in terms of the relative triviality in-volved. For example, seating arrangements at a feast may not be consid-ered a matter of etiquette since the status of the individual is vitally involved, whereas the relation of chief to commoner, with its *noblesse oblige*, may partake more of the nature of etiquette. That is, where rights of status are socially guaranteed and insisted upon, [perhaps] the tendency is to move away from regarding such behavior as etiquette and, instead, to consider it morality, especially where freedom of choice, responsibility and irresponsibility, and voluntary participation are not factors to be considered.

[Thus the behaviors we are accustomed to consider as etiquette have] shifting connotations, [depending on their social context and also depending on the personalities of the individuals concerned.] Personality differences will count in the evaluation of etiquette — a healthy introvert will differ from an extravert in his reaction to etiquette problems. The problem of personality is fundamental and enters into every discussion of value. [So we cannot discover the meaning of etiquette in the particulars of the behaviors in which we observe it. What matters most is the behavioral form's] locus in implication: one's hostility to its tyranny, [say; one's sense of it as] a social duty; one's perfunctoriness [in performing it]; and perhaps one's use of etiquette as a mask for emotional privacy. The actual concrete symbol doesn't matter so much. [What is most important is] the total configuration [in which it is placed. Like other symbolic forms,] etiquette lives in a world of inarticulate implication.

Notes

1. These notes come from the Rockefeller Seminar, where Sapir's lectures were followed by class discussion. The notetaker has: "The following discussion in the Seminar centered around the many aspects of and difficulties involved in the concepts of sign versus symbol. Professor Sapir admitted that his intention was just to use this first lecture on symbols to show the interesting, but also very difficult and complicated field and in a way to clear the ground for the following hour on the same topic."
2. See Sapir (1934c), "Symbolism", for comments similar to the bracketed passage.
3. Participants in the Rockefeller Seminar had evidently been asked to write short essays giving examples of cultural symbols in their home communities.
4. World War I.
5. The notetaker presents Sapir's comment as following upon this statement by Dollard: "As used by the psychiatrist, 'symbol' has the character of affective sense or power which distinguishes it from non-symbolic words, gestures, acts. ... We hit here upon private symbolism. The child, for instance, has a private world which is reshaped by the social environment. To be true, there is no hard and fast line between private and socialized signs and symbols."
6. Beck had been a criminologist in Germany before joining the seminar.
7. The notetaker continues: "A discussion takes place about the distinction between meaning and symbol."
8. One of the notetakers ends his notes on this seminar session with the following: "Professor Sapir asked everybody to try to suggest situations where the sign-implication for two persons may be quite different."
9. The preceding sentence is quoted from Sapir (1934a).
10. The preceding sentence is drawn from Sapir (1938).
11. The preceding sentence is quoted from Sapir (1932a).
12. Sapir (1929b).

13. The preceding three sentences are quoted from Sapir (1929b).
14. The preceding sentence is quoted from Sapir (1929b). The notetaker alludes to "control indices".
15. The notetaker adds: "As to further and detailed information I refer to the study mentioned above which is published in … " (the reference is not given).
16. For the notion of "expressive" as opposed to "merely referential" symbolism, see Sapir (1929b).
17. See Sapir (1929a), "Male and Female Forms of Speech in Yana".
18. The capital *R* presumably represents voiceless *r*. Sapir (1929a) has italic vs. normal *r* to represent this contrast. The notetaker omits the exclamation mark and diacritic, which I add from Sapir (1929a).
19. Note that Sapir indulges in no such speculations in his published work on Yana speech. On the contrary, he suggests that the differences between male and female speech are as conventionalized as anything else in language; see Sapir (1929a). Perhaps in the Rockefeller Seminar he offered his interpretation with more qualifiers and hedges than are indicated in the student notes.
20. The preceding sentence is quoted from Sapir (1929b).
21. The preceding paragraph is quoted from Sapir (1927b).
22. The preceding paragraph is quoted from Sapir (1932a). The text goes on to argue: "We have learned that the individual in isolation from society is a psychological fiction. We have not had the courage to face the fact that formally organized groups are equally fictitious in the psychological sense, for geographically contiguous groups are merely a first approximation to the infinitely variable groupings of human beings to whom culture in its various aspects is actually to be credited as a matter of realistic psychology."
23. In 1934 Sapir had recently written his Encyclopedia article on "Symbolism", Sapir (1934c). The student notes parallel that article so closely as to suggest that he must have read it, or recited it, to the class. For much of the following section I have quoted the article, but it must be understood that the class notes include the same material. Where the student notes add some point I have incorporated it in the text. The quotation from Sapir (1934c) is not quite exact, therefore.
24. Here one noteaker (Mandelbaum) has: "Now flags, mathematics, speech, are symbolic entities in that they have no meaning in themselves. They are significant only in so far as they lead the understanding recipient to wider conceptions." W. Hill has: "symbolism / speech, writing — symbols of reference".
25. A notetaker (LaBarre) has "suppressed attitude, masks?"
26. Siskin's notes have: "(1) symbolizing — always referring to something which is not directly connected with *context* of action."
27. One notetaker (W. Hill) has: "Symbolisms which lie in the unconscious are older than those which are referential symbols, which emerge from condensation symbols when the emotional tinge drops away". LaBarre has: "Condensational older than referential symbols."
28. The preceding sentence does not occur in Sapir (1934c).
29. For a discussion of a similar topic, see Sapir (1927a), "Anthropology and Sociology".
30. Up to this point the text has closely followed Sapir (1934c). It now departs for a while.
31. The preceding two sentences, and the next paragraph, are drawn from Sapir (1934c).

Chapter Thirteen

The Impact of Culture on Personality

1. [May 1933:] The Study of "Culture and Personality"

What problems are worth considering in the field [called] "culture and personality"? What [problems, on the other hand,] do not deserve our spending a great amount of energy trying to solve them?

[Let us begin with a] definition of the field. Culture, [as anthropologists have traditionally conceived of it,] is not the chief object of concern in [this field,] the study [of "culture and personality."] Knowledge of the history of culture, [which is what the traditional approach focuses upon,] can throw but little light on culture's present meaning, [or its relationship to the individuals who encounter it.] For example, a cathedral may have lost all its [original,] intrinsic meaning and have become the mere symbol of a past greatness. On the other hand, to study the problem of the relations of culture and personality means that one does not consider personality as the mere unfolding of a biological organism. So far as the study in point is concerned, then, [the concept of] culture is relevant only if it takes its meaning in the present psychology of the people, [the concept of] personality only if it is referred to its milieu. To be exact, all that can be said about a person is relevant, [and this will include a great deal about the social milieu and cultural background], but it is a question of degree.

The best name for this field of research would really be "social psychology", although this term implies erroneously that there is [such a thing as] an individual psychology. [At any rate, the field which purports to study individual psychology has produced little that has really to do with that subject, should it even prove a useful conception in the long run.] A great deal of what has been written about individual psychology is [actually] a blend of physiology and social psychology.

[Another difficulty, from our point of view, with the field of psychology as it has so far been developed is its preoccupation with scientific objectivity.] In the field of culture and personality, the question of objectivity or subjectivity is not very important. We know, by introspection, that we are always doing some violence to the facts. We cannot get down to an absolute objective level, [and if we could] it would conceal from us the true meaning of what we are studying. Psychology and sociology are the most dangerous disciplines for the field of social psychology, because they are well systematized and their concepts well defined. Their methods are a lure for the social psychologist [because they offer a spurious sense of accuracy and objectivity. They suffer from what we might call the] technical fallacy: bending the knee to established techniques, to protect oneself from scientific mistakes or from the moral blame of intellectual dishonesty, [rather than thinking the situation through.]

Is social psychology a science [anyway? Perhaps it may turn out to be, but in our present understanding of "science"] the term is not flexible enough for the indeterminacy and the great variety of this field. We are concerned with the symbolic interpretation of events, [more than with their physical characteristics; and] one is constantly driven to biographies, to unique events, [rather than to abstract away from these toward the formulation of general laws. In this field] one is concerned with the fate of the development of a certain personality. [You may wonder why I use the word "fate" — perhaps it is a little dramatic, but really] fate is the right word because [it is impossible to pin down definite causes of the way a personality develops. Above all] it is impossible to attribute responsibility for what happens to somebody else. There is a process [of development which from this point of view can only be taken as] inevitable.

[Now, let us return to our initial question. What are the] problems worth considering, [in this field?]

1.1. The meaning of culture

[When I said that we are not principally interested in culture itself as anthropologists have usually studied it, I did not mean we are not interested in it at all.] Culture patterns must be described and their history must be studied. But the emphasis [in the study of culture patterns] must be placed on their meaning. For instance, it is not relevant to say that, in general, sport is important. [Instead,] the importance [or unimportance] of sport must be studied with reference to the life of the people of each culture. [Similarly,] to have a philosophy or a set of moral values [for assessing culture patterns from the outset] is mischievous, in this field. No cultural pattern is either good or evil. What one has to find is its meaning. [We may not accord importance and value to some predetermined mode or aspect of human existence from the very start of our study; for] what is important is the triumph of life, [not some particular way in which it is led.] That is the first problem [in our field, then]: what the generalized patterns [of culture] mean for people in given cultural areas.

1.2. The study of the individual in his milieu

This [type of] study is conditioned by [and dependent upon] our understanding of the meaning of culture. [In a sense culture and the individual go together, because culture can only have meaning for someone. But what we emphasize here is the individual rather than the group as a whole.] The most interesting milieu, [if we wish to understand the impact of culture on the personality,] is that of the very young individual. But [this situation in its full complexity] is often difficult to understand.

[If we take the study of individuals in their particular circumstances seriously, we shall have to recognize that] culture varies infinitely, not only as to manifest content but as to the distribution of psychologic emphases on the elements and implications of this content. According to our scale of treatment, we have to deal with the cultures of groups and the cultures of individuals.[1] [From this standpoint we should find, for example, that] the difference between intra-cultural and inter-cultural conflicts is not real. We have always to deal with inter-cultural conflicts; [it is only the locus of culture that differs.]

1.3. The study of the family

[This is one of our most important areas —] to study the psychological scheme of the affective relationships in the family. Though it would be better to discard the term "psychoanalysis", the psychoanalytic school has probably contributed more than anybody else to the understanding of the personality. A comparative study of families will reveal different distributions of affections and different symbolisms.

[Now] it is often impossible to study "the family" itself [— what one is studying is the relationships of the people in it — just as it is impossible to study the individual in isolation.] Instead of studying individuals alone, we should try to study them in relation to their family. For instance, one could arrive at a perfect understanding of the personality of a political leader only by tracing the mechanisms to which he owes his success back to those he used in his parental home. Any true knowledge of meaning is conditioned by the understanding of this primitive milieu. [In the study of culture,] we are constantly referred to biography.

These three problems − the meaning of culture, the relation of the individual and his milieu, and the distribution of affect in the family and its symbolism − are the three main problems of the field of culture and personality. [Still, there are two further tasks worth mentioning, though they are more long range.]

1.4. Typology of personality

We may look forward to a time when we shall be able to build a typology of personality (from which may come a typology of culture). There are three important determinants of the personality: the genetic process; the maturation [process]; and the early conditioning factors, [the events of] the first two years [of life. If we study a sufficient number of individuals in different milieux] we can expect to discover tangible parallels and establish types of personalities and situations. [It seems to me that this is a task of the utmost importance, for] it is only by means of such a typology of [personal] fates that we can develop a tolerance for [the varying modes of human] life. To try to enter into personalities completely foreign to your own is the most healthy of exercises.

1.5. The reality of certain normal processes

The cultural anthropologist has perhaps developed an excessive sense of relativism. He must see that there are some fundamental meanings which persist everywhere: for instance the affective bonds between the child and its parents or their substitute (the maternal uncle, [or someone else, as the case may be, depending on the particular society and its family arrangements). Though the affective bonds established in child-rearing may be the clearest example I believe there are other fundamentals too − perhaps the sense that] the main task of an individual is to lose himself in the love of others. [But however universal a push toward social success may be, its particular requirements will not be compatible with every type of personality.] Often a social success is an individual failure. [From a certain standpoint] this social success may be interpreted as a reconciliation of ourselves with our fate. Nevertheless, [if that reconciliation demands too much of the personality its results will not take the form of true expressive creativity.] The most expressive creations have been [and must be the results of personality] fulfillment, not of thwarting. [It is these modes of fulfillment that we must seek to understand, not only the pathologies.] Psychic normality is the great task of personality study. [2]

[Psychoanalysis has taken the opposite approach and assumed that its main concern is with the abnormal. Still, the psychoanalysts' achievement has been enormous.] One of the greatest discoveries of modern times is Freud's [revelation that in phenomena which seem to be purely psychic] there is a problem of sexual adjustment. [That is, and this is the important point,] there is no break between the mind and the body. To those [personalities] unable to solve their bodily problems this mischievous separation [of mind and body] gives release: they can fly away from their problems. But although they [may] believe they are flying towards God, [what they are doing is] flying from man. The great task of the future will be to ennoble the body.

The problem of sexual adjustment is sometimes solved by dividing it in two: on the one side is sexual gratification; on the other, appreciation and sharing the life of another. But this appreciation and sharing are only friendship, they are not really love. [So the separation of the two sides of the problem is no true solution; and in any case we should look further into the individual's adjustment to the patterns of the cultural milieu.] The reason for so many sexual maladjustments is perhaps the overdevelopment of the ego in our Western civilization, where the fulfillment of the individual is sought in power, [which for some personalities may not be the compatible avenue.]

[It has not been my purpose here to claim that we have advanced very far into the field that lies open before us, or to convince you of my speculations about what we might find once we got there.] The main purpose of this seminar [3] has been to make you feel deeply skeptical about the biological, the psychological, and the sociological viewpoints about culture and personality. The problems [we encounter in] these sciences spring from the field of the concrete behavior of the people, and that is what we have to study.

2. [May 1934:] The Impact of Culture on Personality

[We have now spent a considerable time discussing conceptions of culture, of personality, and of their possible relationships, as well as the various disciplines that have taken these problems as within their purview. Let us see if we can now summarize our discussion by noting a few] general considerations, [particularly concerning] the impact of culture on personality.

[I have said on several occasions that one must begin] with a study of the cultural patterns in the individual's milieu. [No matter how interested we may be in individuals in their own right, we must not forget that] the individual in isolation from society is a psychological fiction.[4] [It is obvious, for example, that] society classifies individuals in terms of rank, status, and other [attributes and schemes. Although one may question the particular category to which one is assigned] the individual is not allowed to question [the social process of classification itself]. What a personality does, therefore, is only in small measure a function of what he is − of himself. It is culture that makes him what he is − [that makes him, to some degree, a sort of] refraction of society.

[So] the difference between culture and personality is not that the data are different, but that the flow of our interests is different. In anthropology there are two viewpoints, then − the psychological and the sociological − [depending on whether] we wish to hold onto our personality. [Taking] the psychological viewpoint, I wish to hold onto my personality; [taking] the sociological, I do not wish to hold onto my personality. The individual in relation to himself is a personality. The individual in relation to others is part of culture. One sees personality when looking from the inside outward; one sees culture when looking toward the other individual. For in personal relationships, the other person never is himself.

The reason for our interest in personality is that we are never tired of looking and peering into ourselves. Indeed, one may study personality only by [striving at the same time to gain] a deeper knowledge of oneself, and through the growth of selfconsciousness. On the other hand, the personality needs culture in order to give it its fullest meanings. It is the culture of a group that gives the meanings to symbolisms without which the individual cannot function, either in relation to himself or to others.

From one point of view, however, culture is the agreed-upon ghost in the [machine], that catches up the individual and molds him according to a predetermined form and style. [This is the view of culture as the] impersonal, pageant-like "superorganic", as Kroeber [termed it and against which I have engaged in some] polemic.[5] Culture, like truth, is what we make it. [It does not seem to me necessary or suitable to construct as unbridgeable a chasm between individual and culture as there seems to be between the organic and the social.] Social science is not psychology, not because it studies the resultants of a superpsychic or superorganic force, but because its terms are differently demarcated.[6]

[When I have made this point, over the years, I have always begun] to fear misunderstanding.[7] It might almost appear that I considered, with certain psychological students of culture, the fundamental problem of social science to consist of the resolution of the social into the psychic,[8] [or that I have no genuine interest in cultural patterns in themselves.] Of course I'm interested in cultural patterns, linguistic included. All I claim is that their consistencies and spatial and temporal persistences can be, and ultimately should be, explained in terms of humble psychological formulations, with particular emphasis on interpersonal relations. I have no consciousness whatever of being revolutionary or of losing an interest in what is generally phrased in an impersonal way. Quite the contrary. I feel rather like a physicist who believes the immensities of the atom are not unrelated to the immensities of interstellar space.[9]

[Perhaps I should find it a more appropriate image to consider culture not so much as the ghost in the machine, as] a form of collective lunacy. [I would hardly wish to deny that culture patterns influence, even govern, our actions even though I believe they are patterns we ourselves have created. Indeed,] so tyrannical are our methods of mapping out experience that we do not do what we think we do; we do not see what we think we see; we do not hear what we think we hear; we do not feel what we think we feel. We know the functions [of our actions, and the] needs [toward which they are addressed, only] through the activities that try to satisfy them. [It will not do to read a higher purpose into these activities. Perhaps we had best look upon culture as a form of] collective floundering!

[There are many problems I have raised in these lectures whose solutions I must] leave to future investigators. I am not so bold as to suggest anything at all. But as to the reality of the dual problem of seeing the "set" personality — and set alarmingly early, in my opinion — going out into culture and embracing it and making it always the same thing as itself in a constantly increasing complexity of blends of behavior in some sensible meaning of the word "same", on the one hand, and seeing the historically determined stream of culture, which takes us right back to paleolithic man, actualizing itself in given human behavior, on the other — this dual problem set by two opposed directions of interest, is the real problem, it seems to me, of the analyst of human behavior. The difficulty at present is not so much the understanding of the problem as a problem but the convincing ourselves that it is a real one. [10]

Notes

1. The preceding two sentences are quoted from Sapir (1932a).
2. See also Sapir (1932a): "Cultural anthropology is not valuable because it uncovers the archaic in the psychological sense. It is valuable because it is constantly rediscovering the normal."
3. I.e., the Rockefeller Seminar, from which this material derives.
4. This sentence is drawn from Sapir (1932a).
5. See the debate between Kroeber (1917) and Sapir (1917a) on the "superorganic".
6. The preceding sentence is quoted from Sapir (1917a).
7. This sentence, quoted from Sapir (1917a), begins as follows in that text: "At this point I begin to fear misunderstanding." Sapir was misunderstood on this point, or felt himself to be, long after his 1917 statement, as is obvious from his 1938 letter to Kroeber quoted below.
8. The preceding passage, from "It might almost appear", is quoted from Sapir (1917a). The text continues: "of the unraveling of the tangled web of psychology that may be thought to underlie social phenomena. This conception of social science I have as much abhorrence of as Dr. Kroeber."
9. The preceding passage, from "Of course I'm interested", is quoted from Sapir's 1938 letter to Kroeber (n.d. [1938]). The letter continues: "In spite of all you say to the contrary, your philosophy is pervaded by fear of the individual and his reality. You find anchorage — as most people do, for that matter — in an imaginatively sundered system of cultural and social values in the face of which the individual has almost to apologize for presuming to exist at all."
10. The preceding paragraph is quoted from Sapir (n.d. [1930]).

References

Authors other than Sapir

Adler, Alfred
 1929   *The Practice and Theory of Individual Psychology.* Second edition, revised. London: Routledge & Kegan Paul.
 1937   Psychiatric aspects regarding individual and social disorganization. *American Journal of Sociology* 42:773−780.
Alexander, Franz
 1937   Psychoanalysis and social disorganization. *American Journal of Sociology* 42:781−813.
Benedict, Ruth Fulton
 1934   *Patterns of Culture.* Boston and New York: Houghton Mifflin.
Blumer, Herbert
 1937   Social disorganization and individual disorganization. *American Journal of Sociology* 42:871−77.
Boas, Franz
 1891   The dissemination of tales. *Journal of American Folklore* 4:13−20.
 1911   *The Mind of Primitive Man.* New York: Macmillan.
 1916   The development of folktales and myths. *Scientific Monthly* 3:335−43.
Brill, Abraham Arden
 1914   *Psychoanalysis: Its Theories and Practical Application.* Philadelphia and London: W. B. Saunders.
 1921   *Fundamental Conceptions of Psychoanalysis.* New York: Harcourt.
Burrow, Trigant
 1937   The law of the organism: A neuro-social approach to the problems of human behavior. *American Journal of Sociology* 42:814−24.
Butler, Samuel
 1903   *The Way of All Flesh.* London: Grant Richards.
Cooley, Charles Horton
 1902   *Human Nature and the Social Order.* New York: Scribner's.
 1918   *Social Process.* New York: Scribner's.
Cowan, William, Michael K. Foster, and Konrad Koerner, eds.
 1986   *New Perspectives in Language, Culture, and Personality: Proceedings of the Edward Sapir Centenary Conference, Ottawa, 1−3 October 1984.* Amsterdam and Philadelphia: John Benjamins.
Darnell, Regna
 1990   *Edward Sapir: Linguist, Anthropologist, Humanist.* Berkeley, CA: University of California Press.
Dewey, John
 1922   *Human Nature and Conduct.* New York: H. Holt.

Dorsey, George Amos
1903   *The Arapaho Sun Dance; The Ceremony of the Offerings Lodge*. Field Columbian Museum, Publication 75, Anthropological Series vol. IV. Chicago.

Dummer, Ethel, ed.
1927   *The Unconscious: A Symposium*. New York: Alfred A. Knopf.

Fielding, Henry
1749   *The History of Tom Jones, a Foundling*. London: A. Millar.

Flugel, John Carl
1921   *The Psychoanalytic Study of the Family*. London, New York: Hogarth and the International Psychoanalytic Press.

Frazer, James
1917–20 *The Golden Bough*. Third edition, 12 volumes. London: Macmillan.

Freud, Sigmund
1917   *The Psychopathology of Everyday Life*. Authorized English edition, with an introduction by A. A. Brill. New York: Macmillan.
1920   *General Introduction to Psychoanalysis*. Authorized translation, with a preface by G. Stanley Hall. New York: Boni & Liveright.
1923   *The Interpretation of Dreams*. Third edition, with an introduction by A. A. Brill. New York: Macmillan. (First published 1913.)
1928   *The Future of an Illusion*. Trans. W. D. Robson-Scott. New York: Liveright.

Gale, Zona
1928   *Portage, Wisconsin and Other Essays*. New York: Alfred A. Knopf.

Goldenweiser, Alexander
1922   *Early Civilization: An Introduction to Anthropology*. New York: Alfred A. Knopf.

Gorky, Maxim
1912   *The Lower Depths*. Trans. Laurence Irving. London: T. F. Unwin. (First published 1903.)

Graebner, Fritz
1911   *Methode der Ethnologie*. Heidelberg: C. Winter.
1924   *Das Weltbild der Primitiven*. Munich: E. Reinhardt.

Hart, Bernhard
1931   *The Psychology of Insanity*. Fourth edition. New York: Macmillan. (First published 1912.)

Holt, Edwin Bissell
1915   *The Freudian Wish and Its Place in Ethics*. New York: H. Holt.

Hughes, Thomas
1857   *Tom Brown's Schooldays*. Cambridge: Macmillan.

Huntington, Charles Clifford, and Fred A. Carlson
1929   *The Environmental Basis of Social Geography*. New York: Prentice-Hall.
1933   *The Geographic Basis of Society*. (Revision of 1929 edition.) New York: Prentice-Hall.

Huntington, Ellsworth
1915   *Civilization and Climate*. New Haven: Yale University Press.

Jung, Carl Gustav
1922   *Collected Papers on Analytical Psychology*. Constance E. Long, ed. Second edition. London: Bailliere, Tindall & Cox.

1923   *Psychological Types; or, the Psychology of Individuation.* Trans. H. Godwin
            Baynes. New York: Harcourt Brace.

Kantor, Jacob Robert
1922   An essay toward an institutional conception of social psychology. *American
            Journal of Sociology* 27:611−27, 758−79.

Koffka, Kurt
1925   *The Growth of the Mind: An Introduction to Child-Psychology.* Trans. Robert
            Morris Ogden. New York: Harcourt Brace.

Kretschmer, Ernst
1925   *Physique and Character: An Investigation of the Nature of Constitution and of
            the Theory of Temperament.* Translated from the second, revised edition by
            W. J. H. Sprott. New York: Harcourt, Brace.

Kroeber, Alfred Louis
1917   The Superorganic. *American Anthropologist* 19:163−213.

Laufer, Berthold
1924a   *Tobacco and Its Use in Asia.* Chicago: Field Museum of Natural History.
            Anthropology leaflet 18.
1924b   *Introduction of Tobacco into Europe.* Chicago: Field Museum of Natural
            History. Anthropology leaflet 19.

Laufer, Berthold, Wilfrid D. Hambly, and Ralph Linton
1930   *Tobacco and Its Use in Africa.* Chicago: Field Museum of Natural History.
            Anthropology leaflet 29.

Lévy-Bruhl, Lucien
1923   *Primitive Mentality.* Trans. Lilian Clare. London: George Allen & Unwin;
            New York: Macmillan. (First published 1922.)

Lippert, Julius
1886−87   *Kulturgeschichte der Menschheit in ihrem Organischen Aufbau.* Stuttgart: F.
            Enke.

Lowie, Robert
1917   *Culture and Ethnology.* New York: Liveright.
1920   *Primitive Society.* New York: Boni & Liveright.

Machen, Arthur
1927   *The Hill of Dreams.* New York: Alfred A. Knopf. (First published 1907.)

Malinowski, Bronislaw
1923   The Problem of Meaning in Primitive Languages. Supplementary essay in C.
            K. Ogden and I. R. Richards, *The Meaning of Meaning.* London: Kegan
            Paul. Pp. 451−510.
1926   *Crime and Custom in Savage Society.* New York: Harcourt, Brace.
1927   *Sex and Repression in Savage Society.* New York: Harcourt, Brace.

Mandelbaum, David
1941   Edward Sapir. *Jewish Social Studies* 3:131−40.

Mandelbaum, David, cd.
1949   *Selected Writings of Edward Sapir.* Berkeley, CA: University of California
            Press.

May, Mark Arthur
1937   A research note on cooperative and competitive behavior. *American Journal
            of Sociology* 42:887−91.

Mayo, Elton
1937   Psychiatry and sociology in relation to social disorganization. *American Journal of Sociology* 42:825—31.
McDougall, William
1921   *An Introduction to Social Psychology*. Fourteenth edition. Boston: J. W. Luce.
Mead, Margaret
1928   *Coming of Age in Samoa*. New York: William Morrow.
1959   *An Anthropologist At Work: Writings of Ruth Benedict*. Boston: Houghton Mifflin.
Mecklin, John Moffatt
1924   *The Ku Klux Klan: A Study of the American Mind*. New York: Harcourt Brace.
1934   *The Story of American Dissent*. New York: Harcourt Brace.
Newman, Stanley
1933   Further experiments in phonetic symbolism. *American Journal of Psychology* 45:53—75.
Ogburn, William Fielding
1922   *Social Change with Respect to Culture and Original Nature*. New York: B. W. Huebsch.
Ogburn, William Fielding, and Alexander A. Goldenweiser, eds.
1927   *The Social Sciences and Their Interrelations*. Boston: Little and James.
Ogburn, William Fielding, and Abram J. Jaffe
1937   Recovery and social conditions. *American Journal of Sociology* 42:878—86.
Perry, William James
1923   *The Children of the Sun*. New York: E. P. Dutton.
Preston, Richard
1986   Sapir's "Psychology of Culture" prospectus. In William Cowan, Michael K. Foster, and Konrad Koerner, eds., *New Perspectives in Language, Culture, and Personality: Proceedings of the Edward Sapir Centenary Conference (Ottawa, 1—3 Oct. 1984)*. Amsterdam and Philadelphia: John Benjamins. Pp. 533—551.
Rice, Stuart Arthur, ed.
1931   *Methods in Social Science*. Chicago: University of Chicago Press.
Rickert, Heinrich
1899   *Kulturwissenschaft und Naturwissenschaft: ein Vortrag*. Freiburg i. B. (Fifth edition published 1925.)
1902   *Die Grenzen der Naturwissenschaftlichen Begriffsbildung*. Tübingen: J. C. B. Mohr. (Fifth edition published 1929.)
Rivers, William Halse Rivers
1920   *Instinct and the Unconscious*. Cambridge (U.K.): Cambridge University Press.
Roheim, Geza
1932   Psychoanalysis of primitive cultural types. *International Journal of Psychoanalysis* 13:1—224.
1934   *The Riddle of the Sphinx*. London: Hogarth.
Saussure, Ferdinand de
1922   *Cours de linguistique générale*. Second edition. Edited by Charles Bally and Albert Sechehaye. Paris: Payot. (First published 1916.)

Schilder, Paul
  1937   The relation between social and personal disorganization. *American Journal of Sociology* 42:832−39.
Schmidt, Wilhelm
  1924   *Volker und Kulturen*. Regensburg: J. Habbel.
  1926−35   *Der Ursprung der Gottesidee*. Münster: Aschendorff.
Slight, David
  1937   Disorganization in the individual and in society. *American Journal of Sociology* 42:840−47.
Smith, Grafton Elliot
  1915   *The Migrations of Early Culture*. London, New York: Longmans, Green.
  1930   *Human History*. London: J. Cape.
Spengler, Oswald
  1922−23   *Der Untergang des Abendlandes*. Munich: Beck.
Spier, Leslie
  1939   Edward Sapir. *Science* 89 (2307):237−38.
Spier, Leslie, Alfred I. Hallowell, and Stanley Newman, eds.
  1941   *Language, Culture, and Personality: Essays in Memory of Edward Sapir*. Menasha, WI: Edward Sapir Memorial Fund.
Sullivan, Harry Stack
  1937   A note on the implications of psychiatry, the study of interpersonal relations, for investigations in the social sciences. *American Journal of Sociology* 42:848−61.
Teggart, Frederick John
  1918   *Processes of History*. New Haven: Yale University Press.
Thurnwald, Richard
  1932   *Economics in Primitive Communities*. London: Oxford University Press.
Thurstone, Louis Leon
  1929   *The Measurement of Attitude*. Chicago: University of Chicago Press.
Trotter, Wilfred
  1916   *Instincts of the Herd in Peace and War*. New York: Macmillan.
Tylor, Edward Burnett
  1871   *Primitive Culture*. London: John Murray.
Veblen, Thorstein
  1899   *Theory of the Leisure Class*. New York: A. M. Kelley.
Wissler, Clark
  1923   *Man and Culture*. New York: Thomas Y. Crowell.

Publications and manuscripts by Edward Sapir

(Works that appear in *The Collected Works of Edward Sapir* are indicated by the appropriate volume number following the entry.)

  1912   Language and environment. *American Anthropologist* 14: 226−242. *CWES* I.

1913   A girls' puberty ceremony among the Nootka Indians. *Transactions, Royal Society of Canada*, Third series, 7:67–80. *CWES* IV.

1915a   *Abnormal Types of Speech in Nootka*. Canada, Department of Mines, Geological Survey, Memoir 62, Anthropological Series 5. *CWES* VI.

1915b   *A Sketch of the Social Organization of the Nass River Indians*. Canada, Department of Mines, Geological Survey, Museum Bulletin 19, Anthropological Series 7. *CWES* IV.

1915c   The social organization of the west coast tribes. *Transactions, Royal Society of Canada*, Second Series, 9:355–374. *CWES* IV.

1916   *Time Perspective in Aboriginal American Culture: A Study in Method*. Canada, Department of Mines, Geological Survey, Memoir 90, Anthropological Series 13. *CWES* IV.

1917a   Do we need a 'superorganic'? *American Anthropologist* 19:441–447. *CWES* III.

1917b   Psychoanalysis as pathfinder. Review of Oskar Pfister, *The Psychoanalytic Method*. *The Dial* 62:503–506. *CWES* III.

1921   *Language: An Introduction to the Study of Speech*. New York: Harcourt, Brace. *CWES* II.

1922   Sayach'apis, a Nootka trader. In Elsie C. Parsons, ed., *American Indian Life*. New York: B. W. Huebsch. Pp. 297–323. *CWES* IV.

1923a   An approach to symbolism. Review of C. K. Ogden and I. A. Richards, *The Meaning of Meaning*. *The Freeman* 7:572–573. *CWES* III.

1923b   Two kinds of human beings. Review of C. Jung, *Psychological Types*. *The Freeman* 8:211–212. *CWES* III.

1924a   Culture, genuine and spurious. *American Journal of Sociology* 29:401–429. (Part 1 previously published in 1922 in *The Dalhousie Review* 2:165–178; Part 2 previously published in 1919 in *The Dial* 67:233–236 and in 1922 in *The Dalhousie Review* 2:358–368.) *CWES* III.

1924b   The grammarian and his language. *The American Mercury* 1:149–155. *CWES* I.

1924c   Racial superiority. *The Menorah Journal* 10:200–212. *CWES* III.

1925a   Are the Nordics a superior race? *The Canadian Forum* (June), 265–266. *CWES* III.

1925b   Sound patterns in language. *Language* 1:37–51. *CWES* I.

1927a   Anthropology and sociology. In W. F. Ogburn and A. Goldenweiser, eds., *The Social Sciences and Their Interrelations*. Boston: Houghton Mifflin. Pp. 97–113. *CWES* III.

1927b   Speech as a personality trait. *American J. of Sociology* 32:892–905. *CWES* III.

1927c   The unconscious patterning of behavior in society. In E. Dummer, ed., *The Unconscious: A Symposium*. New York: A. A. Knopf. Pp. 114–142. *CWES* III.

1928a   Psychoanalysis as prophet. Review of Sigmund Freud, *The Future of an Illusion*. *The New Republic* 56:356–357. *CWES* III.

1928b   The meaning of religion. *The American Mercury* 15:72–79. *CWES* III.

1929a   Male and female forms of speech in Yana. In St. W. J. Teeuwen, ed., *Donum Natalicium Schrijnen*. Nijmegen-Utrecht: N. v. Dekker & van de Vegt. Pp. 79–85. *CWES* V.

1929b	A study in phonetic symbolism. *Journal of Experimental Psychology* 12:225–239. *CWES* I.
1930	Original memorandum to the Social Science Research Council from the Conference on Acculturation and Personality. *Proceedings, Second Colloquium on Personality Investigation; Held under the Joint Auspices of the American Psychiatric Association and of the Social Science Research Council.* Baltimore. *CWES* III.
1931a	Communication. *Encyclopedia of the Social Sciences* 4:78–81. *CWES* I.
1931b	Custom. *Encyclopedia of the Social Sciences* 4:658–662. *CWES* III.
1931c	Dialect. *Encyclopedia of the Social Sciences* 5:123–126. *CWES* I.
1931d	Fashion. *Encyclopedia of the Social Sciences* 6:139–144. *CWES* III.
1932a	Cultural anthropology and psychiatry. *Journal of Abnormal and Social Psychology* 27: 229–242. *CWES* III.
1932b	Group. *Encyclopedia of the Social Sciences* 7:178–182. *CWES* III.
1933	Language. *Encyclopedia of the Social Sciences* 9:155–169. *CWES* I.
1934a	The emergence of the concept of personality in a study of cultures. *Journal of Social Psychology* 5:408–415. *CWES* III.
1934b	Personality. *Encyclopedia of the Social Sciences* 12:85–87. *CWES* III.
1934c	Symbolism. *Encyclopedia of the Social Sciences* 14:492–495. *CWES* III.
1936	The application of anthropology to human relations. In N. D. Baker, C. J. H. Hayes, and R. W. Strauss, eds., *The American Way.* Chicago and New York: Willett, Clark. Pp. 121–129. *CWES* III.
1937	The contribution of psychiatry to an understanding of behavior in society. *American Journal of Sociology* 42: 862–870. *CWES* III.
1938	Why cultural anthropology needs the psychiatrist. *Psychiatry* 1:7–12. *CWES* III.
1939a	Psychiatric and cultural pitfalls in the business of getting a living. *Mental Health* (publication of the American Association for the Advancement of Science) 9:237–244. *CWES* III.
1939b	Songs for a Comox dancing mask. Edited by Leslie Spier. *Ethnos* 4:49–55. *CWES* IV.
1939c	(with Morris Swadesh) *Nootka Texts: Tales and Ethnological Narratives with Grammatical Notes and Lexical Materials.* William Dwight Whitney Linguistic Series, Linguistic Society of America. Philadelphia. *CWES* XI.
1946	(with Morris Swadesh) American Indian grammatical categories. *Word* 2:103–112. *CWES* V.
1959	Letters to Ruth Benedict. In M. Mead, (ed.), *An Anthropologist at Work: Writings of Ruth Benedict.* Boston: Houghton Mifflin.
1980	[1938] Letter to Philip A. Selznick, 25 October 1938. In G. Stocking, "Sapir's last testament on culture and personality", *History of Anthropology Newsletter* 7:8–11. *CWES* III.
n.d.	[1926] Notes on psychological orientation in a given society. Social Science Research Council, Hanover Conference. (Hanover Conference transcripts, Dartmouth College.) *CWES* III.
n.d.	[1930] The cultural approach to the study of personality. Social Science Research Council, Hanover Conference. (Hanover Conference transcripts, Dartmouth College.) *CWES* III.
n.d.	[1938] Letter to A. L. Kroeber, 25 August 1938. University of California, Berkeley, Bancroft Library (Kroeber papers).

Index